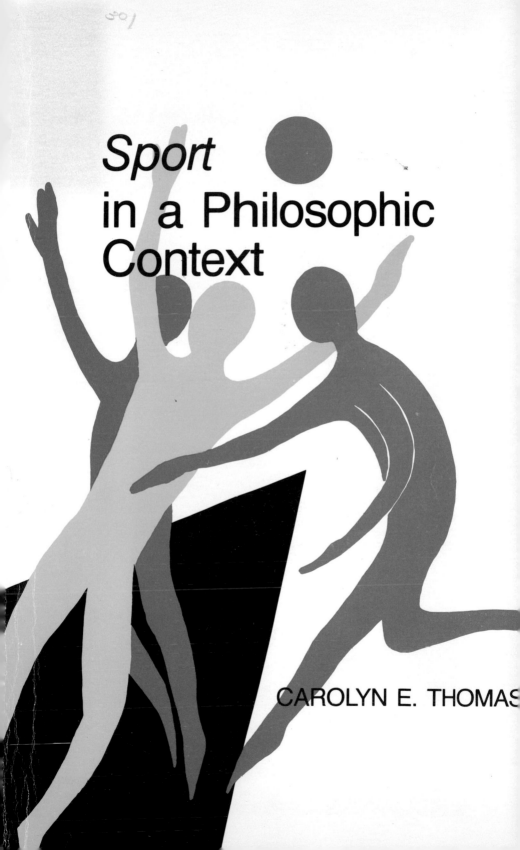

Sport
in a Philosophic
Context

CAROLYN E. THOMAS

Sport
in a Philosophic Context

Sport
in a Philosophic Context

CAROLYN E. THOMAS, PH.D.

Associate Professor, Department of Physical Education
State University of New York at Buffalo
Buffalo, New York

Lea & Febiger • *Philadelphia*   1983

Lea & Febiger
600 South Washington Square
Philadelphia, Pa. 19106
U.S.A.

Library of Congress Cataloging in Publication Data

Thomas, Carolyn E.
  Sport in a philosophic context.

  Includes bibliographies and index.
  1. Sports—Philosophy.   I. Title.
GV706.T49   1983   796'.01   82-12662
ISBN 0-8121-0871-X

GV
706
T49
1983

PRINTED IN THE UNITED STATES OF AMERICA

PRINT NUMBER   3   2   1

This is for Diane Albright and Diane BeBacy, two master teachers who taught me that action is superior to words and that attention to process is the bigger payoff. And, this is for my Dad who never understood what I wrote but who knew more about winning and losing than any coach or athlete or philosopher I ever met.

Foreword

It is highly gratifying to introduce the reader to the author of this work and to take a certain amount of pride in doing so. It is especially rewarding for a professor to see the potential of a former student coming to fulfillment. Ten years ago I was impressed with the ease with which Carolyn Thomas made the transition from student to colleague. With this work, I believe she may be aptly referred to as "distinguished colleague."

For the most part, those of us involved with theorizing about physical education and sport have been content to deal with particulars and specific topics of personal interest. However, Dr. Thomas has undertaken a more ambitious task. She comes to grips with the various issues and problems that comprise the theoretical realm of sport and physical education in a logical and sequential manner. Her intention is to point us, with clarity, in the direction of order, and this makes a great deal of sense. One will find here neither grand schemes nor elaborate solutions. Rather, we are presented with an overview of the field which is both timely and long overdue. Those of us in physical education and philosophy who have been asking questions and debating problems along these lines for more than 20 years have extended, rather indiscriminately, our efforts in so many directions we cannot but find it useful to pause and review what has been happening in this time period.

The field of sport philosophy is a relatively young one. Publication of *Zen in the Art of Archery* by Eugen Herrigel in 1953 and *Man, Sport and Existence* by Howard Slusher in 1967 may be regarded as milestones when one wishes to identify the beginnings of this era. It is not necessarily what these authors said as much as the fact that they called attention, in their own way, to the relationship between sport and philosophy and, in so doing, stimulated and motivated others to follow suit. Thus, we have seen in these two to three decades the development of a rather substantial body of literature devoted to the theoretical aspects of sport. In effect, this literature may be looked upon as both the reflection and the creation of a new area of inquiry. The Philosophic Society for the Study of Sport and its publication, *The Journal of the Philosophy of Sport*, are probably the most visible manifestations of this activity. However, although journals provide us with a sense of current interests, they do little to offer a broad, general view of a field. Dr. Thomas's work aids us immeasurably by offering us a larger picture of the philosophic nature and implications of sport. What is presented here will undoubtedly challenge some of our beliefs and provoke discussion because it calls attention to the dilemmas we face as participants, spectators, and teachers. Those of us struggling to understand the seemingly universal nature of our romance with, and compulsion to engage in, sport and physical activity should be pleased by the mature nature of the work being done.

For a person not well acquainted with this area of inquiry, the juxtaposition of sport and philosophy may appear unusual. However, it becomes readily apparent that the philosophical categories of ethics, aesthetics, metaphysics, and epistemology all have relevance to the study of sport. For the sports philosopher, *Sport in a Philosophic Context* offers an excellent example of a talented thinker's attempt to present contemporary concerns philosophically in a way that has relevance and meaning. I find this approach to be most appropriate because it is the realm of meaning which the author continually emphasizes. The importance, relevance, and inevitability of meaning to be found in the world of sport are probably the most important factors that the author calls to our attention. In this sense, Dr. Thomas shows remarkable consistency, for it was in the spring of 1972 that she presented me with a compelling experiential description of skydiving clearly and graphically illustrating the importance of this dimension.

In a sense, I view this foreword as a dedication to the seeker in all of us, to those who ask questions, to those who recognize the importance of seeking new beginnings. This is my interpretation of *Sport in a Philosophic Context*. A foreword also signifies moving ahead, assuming a stance that connotes activity, action, and movement. It implies an optimism, a refusal to stand still. It is a stimulus to seek out, discover, create, and recreate. This too may be regarded as the nature of this work, and it is an admirable task which Carolyn Thomas has set for herself. I regard it also as a challenge to discover for ourselves the order or structure "out there" so that we may render it compatible with our own way of doing things.

Seymour Kleinman
Ohio State University
Columbus, Ohio

"For once in his life he is utterly alone. The situation is all important, immediate and irrevocable."

Bannister

"Here the training, mobility, and versatility all converge to achieve a degree of attention that eliminates all extraneous perception and pinpoints one decisive moment."

Wenkert

"Within this performance, he cannot delude himself about his own capabilities. Neither can he escape his own feelings as they are revealed to him within the performance. . . . He must act in terms of those feelings even as he is experiencing them."

Metheny

Preface

This book was undertaken mostly out of a frustration with teaching the philosophy of sport to undergraduates who had either little background in philosophy or little background in sport. While the past decade has produced a great deal of literature in sport philosophy, much of it has been written by philosophers and sport theorists for colleagues rather than for students. As a result, the ideas that are exciting and challenging have found a small cadre of readers. In addition, the literature is not yet easily accessible to teachers. Consequently, the intent of this effort is to bring together the many diverse topics that now comprise the philosophy of sport and to use the existing literature to provide an overview suitable for the student and nonphilosopher audience. This attempt at reducing complex ideas to a readable state for the novice runs the risk of simplifying to a point of generalizing. However, I risk this in trying to provide a teaching tool and reference that will serve as a point of departure for students of sport who are not philosophers to "get into" the "solid" literature in sport philosophy.

Writing an overview usually creates an unevenness in quality and quantity among topics. I can level this criticism at myself, but in an era of ultraspecialization I am one of the leftover generalists. Reworking the original Thomas design is probably a waste of time—something about old dogs and new tricks. At any rate, I admit to knowing less about some topics than others and even less about several others. However, I think each topic is covered sufficiently to provide information and questions about sport that may not have been previously considered by student readers. The suggested readings at the end of each chapter were selected for three reasons: (1) they are accessible; (2) they are readable; and (3) they complement, supplement, or reinforce material in the chapter.

There is a definite bias in my approach. After an athletic career spanning three decades (kindergarten through university), 18 coaches (including my Dad and a Vince Lombardi look-alike), and injuries (both physical and psychologic) that live on after trophies have been thrown out and the newspaper clippings have yellowed, I value experience as a source of knowledge. This is not to say that logic, linguistic analysis, or observation are invalid. But as a nine-year-old in Michigan shoveling snow off the backyard basketball court so I could practice my free throws, and as an old-enough-to-know-better golfer who cheats, I think I understand sport in its most fundamental philosophic context. As a former coach and athletic director, I know the potential for winning and losing, what is possible to risk ethically, professionally, and personally. I know the potentials for manipulation, for creating a "good" experience, for diminishing or enhancing the possibility of meaning and self-understanding, for responsibility or irresponsibility. From playing, I know about things that others who have not played can only discuss: compassion, losing, quitting, pressure, coolness under fire, cheating, dedication, frivolity, glory, and despair. My bias will be evident and some of my analyses will suffer as a result of it. I will not apologize but only will promise to get better at my analytic skills in the next season of my career.

I wrote from two basic assumptions: (1) people do not voluntarily engage in meaningless activities and (2) meaning is highly individual and often difficult to communicate. People in North America are fascinated with sport but do not know why. They denounce and glorify it in the same breath. People want sport to be valuable and meaningful but do not understand its value, meaning, or potential in a society that values work, utilitarian productivity, and more serious endeavors. My belief in writing this overview of sport from a philosophic perspective is that both experience *and* discussion will foster a greater understanding of a prevalent but little understood social phenomenon.

Any manuscript has many invisible contributors. I sincerely appreciate the extra duty of Mildred O'Gorek, Chris Middler, Marcia Sickau, and Terri Tripi in preparing the various drafts. Dr. Kathy Erlmer provided some background for Chapters 8 and 10. Harry, Diane, Kathy and the State University of New York at Buffalo helped me find the block of time necessary for this project; Plato and Jan substituted for me in my absence. To all of these people I extend my thanks. I am indebted to my teachers, Jean Friedel, Marion Broer, Mabel Locke, and Sy Kleinman, who with their differing perspectives on sport planted many of the seeds of my thinking. The two photographs were taken by Thomas Buchanan, Office of Public Affairs, State University of New York at Buffalo.

I needed the time to be alone to think, to make peace, and to put some thoughts on paper. This book is a by-product of that process. Why does man play? Why does man create or strive? After all this thinking, I still do not know if there is one or even an answer. Perhaps to be able to say: "I am free or I am strong or I am unique." Perhaps only to say: "I am." I think the best things happen—the most foolish and the most wise— when someone is moved by a vision of excellence. In the free, wild, and useless energy with which man surpasses himself, he demonstrates he is more than a creature of habit. In the ashes there is fire, and I sincerely believe that in sport there is the reality of life.

Rainbow Springs, Florida   Carolyn Thomas

Contents

Chapter 1

INTRODUCTION

CONCEPT OF PHYSICAL EDUCATION

Physical education is generally construed as being concerned with physical fitness, physical skill development in a variety of basic and "sportlike" activities, as the learning of body awareness and grace through dance and rhythmic movement, psychosocial development as a result of participation in games and play settings, and as a physical problem-solving environment. Traditionally, it has been aimed at fostering value-related behaviors through the competitive, cooperative, and decision-making process involved in the sport, dance, and exercise forms that comprise contemporary physical education.

There is an ambiguity in trying to explain *what* physical education is owing to a variety of programs from pre-school through university. What physical education is perceived as may depend on where you live: the activity emphasis may be swimming in Southern California, field hockey in Pennsylvania, ice hockey in New York, tennis in Florida, skiing in Colorado. Yet the sport, play, games, exercise, and dance that form the nucleus of physical education have been, in one form or another, a significant participatory aspect of all cultures both currently and historically.

The nature of American physical education has changed dramatically in the past century. From its beginning focus on gymnastics and calisthenics that were highly militaristic, physical education programs have followed closely the many changes in twentieth century educational thought. The addition of a variety of sports, games, and dance activities are now seen as complements to the strong exercise component.

Attention given to noncompetitive types of movement activities has taken the form of movement education in elementary schools, lifetime sports and outdoor pursuits in secondary schools. The integration of health concepts at all levels has served to form the present curriculum in physical education. Objectives have shifted from a perspective adhering to strict physical development to the incorporation of beliefs that physical activity serves the development of the "whole person." While the *kinds* of activ-

1

ities included in a physical education program have varied over the years and still receive different emphases in programs today, exercise, dance, sport, play, and athletics remain the basic movement forms around which programs of physical education are built.

Many of the fundamental movement skills (running, jumping, throwing, striking) that are learned in early physical education experiences provide the student with the basics to learn more complex skills. Usually these complex skills are found in sports and games incorporated into school programs in the late elementary grades. In a culture providing many opportunities to play and to watch sporting events, there appears to be interest and motivation in learning sports skills of one kind or another. Sport sociologists have looked at how the culture can influence what people choose to do in terms of their play and games. Sport, by its competitive nature, is closely aligned with the values and activities of North American culture. Consequently, of all the movement forms in the school physical education program, sport has gone beyond the school program of physical education and found its way into the American life style either indirectly or directly.

While dance and exercise are certainly not of less value than sport either in physical education programs or in postschool years, these movement forms have not captured the attention nor stimulated the participation that sport has in the last half of the twentieth century. Only in the past decade have large numbers of people developed a strong interest in becoming physically fit after they leave school. Yet this recent fitness development has not been an end in itself in the same way as has sport. Many people want to be "fit" so they can play tennis better or run faster in 10K races or "fun runs." In many instances, fitness takes on "sportlike" characteristics. Again, this is not to downplay exercise but to point out the strong sport orientation pervading our society.

Similarly, there is a growing interest in dance as a performing art; yet the participation of Americans in structured dance is minimal and the dance skills learned in physical education are infrequently carried into lifetime activities. Except for "jazzercise," "disco," or some Saturday night "boogies," dance skills may serve body awareness objectives but are more applicable to participation as an informed and educated viewer.

The cognitive, affective, and motor objectives of physical education that lead to such outcomes as physical development, skill development, self-understanding, and emotional and social development capture the essence of what physical education is. Use of the movement forms of sport, dance, and exercise may characterize programs of physical education in an infinite number of variations, but the sport form in its educational, amateur, and eventual professional manifestations can be viewed as the primary movement medium—particularly at the secondary and university levels in North America.

SPORT, PHYSICAL EDUCATION, AND THE ACADEMIC DISCIPLINE

Those who would use physical activity to change behavior—whether it be cognitive, affective, or psychomotor—we may term physical educators. On the other hand, those whose objective is to understand the phenomenon, we may consider members of a discipline . . . (199)

A profession has service as its primary motivation and can be defined as the *application* of knowledges and principles to situations demanding techniques of practical application. From its inception as a profession in the latter decades of the nineteenth century, physical education has been concerned with the application of knowledge from a variety of sources to the teaching and coaching of physical activities. Beginning with a primary emphasis on Swedish and German gymnastics and later incorporating a variety of sports, games, and rhythmic activities into their school programs, physical educators extracted knowledge from physiology, anatomy, psychology, sociology, and pedagogy to apply to the teaching of sport, dance, exercise, and games. Current sport-related professions might include teaching, coaching, athletic training, sports administration, recreation leadership, cardiac health science.

Singer (378:19) suggests that a profession has the following characteristics:

1. A profession encompasses activities that are beneficial to mankind.
2. A profession demands intensive training and education of its membership.
3. A profession is structured to control its membership, characteristically giving a series of tests leading to a license.
4. A profession maintains a code of ethics or standards of conduct to which individual professionals must adhere to sustain continuous membership.
5. The membership of a profession assumes responsibility for the manner in which a professional task is conducted.
6. The membership of a profession imposes a self-monitoring system.
7. A profession is centered around an organized association to administer the varied ethical systems, educational requirements, and monitory methods.

On the other hand, a discipline has curiosity as its primary motivation. Franklin Henry was the first to write an overview of what the discipline of physical education might be. In 1964, he defined a discipline as:

. . . an organized body of knowledge collectively embraced in a formal course of learning. The acquisition of such knowledge is assumed to be an adequate and worthy objective as such, without any demonstration or requirement of practical application. The content is theoretical and scholarly as distinguished from technical and professional. (162:332)

Singer (378:18) suggests an academic discipline has (1) a focus, (2) structure, (3) a body of knowledge, and (4) distinctive modes of inquiry.

Until the early 1960s, physical education which included sport was considered primarily a profession. As early as the 1930s, however, there were a number of scientific inquiries that did not have specific professional applications. Henry's advocacy of a "scholarly field of knowledge basic to physical education" served to prompt a number of prominent professionals in physical education to identify the body of knowledge unique to human movement. By 1966, exercise physiology, biomechanics, motor learning/ sport psychology, sociology and sport education, history and philosophy of physical education, and administrative theory in athletics and physical education had been identified as the six subdisciplines which would contribute to the body of knowledge of human movement. This body of knowledge would then serve as the basis of the academic discipline of physical education.

The study of sport, exercise, and play has served as the primary focus for the various subdisciplines in physical education during the past 15 years. During that time, increased sophistication in research and the development of modes of inquiry specific to the study of human movement have become evident in the physical education literature. Academies within the national professional organization, the American Alliance for Health, Physical Education, Recreation and Dance (AAHPERD) offer the professional membership both knowledge of a disciplinary nature as well as techniques related to a variety of professional applications. In addition, a number of learned societies have developed during the past decade to foster research and exchange of information related to disciplinary concerns in sport philosophy, sport psychology, sport history, sport sociology, sport administration, and sports medicine. These societies in their study of the sport or exercise phenomena are often geared to the advancement of the body of knowledge in a disciplinary rather than a professional manner. The Philosophic Society for the Study of Sport has its primary focus on philosophic investigations, speculation, and analyses related to sport.

Kroll (221:125) has argued that "To qualify as a profession, physical education needs most to establish the fact that its emphasis is on the intellectual aspects of the performance of its skilled and practical service to society." The implication is that the professional involved in the teaching, coaching, administration, or therapeutic use of sports, games, exercise, dance and/or play needs to have a sound understanding of them from a disciplinary base grounded in a growing body of knowledge. Siedentop's (375:75) advocacy that "there can be no doubt that professional physical educators must rely more directly on a theoretical and empirical base as they use their skills in the service of students" points to a direct relationship between the academic discipline of physical education and the professional options related to sport and physical education.

Table 1–1.   Theoretical Framework for Physical Education

HUMAN MOVEMENT THEORY	ACADEMIC DISCIPLINE
"What is Human Movement?"	"What Do We Know About Human Movement?"
Speculative knowledge which depends on:	Descriptive knowledge which depends on:
1. Direct movement experiences 2. Descriptive knowledge 3. Philosophic tools	1. A perspective on movement (human movement therapy) 2. Direct movement experiences 3. Related disciplines and tools of inquiry

Physical
Education
Theoretical
Framework

THEORY OF PHYSICAL EDUCATION
"What Should We Teach?"
Prescriptive knowledge which depends on:
1. Practical function
2. Knowledge from philosophy and educational philosophy
3. Speculative knowledge (human movement theory)
3. Descriptive knowledge (academic discipline)

From Fraleigh, W.P.: Lecture Notes, PHE Philosophic Perspectives. Brockport State College, September 1973.

Fraleigh (113:2) explained the possible relationship between the disciplinary and professional aspects in a paradigm he called a "Theoretical Framework for Physical Education" (Table 1–1). It was comprised of three dimensions that were interrelated in the development of a body of knowledge and then the subsequent use of that information to prescribe various programs of human movement in diverse settings.

Fraleigh's concept is that human movement theory serves as the basis for both the academic discipline and the profession of physical education. It is based on his belief that even though answers to the question "What is human movement?" may be speculative, a sound human movement theory will provide a conceptual structure and groundwork for logical inquiry aimed at the definition and significance of human movement in our existence. Then, by using analytic and speculative means it is possible to attempt to describe what we know about various forms of human movement. The academic discipline is seen as a conceptual structure of statements and as a logically organized inquiry that aims at a description of the human movement phenomena. After human movement in its forms of sport, dance, exercise, and play have been defined and described, it is then possible to prescribe what we teach or what kinds of professional applications are appropriate in a given situation. So the professional aspects of physical education which include direct guidance of a program stem from the discipline. In Fraleigh's model, the academic discipline serves to assist in providing operational recommendations for the selection of program objectives and other pedagogic functions.

The evolution of academic discipline in the past 15 years has served three major purposes. It has aided in achieving the academic status and respectability that was sought by physical educators when they initially became attentive to the potential of a body of knowledge unique to human movement. Basic researchers in the subdisciplines of sport and physical education have gained alliances with other academics, scientists, and social scientists and stimulated both their interest in and respect for the contributions of human movement to man's existence. Physical educators have outgrown the "dumb jock syndrome" by developing a growing body of knowledge about sport, dance, exercise, and play that relies on sound modes of inquiry.

Secondly, the academic discipline has generated information that has the potential to improve the professional approaches of a wide range of practitioners. While disciplinary research is generally value-free and often is not directly related to practice, a sincere effort has been made to translate theory into practice in order to improve professional applications at all levels. The third benefit of the academic discipline has been in the production of research that has, in turn, stimulated the acquisition of funds, facilities, and public support to carry on even more research. This has fostered the refinement of equipment and the ability of physical educators to address movement-related problems that would have been difficult or impossible without such "soft money" funding.

THE NATURE OF THE SPORT WORLD

People have primary drives to satisfy their most elementary needs of food, shelter, and material things. While the search for subsistence is arduous, even to civilized man, the search for personal meaning or a purpose in life is even more difficult. Yet it is this search for self and/or for the meaning of existence that has produced some of man's most creative endeavors: his myths, his religions, his works of art, his philosophic systems, his scientific theories, and his games. The sport form, like many of man's other creations, has been described as a sort of "world." When we are engaged in sport we are separate from the other aspects of our life and involved in something that is considered nonutilitarian, that is, it is not absolutely essential in order to live, or subsist. Any one individual may exist in several "worlds." These "worlds" may be functional such as a family world or a work world, or they may be nonutilitarian worlds such as hobbies, music, or sport.

Metheny has examined the nature of sport as a nonutilitarian mode, fashioned after the task of Sisyphus. Her 1968 work, *Movement and Meaning*, (271) has withstood a decade of sophisticated and critical thought and examination to become a classic description of sport. Metheny has maintained that sport provides a world in which the freedom to act is guaranteed because the rules eliminate the demands of necessity which usually characterize the functional work or family worlds. If we define as unnecessary and futile a task that produces nothing of material value, sport is seen as being outside our functional worlds. "All sport forms are governed by an elaborate code of rules in which every task of Sisyphus is described, defined, and denoted in explicit terms."(271:60) "The only question left unanswered," she says, is: "How well can the performer do what is prescribed by these rules."(271:60) It is a task, or as Huizinga (174:28) notes, an activity or occupation that is voluntary "according to rules freely accepted but absolutely binding, having its aim in itself (and) different from ordinary life."

Similarly, Weiss speaks to both the nonutilitarian nature of the sport world as well as to the commitment of the athlete to his world:

> The athlete's world is set over against the everyday world. Economic demands and the satisfaction of appetites are for the moment put aside. . . . Artists and historians similarly bracket off their distinctive, dynamic spatio-temporal worlds. What he [artist or athlete] is and what he does is for the moment, thereby severed from the rest of the world. (437:243, 245)

One concludes from such writers as Metheny, Weiss, and Huizinga, among others, that the sport experience is separate and apart from the everyday world in conduct, intent, and in its nonutilitarian and absurd functions. It becomes a "world apart" for the participant.

The first apparent task in any discussion of sport is that of definition. In addition to sport being a separate "world" for the participant, it is also a personal experience and different each time an individual engages in it. "If the sport experience was the same each time, we can only assume that eventually it would become boring rather than interesting." (98:44) Kleinman says that in sport, elements of challenge and the primary element of the individual keep it a "new" experience each time and prohibit establishment of a set of necessary and sufficient properties which define sport. (209:30)

However, in light of Metheny's (275:60) insistence that definition is necessary to avoid sweeping generalizations, sport will be considered to be an artificially specific situation in which the individual, alone or with others, physically moves over time and space to perform a series of actions that will achieve some arbitrary standard or fulfill a predetermined intent. The individual may move with and/or against others, objects, or the environment in an *attempt* to achieve a standard or to fulfill an intent. The inclusion of gross bodily movement in some spatial-temporal sequence is an attempt to eliminate board and card games which often have been considered in other definitions of sport. The inclusion of fulfillment of intent rather than achievement of a standard as the sole criterion in outcome is an attempt to consider and to include recreational sport activities that do not have standards or scores, e.g., skydiving, skiing, mountain climbing. It also should be noted that sport is defined as the *attempt* to achieve or fulfill, allowing for unsuccessful achievement or fulfillment.

Gerber (135:3) indicates that a definition of sport must be "general enough to include all activities one wishes to accept as sport and specific enough to exclude all activities which one rejects as non-sport." Definitions are often difficult to formulate because they rely on some social agreement or consensus, exactness in the use of words, and precision in the application of language, particularly when one of the objectives is to exclude things that are, in this instance, "non-sport." Her definition goes as follows:

> Sport is a human activity that involves specific administrative organization and a historical background of rules which define the objective and limit the pattern of human behavior; it involves competition or challenge and a definite outcome primarily determined by physical skill. (136:vi)

Another technique in trying to understand the nature of sport has been to set up categories or classification systems. As you will note from the following attempts at classification, sport is often interlocked with dance/rhythmic activities, games, play, and exercise. To some extent, however, sport is play, it is a game on many occasions, incorporates an exercise component, and, if technically well-done, it can have dance-like qualities. Loy (249:38–47) looked at sport as a game occurrence, compared the qualities ascribed to play (Huizinga, 174 and Caillois, 52) and then noted the similarities as they applied to sport. These sport characteristics included:

1. Free: participation is voluntary.
2. Separate: it is spatially and temporally limited and set apart from "real world".
3. Uncertain: the end result is in doubt at the outset.
4. Unproductive: nonutilitarian. It does not result in the creation of material goods.
5. Governed by rules.
6. Make-believe: outside "real" life and has a pretending quality.

Loy, like Slusher (382:33–36), also identified competition, or the contention of interest, as a primary ingredient of the sport medium. Physical skill and strategy as opposed to chance are also noted by Loy as primary to sport. "Although chance is also associated with sport, its role in determining the outcome of a contest is generally held to a minimum in order that the winning side can attribute its victory to merit rather than to a fluke of nature." (249:41) Loy further suggests that physical prowess often separates an event called "sport" from a game. He subsequently defines sport as "an institutionalized game demanding the demonstration of physical prowess."(249:41)

Caillois (54) has set up a categorization of play in which it is possible to view sport in the broader context of play and games. His four categories consist of:

Agon: This includes competitive games, mostly sports, in which the player is active in attempting to direct the outcome of the contest (game). It takes on many work-like attitudes and superiority is the desired outcome. There is a rivalry presupposed and the players go against each other. An adversarial relationship is important and the "other" is historically one-to-one rivalry.

Alea: As contrasted to the competitive games of the agon, chance is the chief characteristic of the alea. The player becomes passive and surrenders to a destiny where the outcomes of the game are beyond control of the player. Lotteries, dice games, roulette, horse or jai alai betting are examples of games where chance rather than player skill is the central controlling factor in the outcome. The "sporting element" may be found in a vicarious involvement in things the player cannot do, e.g., being a jockey. So in studying the horses or the players before the race or the game, the player can "play the horses" or "play jai alai."

Mimicry: The agon bears some relationship to mimicry in that thinking of play as mimicry involves a suspension of reality and a kind of fantasy. Mimicry is very characteristic of children's games, e.g., playing house, playing war, or other games which aim to imitate adults. The pleasure of mimicry lies in being, or passing for, another. In the sport context, elements of mimicry exist not as part of the structure of the game but often as "game within a game." The solitary basketball player practicing in the gym moves into "sky-hook" like Kareem or reverse dunks while imagining himself to be Dr. J. The mind games of a weekend golfer stepping up to a short $50,000 putt thinking of the gallery on the eighteenth green are forms of mimicry. The mimicry of the Littler Leaguer who spits like the pros while leading off second or knocks nonexistent dirt off his spikes at bat is not related directly to sport in terms of outcome but is mimicry that becomes integrated in the overall process of playing the sport.

Ilinx: The last kind of play consists of those activities which involve the pursuit of vertigo and which create an "induced panic." Sometimes they are part of sporting events and sometimes they are not. Vertigo is a pleasurable sensation for many brought on by speed, high places, and disturbances in equilibrium. Downhill skiing, mountain climbing, gymnastic activities, and motocross are examples of vertigo (ilinx) pursuits.

In general it is possible to say that sport is often a form of play but when taken very seriously it can cease to be play. It is also possible to say that sport can take the form of a game but that some games do not classify as sport if the contest element is missing or if chance outweighs the physical skill component. In addition, sport is not always a game setting. When the contest is against a river, against a clock, or against oneself, it may be sport but may not be a game.

RELATED MOVEMENT FORMS

In attempting to understand what sport is and why it is often selected as the preferred participatory movement form, it seems appropriate to provide some background about the other movement forms, specifically, dance, exercise, and athletics. While each of these forms is distinct from sport in its attention to structure, focus, degree of competitiveness, and purpose, there are also some similarities.

Dance

Dance is most clearly identified historically as a creative performing art in which the body is the instrument and physical movement is the medium. It generally represents three areas in an educational context: ballet, modern, and folk. Dance may be viewed as highly structured in its adherence to line, shape, and technique, particularly in the ballet form. It may represent cultural heritage and varying patterns of style and costume typically found in square, round, or folk dance. Or, it may represent a true expressive and extemporaneous medium as in modern dance. Fraleigh captures the variation in potential when she states:

> Dance is my creation, my body, my movement. Some dances are more me than others and in some I cannot find myself at all. Dances evoke varying levels of involvement. (108:69)

The focus of the dancer is on the body in much the same way that the focus of the diver is on the body. From this standpoint, a great deal of body awareness is essential, as the body is *the* medium for accomplishing the choreographic task. The audience watches the body and not, for example, a basketball. The body as the primary instrument of expression demands a great deal of "athletic" ability, body awareness, and perfection of technique, for as the body goes, so goes the dance. In this regard, dance may be the most communicative movement form, since the movement medium is the message without any reliance on external implements either to accomplish the task or to divert audience attention.

Cheney provides a succinct but inclusive description of dance:

> Movement, the essence of dance, is also, of course, shared by sport. Dance deals with time, space, and energy; it is organized rhythmically, spatially, and dynamically; it is concerned with economy, efficiency, control, and meaning. Balance, compensation, elevation, momentum, coordination, opposition, sequence, climax are involved. It is a form of expression; it is communication; it is performance; it is occasionally an aesthetic experience. (63:124)

Exercise

Exercise as a movement form is most closely associated with physical fitness. It is probably impossible to have sport without some element of exercise or training, since good physical fitness is often a prerequisite for efficient and optimal sport performance outcomes; yet the exercise form independent of sport involvements has a validity and participatory following of its own. While the *means* to achieve fitness and exercise protocols have changed over the years beginning with gymnastics and calisthenics and proceeding to circuit weight training, Nautilus, and aerobic/anaerobic programs, the objectives have not changed markedly. The primary health and fitness objectives have been to increase circulatory-respiratory capacity, flexibility, muscular endurance, and strength. In addition, development of such factors as coordination, agility, power, balance, reaction time, and speed are desired objectives in enhancing motor performance. Some fitness parameters are developed specifically for performance in a sport activity. However, as an exercise movement form, total fitness is the primary goal. In much the same way as dance, attention is given to the body as the medium of expression. A physically fit body becomes an end in itself, and exercise becomes the means to express this objective.

Athletics

In many respects, athletics and sport are viewed by the general public as synonymous terms. The primary difference may be one of degree of emphasis on or concern with the outcome(s). All of the characteristics attributed to sport (competitiveness, contention of interest, physical skill, and prowess) also can be attributed to athletics, yet athletics is what might be called an extension, or intensification, of sport.

The most notable distinction between sport and athletics has been made by Keating (191) in his attempt to establish moral categories. He argued that "sport" had become the descriptor for radically different activities ranging from those agonistic endeavors designed to establish superiority to those who seek only a pleasant diversion. Consequently, his distinction maintains that:

> In essence, sport is a kind of diversion which has for its direct and immediate end fun, pleasure, and delight and which is dominated by a spirit of moderation and generosity. Athletics, on the other hand, is essentially a competitive activity, which has for its end victory in the contest and which is characterized by a spirit of dedication, sacrifice, and intensity. (191:266)

This distinction is not to suggest that sport lacks seriousness or commitment but merely points to the difference between the main emphasis in sport and in athletics. Briefly, sport may be characterized by the adage: "It isn't that you win or lose but how you play the game," whereas athletics may be more closely but not exclusively identified with "Winning isn't everything, it's the only thing." While the outcome per se, winning, may not be a moral right/wrong question in that it is the object of any endeavor we call sport, the emphasis placed on outcome may most clearly distinguish what we call sport from what we call athletics.

SIMILARITIES AMONG MOVEMENT FORMS

All of the movement forms used by physical educators and numerous others have one common denominator: structured human movement. A paradigm by Abernathy and Waltz (1:4) gives an overview of the complexities and variables that impact on an individual movement form (Table 1–2).

Looking at sport, dance, exercise, and athletics and the biomechanical skill demands that are made, it is easy to note either visually or with the aid of electromyography that there are many similarities in the movement patterns among all forms. Broer (39) notes, however, that while the mechanics of many movements are the same or similar, the intent of the movement determines its placement into a particular movement form. For example, the leap of a dancer and the leap of a wide receiver in football may be mechanically identical and require basically the same energy demands. In one instance, however, the leap may be a stylized expression classifying it as a dance movement. The functional and goal-directed leap of the football player to catch a ball makes style or expression irrelevant and places it in a sport/athletic mode.

Another scientific approach to looking at cross-form movement patterns is the effort/shape system of identification and notation pioneered by Rudolph Laban. Laban's analysis is not only in terms of mechanical analysis but is also based on the space, time, and flow of the movement. His eight categories—float, dab, flick, press, punch, wring, glide, and slash—were an attempt to look at qualitative aspects of movement regardless of the movement form. Extrapolations from his findings would indicate that sport, dance, and exercise share common space/time/flow movement qualities. For example, the pressing qualities of a football blocker, an exercise bench press, or a stylized choreographic move may be similar in qualitative effort/shape pattern, but despite the similarity, it is the *intent* of the movement that classifies it as sport, dance, or exercise.

A second way of looking at cross-form similarities lies in examining or comparing the characteristics of structured movement forms. What Huizinga describes in the following passage is the nature of play, but it also fits the movement forms of sport, dance, and exercise:

> a voluntary activity or occupation executed within certain fixed limits of time and place, according to rules freely accepted but absolutely binding, having its aim in itself and accompanied by a feeling of tension, joy, and the consciousness that it is different from ordinary life. (174:28)

Table 1–2.   A Human Movement Theoretical Scheme

Human Movement is initiated by

PURPOSE

to achieve—to communicate—to express—to relate

is restricted by

PHYSICAL LIMITS

the limits	the limits
of body potential	of environmental laws
(structure, function)	(gravity, motion, force)

and modified by

MOVEMENT EXPERIENCES

conditions, habits, skills, style, knowledges

PERSONALITY STRUCTURE

attitudes, traits, emotions, constructs, goals

PERSONAL PERCEPTION

of self, of others, of universe

SOCIAL-CULTURAL ENVIRONMENT

customs, expectancies, roles, models, patterns

PHYSICAL ENVIRONMENT

sounds, space, equipment, weather, time

the Process of Moving

Occurs through space, in time, with quality (level-tempo-force). Can be described in terms of its own components: dimensions, basic movements, fundamental skills; its design, pattern, and style. Can be used to control equilibrium—to give and receive impetus. May or may not be efficient in terms of mechanics and purpose. Is perceived variantly with occurrence, the mover, and observers.

and

IS A MODIFIER OF ITS OWN DETERMINANTS

From Abernathy, R., and Waltz, M.: Toward a discipine: first steps first. Quest, 1:4, 1964.

Huizinga has noted a number of features common to play as well as to other more structured movement forms: voluntariness, spatial-temporal characteristics, arbitrary rules, nonutilitarian qualities, affectivity, and the fact that it is marked off from everyday and ordinary experience.

All movement forms share the common element of voluntary participation by the performer. Voluntary involvement means freedom from external force and a choice by the performer to participate. However, it may be feasible that the performer will participate due to an internal compulsion, or drive, which may, in a way, make participation an involuntary function. In the case of sport or dance being an individual's occupation, there is, for example, evidence in the baseball history of Boston's Jimmy Pearsall or Detroit's Willie Horton and in the dance history of Isadora Duncan to suggest that the option not to perform or to leave in the midst of a performance is available to the performer. The "scratch," the "bench," and the "understudy" are integral parts of the sport and dance worlds.

Dance, exercise, and sport experiences are characterized by the structures of time and place. Sport and athletics have their courts, fields, and stadia, dance has its stages and concert halls, and exercise has its prescribed place. Most sports are marked off in periods, quarters, or halves, or at least, in such cases as mountain climbing and skydiving, by a definite beginning and ending. Dances are also characterized by temporal separation into acts, measures, beats, or in the case of extemporaneous dance by a beginning and an ending. Similarly, exercise is often separated into times, bouts, and repetitions that establish the protocol and there is definite start and stop time.

Structured movement experiences share the commonality of being "outside" of daily experiences. As noted previously, they are all capable of being separate "worlds." None of these forms are essential to an individual's lifestyle. If we choose not to participate, it will have little effect on our work-life, our love-life, the price of groceries, or the rise and fall of the stock market. In this sense, these movement forms are nonutilitarian. This does not mean they are unimportant but only that they are "extras" when we consider the essentials of daily subsistence.

Every movement form is bound by certain arbitrary rules. Some of these rules are written and some are simple tacit, or understood, agreements. These restrictions may take the form of the previously mentioned spatial and temporal dimensions, or they may be rules of conduct, agreements about scoring systems, the time of the event, or a self-imposed exercise technique or pattern. Rejection of these rules or failure to comply fully can result in a variety of individual penalties, expulsion, inhibition of others' performances, or ineffective execution. A good analogy might be that even in jazz improvisation, everyone must play in the same key.

In addition to rules, there is some form of task definition in every movement form. The explicitness with which the task is defined is probably clearest in the sport/athletic forms. Dance often may appear taskless; however, the choreographer sets the task by defining the steps, the music, and the pattern. The goal is expression or communication through movement. Exercise tasks may be loosely delineated, i.e., running for 30 minutes, but they also can be very explicit. Use of Nautilus equipment, for example, is highly delineated in terms of technique.

In addition to these factors initially highlighted by Huizinga, outcome is a common thread joining sport, athletics, dance, and exercise. All these movement forms are, in one way or another, concerned with an outcome. Competition, whether direct or indirect, against self, others, or some arbitrary standard, is a dominant characteristic of sport and athletics. There is present an intent and desire to win if winning is a possibility in a specific activity; to achieve what has not been achieved, or to attain some standard of excellence whether the standard is internally or externally imposed are other ways of "winning." It is a relative matter, the victory being over self and previous performance or over fellow competitors of comparable standard rather than against an arbitrary standard or a record. Similarly, the dancer has an intent and desire to reach goals of achievement and excellence. Despite the absence of a scoring system, there is an internal competitiveness to do well or to express what was intended. Within this context of *self-imposed* competition, little distinction can be made between the dancer and the athlete. The product of these efforts, be it a score or a choreography, is similarly "measured" and evaluated, albeit with different tools and scales, by outside observers and critics, as well as by the performer. In exercise, the performer sets specific goals and basically evaluates physical development against those goals over a period of time to measure success or failure. Weight loss, decreases in body fat, or increases in strength or endurance can all be measured or evaluated as success or failure. New goals or objectives can be established for continued improvement or for basic maintenance.

In addition to the competitive component, an expressive function manifests itself in all of the movement forms. In sport and athletics this may take the form of expressions of excellence, superiority, achievement, intelligence, strategy, emotional release, or self-actualization. Some of these expressions may be visible to the spectators, but others may be known only to the performer with the result that expression often is a subjective experience. The dance form may be symbolic or preverbal expressions of ideas or feelings or attempts to portray the condition of mankind. On the other hand, the expressions may be a simple exploration of the potentials of time, space, or shape. Some expressions will be easily interpreted by an audience; others will remain subjectively personal to the performer.

Exercise is an expression of an individual's choice either to exercise or not to exercise. The body and its condition, fit or unfit, makes a statement about how the person feels about his/her body. In general, our movement, regardless of where it occurs, makes an unintended statement about each of us and about our feelings by the very manner in which we move. Each of the movement forms allows for both intended and unintended movement expression. A winner comes off the field differently from a loser. A healthy and confident person moves differently from one who feels badly about his/her body.

DIFFERENCES AMONG MOVEMENT FORMS

The most obvious difference among movement forms is intent. Although there may be a number of similarities among sports, athletics, dance, and exercise, it is the differences in intent which attract participants to a preferred form. For example, some aspect of competition may be inherent in each of the forms. However, if an individual is given over to self-testing rather than to a need to demonstrate superiority, then sport or exercise would meet this need better than athletics.

Next to intent, previous experience and opportunity to learn specific skills may play a large role in selection of a movement form. Similarly, instruction and the attitudes of significant others may direct an individual toward or away from a particular form. Sex role stereotyping still influences the kinds of activities seen as appropriate for girls/women and boys/men. Often this limits experiences and opportunity and discourages the choice of certain activities or certain movement forms. Girls have been systematically discouraged from weight training, contact sports, and highly competitive athletics and encouraged to take dance activities. The expressive/aesthetic qualities and the ability of dance to develop grace, rhythm, and body awareness have been traditionally viewed as more in keeping with the feminine role. Conversely, males have been discouraged from engaging in dance forms and have been encouraged to pursue forms that allow for demonstrations of aggressiveness, achievement, and dominance, all of which are viewed as integral to the masculine role.

As previously noted, the kind of competition is important in an individual's selection of a movement form. Excellence, mastery, dominance, superiority, success, self-testing are all competitive modes, but different movement forms meet different needs. Even within forms, ballet versus jazz or football versus swimming pose some diverse options in meeting competitive needs. Individual preference for the expression of competitiveness plays a large part in selection of a movement form. Personality structure, which is based on numerous factors, may influence the selection of an activity. Is the person seeking social, fitness, aesthetic, cathartic, vertigo, arousal, challenge, dominance, or expressive outlets? The individual's need structure as it relates to psychologic makeup often influences choice. For example, the aesthetic needs may be met in athletics but probably not as well as in dance or exercise. Challenge needs may be met in dance but probably not as well as in sport or even athletics.

Expression, like competition, is possible in all forms, but the *kind* of expression possible in dance varies greatly from that possible in athletics. What the individual is comfortable with and what expressive outlets are being sought will be determinants in the choice of activity. For example, focus either *on* the body or *away* from it during the expression may be a source of discomfort or comfort for the performer. Many athletes, because they use and depend on implements, a basketball for example, focus away from the body and on the ball, teammate, opponent, and basket. It is expected by the player that the spectator does the same. The basketball player pays little attention to the body and when asked to execute well-skilled movements without the ball often feels awkward when it is perceived that the spectator attention is drawn to his/her body rather than toward the ball. When the body is not the primary instrument of expression, little attention is given to it. On the other hand, the dancer, the diver, the gymnast, and the exercise participant focus *on* rather than away from the body as the primary expressive mode. Placing a skilled athlete in a dance setting is often awkward because there is nothing to work with except the body. Putting the dancer in a sport/athletic setting creates the reverse problem—what to do with the sporting implements.

Many individuals prefer highly structured situations with rules and strategies clearly spelled out, but others prefer to define their own situations and/or apply creative and personal insights as the project develops. Athletics and some forms of dance (ballet, folk) often are highly defined structures in terms of rules and/or technique, whereas exercise can be loosely or highly structured as can other forms of dance, e.g., jazz or modern. Sport structures are variable but offer greater opportunities for personal definition than do athletics because of the emphasis on process in sport. Again, preference for one or the other of these kinds of differences leads to choices of a participatory movement form.

Although there are many other general and specific differences among the four movement forms, the last major difference influencing participation is the effort/shape dimension. Many differences exist within forms, between wrestling and tennis, for example. However, the space/time/flow requirements of dance which may be often indirect and light (toward the floater end of the spectrum) are often unattractive to individuals who are more comfortable with activities requiring strong and direct movements. Leaping lightly across the floor or delicately executing five steps of a folk dance may be difficult for a football player, since the preferred patterns of the individual and the requirements of football may be in direct opposition to those patterns necessary for successful dance.

RELATIONSHIP OF SPORT AND PLAY

Numerous attempts have been made to define play, some of which deal with its essence and tend to contrast play and sport, play and work, the play-world and the "real world." Other attempts center on the instrumental functions of play and view it in terms of the social or psychologic contributions it has made in various cultural settings. Still other definitions center around attempts to explain the motivations that prompt people to seek out play experiences. We know that play exists in many varieties, and each of us understands play in many forms. Our experience-base provides us with ample evidence of its substance. While it is common to see animals of all species "play," only man recognizes and organizes his quest for play and contest.

One of the most common ways to view play is as opposite to work; yet we know of times when man is simultaneously working and playing so that polar classifications may not be helpful. Millar (278:21) suggests that "Perhaps play is best used as an adverb; not as a name of a class of actvities." Huizinga's (174) concept of play, upon which many definitional attempts rest, would place work activities outside the realm of play. He suggests, as previously noted, that play is free and voluntary, spatially and temporally separate, uncertain in its outcome, unproductive in a utilitarian sense, and has a make-believe quality outside of ordinary life. In this same light the classic work by Caillois, *Man, Play and Games,* proposes that a suspension of reality is implicit in the play setting. These qualities of play, delineated by both Huizinga and Caillois, would seem to preclude work as a playful activity.

Sport has elements of play but goes beyond the characteristics of play in its rule structure, organization, and criteria for the evaluation of success. As such, play becomes a necessary but not sufficient condition for sport, and elements of work can be seen as integral in sporting ventures. Keating's distinction between sport and athletics noted earlier also has significance here in that he views sport in close alliance with play, i.e., "in essence, sport is a kind of diversion which has for its direct and immediate end fun, pleasure, and delight which is dominated by a spirit of moderation and generosity." (191:265) Athletics is viewed as taking on considerably more the characteristics of work activities. It is "essentially a competitive activity, which has for its end victory in the contest and which is characterized by a spirit of dedication, sacrifice, and intensity." (191:265) Schmitz (368) cites three abuses that can kill the spirit of play within sport/athletic activities. The first abuse he considers is the exaggeration of victory, which is clearly the goal of athletics and which alienates it from playful activity. The second abuse is that of efficiency of technique and performance, which is aligned with the goals of athletics but is antithetic to the creative, spontaneous, and pretending qualities of play. The third abuse is the presence of spectators, which leads to exploitation of the play setting and the establishment of standards that may be in conflict with the spirit of play. Yet, we know that the spirit of play exists even among professional athletes and although play is not the central focus of athletics, it is this spirit that can make the game fun and the work more bearable.

The examination of the play phenomenon by Schmitz and others has pointed out that "sport (and athletics) is primarily an extension of play, and that it rests upon and derives its central values from play."(368:25)

THE NATURE OF THE PHILOSOPHIC PROCESS

The philosophic process has some confounding properties. Its aim is to provide direction and to clarify words, issues, and actions. It is also given over to raising questions and speculating and often resists giving us "the" answer. We are often put off by the abstractness of the vocabulary of philosophers and the obvious delight they sometimes take in "twisting" words or ideas. But, in a sense, that is their form of "play."

One of the main goals of philosophy is to clarify and help people sort out their beliefs so that the behavior which stems from those beliefs is sound and consistent. Developing a philosophic position is more than just having an opinion about something, since opinions are often emotional, irrational, or not grounded in logical premises. The sorting process also aids in identifying the basis of issues and providing definition for words and concepts so that discussion of ideas and issues may be facilitated in an intelligent fashion.

A second major goal of philosophic inquiry is to seek out wisdom and truth. These "truths" may be related to our moral conduct, to the nature of things and ideas, or directed inward toward potential self-understanding. To arrive at truth, two fundamental processes take place: analysis and speculation.

Analysis, or analytic philosophy, is grounded in logic which most simply can be considered as the exact relationship of ideas. In Chapter 3, analytic methods will be explained. Analytic attempts to look at relationships occur by breaking ideas or issues or concepts into smaller parts for examination. The smaller parts are analyzed for their internal relationships and logic and then recombined into a whole in an attempt to explain various phenomena. On the other hand, speculation raises questions about new possibilities once certain "knowns" have been determined. Speculation tends to examine potentials, what could be or what should be, rather than focusing on actual happenings.

Osterhoudt (308:2) suggests that philosophy should lead to a level of "informed understanding." He says, "it is the notions and principles by which we understand and live the most general and fundamental aspects of our lives. It seeks to recognize in all things, however desperate and repugnant they may seem at first glance, an underlying relation to one another and ultimately to all other, or the whole of things." (308:2)

In addition, Hocking gives us an overview of what the role of philosophy is:

> To inquire what the grounds on which beliefs are held, and what grounds are good grounds. It may find a normal place for prejudice, distinguishing

justifiable from unjustifiable prejudice. It may, in some cases, sanction authority as a ground for belief, leading us to discriminate between a good authority and a bad one. It may advise us in other cases to rely on intuition, offering some way of telling a true intuition from a false one. A large part of its business is to inquire what reason can do and what it cannot do in the way of supporting belief. It holds that we cannot, as human beings, remain satisfied with dumb tenacity in holding our beliefs. (171:6)

In much the same way that analysis and speculation characterize the philosophic process, investigation and inquiry may best characterize the nature of its outcomes. Investigation is somewhat like scientific method in that it assumes there is an answer or product that can be derived if strict methods are followed. It often results in facts and axioms that terminate any further interrogation or argumentation. The responses are complete, and if the process was logical, then the response is also satisfactory. Inquiry, on the other hand, often stems from the incompleteness of answers and assumes only tentative answers to abstract problems related to such matters as freedom, love, and justice. Inquiry permits degrees of enlightenment and assists in achieving understanding that does not end questioning but often compounds the process. Inquiry results in a "the more you know the more you realize there is to know" kind of dilemma.

In short, the role of philosophy and philosophic inquiry is to force reflection on those things we believe and to aid in the development of a sound and systematic basis for our behavior. It encourages speculation about what may seem intuitive or emotional and aids us in organizing our thoughts and ideas about what we know and what is beautiful in our lives. When you question the behavior or actions of yourself or others, you are at the threshold of philosophy and starting the quest for understanding.

BRANCHES OF PHILOSOPHY

Metaphysics

The most general branch of philosophy is concerned with answering the question: What is reality? A metaphysical position in an overall philosophic system, pragmatism, for example, usually sets the tone and serves as the basis for further reflections on epistemology, ethics, and aesthetics. Within metaphysics is a subdiscipline, ontology, which concerns itself with the general nature of existence. Ontology examines the nature of being and man's relationship to God and nature. It also relates to inquiry and investigation about the nature of self, mind-body relationships, and the nature of man's freedom and necessity.

With regard to sport, metaphysics and ontology examine such diverse topics as dualism and embodiment and the impact of these concepts on how the body and its activities are viewed (Chapter 2). In addition, religious overtones, man's relationship to others, his search for a meaningful existence via the sport experience, and the quest for freedom from deterministic necessity or the seeking of the personal freedom to be creative and self-determined fall within the metaphysical/ontological branch of philosophy. Questions and examinations related to the nature of sport and human movement and their potential as a medium of expression, harmony, and communication with self and others become metaphysical concerns. Kleinman summarizes:

> For the theorists in physical education, the questions concerning body and mind have always posed a distinct problem. Is mindful activity separate and distinct from physical activity? Is it the responsibility of the physical educator to develop minds as well as bodies? Are bodies subservient to minds? It becomes obvious that the familiarity with the problems of metaphysics will enable the physical educator to establish better grounds for his beliefs about his own discipline. (205:322)

Epistemology

As the study of the nature of knowledge, epistemology directs its attention to examining the origin, limitation, and acquisition of knowledge. The various ways of knowing include: reason, i.e., inductive and deductive logic; experience; intuition; problem solving; and divine revelation. Chapters 3, 7, and 8 will examine methods of investigation used in the acquisition of knowledge, the role of sport in acquiring self-knowledge, and the development of knowledge about the "world" and "others."

Relative to the sport experience, epistemology is concerned with the learning potential that the sport experience provides, with how some people learn, with the kind of self-understanding sport may foster, and with what we can come to "know" about the world around us and about other people as a result of our playing. Knowledge acquired as a result of direct experience, observations, and reflection is the concern of epistemology. Theories about the nature of knowledge can aid us in more effectively learning skilled movement as well as the ways in which sport is a medium for acquiring knowledge.

Ethics

Within the broader category of axiology, which considers the general nature of value, ethics relates to a variety of judgments concerning moral behavior: right/wrong, good/bad, moral/immoral. Ethics is the study of criteria and potentiality as they relate to moral conduct. Our actions and preferences are indications of an underlying ethical framework. Ethics assists in establishing principles which will guide decision-making based not on actuality—what is—but on potentiality—what *should* be.

Many ethical questions are directly related to sport. As a rule-bound activity in many instances, breaking written and unwritten rules and codes of behavior are the most obvious ethical concerns. The nature and intensity of competition, which is part of sport, often leads to ethical questions related to the appropriate emphasis on ends versus means. Sportsmanship, winning, gambling, player and owner rights, and coaching techniques all fall to ethical scrutiny in the sport setting. Chapter 10 will treat ethical concerns related to sport.

Aesthetics

A second subdiscipline of axiology, aesthetics, relates to concerns about the nature and form of beauty as it is present in a variety of art forms. In addition, it is the branch of philosophy which attempts to establish criteria for making aesthetic judgment. Osterhoudt synthesizes its function as studying ". . . the form, content, and subject matter of the arts; the role of intellectuality (contemplation) and emotionality (feeling) in the arts; the nature of the aesthetic experience and pleasure; the moral, social, political, didactic, and cultural significance of the arts; the relation of the art product (work of art) to the process by which it is created; the role of technique and expression (creativity) in the arts; the role of the artist, performer, and audience in the arts. . . ." (309:303).

In the sport context, attention to sport as an art form, creativity, audience and performer perceptions of aesthetic experiences have all been viable topics. Criteria for judging forms, technique, style, and beauty in a variety of sports requiring criticism have also employed application of the aesthetic dimension of philosophy. Specific sport applications will be examined in Chapter 9.

DISCUSSION QUESTIONS

1. From your experience, identify factors that have fostered the growing popularity of the sport form in our society both in schools and in extraschool settings.
2. The "fitness boom" of the past five years—jogging, health clubs, commercial racquetball and tennis centers—may or may not be here to stay. What health or social factors may be influencing the general population to exercise? What has been the "turn-off" to physical fitness over the years?
3. Dance has been relegated to a relatively low status in educational settings and subsequently in both its participatory and spectator forms. What factors may have influenced this low level of interest in dance activities?
4. In what ways are elements of play evident in the sport and athletic forms? In what ways are sport and athletics similar and different?

DIRECTED READING

Caillois, R.: The classification of games. *In* Sport and the Body, 2nd ed., edited by E.W. Gerber and W.J. Morgan. Philadelphia, Lea & Febiger, 1979, pp. 30–37.

Harper, W.: The philosopher in us. J. Phys. Educ. Rec. Dance, 53:32–34, 1982.

Henry, F.: Physical education: an academic discipline. J. Health Phys. Educ. Rec., 37:7, 1964.

Huizinga, J.: The nature of play. *In* Sport and the Body, 2nd ed., edited by E.W. Gerber and W.J. Morgan. Philadelphia, Lea & Febiger, 1979, pp. 18–21.

Keating, J.W.: Sportsmanship as a moral category. *In* Sport and the Body, 2nd ed., edited by E.W. Gerber and W.J. Morgan. Philadelphia, Lea & Febiger, 1979, pp. 264–271.

Loy, J.W., Jr.: The nature of sport: a definitional effort. *In* Sport and the Body, 2nd ed., edited by E.W. Gerber and W.J. Morgan. Philadelphia, Lea & Febiger, 1979, pp. 38–47.

Metheny, E.: Athletics in the studio. *In* Connotations of Movement in Sport and Dance. Dubuque, W.C. Brown, 1965.

Suits, B.: The element of sport. *In* The Philosophy of Sport, edited by R.G. Osterhoudt. Springfield, IL, Charles C Thomas, 1973, pp. 48–63.

Suits, B.: Words on play. J. Philos. Sport, 4:117–131, 1977.

Chapter 2

METAPHYSICAL CONSIDERATIONS

Contemporary attitudes, beliefs, and values that individuals or groups hold are not generated in an intellectual vacuum devoid of history, education, or socialization. If a person values physical activity or chooses to take care of his/her body, then that behavior has certain roots. Many of the attitudes our society has toward physical education and sport stem from attitudes that have developed about the worth of the body and its activities in contrast to the worth of the mind and its activities. These metaphysical arguments about the nature and relationship of the mind and body have been on-going for centuries and have had an impact on education, as well as on attitudes that dictate behavior related to physical activity. Relative to physical education, Fairs (93) has pointed out that the role of physical education in a society is culturally determined by the mind-body relationship. If the mind and the body are considered separate, then the body is considered the enemy of reason and subsequently disparaged. If the mind and the body are viewed as having only a contingent relationship, then the body is viewed as subservient to the mind. However, says Fairs, if the mind and body are considered to be integrated, then the body will have esteem and value.

Many complex arguments support what are called the concepts of "dualism" (mind/body separation) and "embodiment" (mind/body integration). The dualist, for example, reasons that since men can think, feel, desire, and choose and since such things cannot be asserted of bodies (such as a table) then men are not bodies. Yet it cannot be denied that men *have* bodies. Hence, many arguments which have raged over the centuries are based in part on language. For example, as Taylor (405) points out, it is just as good reasoning that since men think, feel, desire, and choose and since men are bodies (i.e., they are living, animal organisms having essential material attributes of weight and size), then *some* bodies think, feel, desire, and choose. While it is interesting to a philosopher to follow the intricacies of these kinds of arguments, it will be the focus of this chapter to present a less complex overview of the major ideas that represent the dualism and embodiment concepts as they have influenced current attitudes and practices related to sport and physical education.

RATIONALIST DUALISTS

One of the earliest dualists was Plato* (427–347 B.C.) who was also considered one of the originators of the philosophic position of idealism. Idealism,† or more accurately "ideaism," emerges in Plato's writing as both a dominant theme and as a statement about the value of the mind in its relationship to the body.‡ Plato did not hold the body in high regard but rather proposed that reality is most accurately known through ideas or what he called "Platonic Forms." He argued that perfection and reality are known only by the mind and that the body often serves as an impediment to knowledge.

> And thought is best when the mind is gathered into herself and none of these things trouble her—neither sounds nor sights nor pain nor any pleasure—when she takes leave of the body, and has as little as possible to do it, when she has no bodily sense or desire, but is aspiring after true being? (324:119)

Plato does not deny the existence of the body but worships the pursuits of the intellect. "Who are the true philosophers? Those, I said, who are lovers of the vision of truth'." (324:434) He clearly distinguishes between the mind and the body and establishes the subservient nature of the body in all its endeavors. "We make the nearest approach to knowledge when we have the least possible intercourse or communion with the body. . . ." (324:121) Intellectual activities are self-validating and not dependent on physical senses which can be deceptive. Plato argues that the true philosopher (the most worthy citizen is the philosopher king) is not concerned with worldly pleasures nor physical experiences in his search for truth, justice, beauty, and reality. In fact, the body is the source of much that inhibits thought in that it often distracts the mind in its pursuit of reality.

> . . . while the soul is infected with the evils of the body, our desire will not be satisfied, and our desire is of the truth? For the body is the source of endless trouble to us by reason of the mere requirement of food; and is liable also to diseases which overtake and impede us in the search after true being: it fills us full of loves, and lusts, and fears, and fancies of all kinds, and endless foolery, and, in fact, as men say, takes away from us the power of thinking at all. (324:120)

Yet, while Plato did not value the body nor its activities as important in and of themselves, he did advocate discipline and sound physical health.

---

*An excellent examination of Plato's thought on physical education appears in *Innovations and Institutions in Physical Education* by E. W. Gerber, Philadelphia, Lea & Febiger, 1971, pp. 7–13.

†Idealism is the metaphysical theory that the essential nature of reality lies in consciousness or reason.

‡The major writings by Plato directed at his concerns for bodily welfare are *The Republic, Phaedo,* and *The Dialogues.*

Despite his views that the body was, at best, a diversion, he realized that an unfit body could be an even greater inhibitor of the more worthy intellectual endeavors. Subsequently he was careful to prescribe appropriate education for the body and to advocate that attention be given to the training of the body.

> Gymnastic as well as music should begin in early years; the training in it should be careful and should continue through life. Now my belief is not the good body by any bodily excellence improves the soul, but, on the contrary, that the good soul, by her own excellence improves the body. . . . (324:259)

Plato also realized that many citizens would be guardians of the state and that these guardians, or soldiers, must rely on their physical prowess to serve and protect the republic. In general, guardians were considered to be those who did not have the capabilities to become philosopher kings.

> Then, I said, a finer sort of training will be required for our warrior athletes, who are to be like wakeful dogs, and to see and hear with the utmost keenness; amid the many changes of water and also of food, of summer heat and winter cold, which they will have to endure when on a campaign, they must not be liable to break down in health. (324:260)

Plato's recognition of the body as necessary was tempered by his many cautions about training to excess. Yet he realized that an unfit citizenry is susceptible to being conquered in war and that an unhealthy body serves only to get in the way of more worthwhile intellectual pursuits. These writings by Plato and others have served as the nucleus for the nationalistic attitudes of many countries, including the United States, for over 2000 years. His belief in the second class status of the body has further served to influence educational positions related to the importance of physical education in the schools and the status of athletics and physical education as "frills" in the curriculum and to set an undertone for the "dumb jock" syndrome which still lingers:

> Do you not observe that these athletes sleep away their lives, and are liable to most dangerous illnesses if they depart, in ever so slight a degree, from their customary regimen? Did you never observe the effect on the mind itself of exclusive devotion to gymnastic . . . producing a temper of hardness and ferocity . . . I am aware that the mere athlete becomes too much of a savage. . . . (324:262)

Historians Bennett and Van Dalen (28:47) note that "the Greeks gave physical education a respectability that it has never since achieved." The Greek ideals of balance and harmony have filtered down through the centuries in aesthetic ideals committed to bodily symmetry and beauty; yet the ideal of the totally integrated man was lost in Greece. Rather we saw a strong militarism in Sparta, a priority to civic and cultural pursuits in Athens, and the writings of a "philosopher king" advocating intellectual pursuits as the priority of the "republic." Any respect for the body was grounded in the need for civil protection and in the concept that a healthy citizenry can accomplish its more important civic and intellectual tasks if the body is fit. Therefore, although the Greeks handed down a heritage of physical education, it may be that such a heritage was the "right thing for the wrong reasons," for in no way was the body or its functions viewed as important in and of itself.

A second dualist who greatly influenced philosophic thought was René Descartes (1596–1650).* His ideas on the nature of reality and on the mind-body relationship were influential in the indirect formulation of educational objectives, although Descartes was not an educator concerned with the direction of education. Descartes viewed the mind and the body as separate and as having mutually exclusive properties. Thinking was considered to be the essential element in man's existence, whereas bodies and their actions were somehow of lesser significance. Like Plato, he viewed the mind as the primary means to knowledge and therefore of greater importance. He also argued that the senses and the body are deceptive.

> Everything which I have thus far accepted as entirely true has been acquired from the senses or by means of the senses. But I have learned by experience that these senses sometimes mislead me, and it is never prudent to trust wholly those things which have once deceived us. (73:76)

Descartes' belief that all things must become subject to doubt and be examined rationally rather than experientially is the basis for his investigations. The distrust of the senses and reliance on intelligence serve to reinforce, from a different perspective, many of Plato's ideas about the subservience of the body to the mind. All is false until proven true and truth is in rationality. He turned his examination toward attempting to prove his own existence, and the famous statement "I think therefore I am" was born. For Descartes the mind is a necessary and sufficient condition for existence. By maintaining that the properties of mind are totally different and noncomplementary to those of the body, he sets about to find the proof of his existence.

> What then am I? A thinking thing that doubts, understands, affirms, denies, wills, refuses, imagines, and perceives. Assuredly it is not little if all these properties belong to my nature.

> Thus we perceive that thought is a property of mind, and it is distinguished from what is referred to as the body. In addition, the absolute distinction of mind and body is confirmed, since it is readily seen that the body can only be conceived as something that is divisible. While on the other hand, mind cannot be conceived unless as indivisible. For we are not able to conceive the half of a mind as we can of any body however small. Therefore, the

---

*Descartes' major writings concerned with the dualist nature of the mind and body are *Discourse on Method* and *Meditations*.

natures of those two substances are held to be not only as diverse but even in some measure contrary to each other. (Meditation II)

The body is not essential while the "I" is lodged in thought. Experience is mundane, and it will not discover the truth nor provide the basis for existence. Cartesian dualism carried into education a subtle mandate for the development of rational and intellectual reasoning skills at the expense of subject matter, including physical education, which was not so directly aimed at the acquisition of intellectual skills. The relative unimportance attached to understanding the body or promoting its activities for its own sake remains a strong sentiment in the academic community of the late twentieth century. The mutual exclusiveness of the mind and body also remains in our propensity to separate theory and practice, work and play, to be skeptical of intuition and experience, and to rely instead on logic and science to provide the "correct" answers. The role of sport and physical education in education has not been a primary concern among academics who remain separatist and hierarchical in their Cartesian view of the mind-body relationship.

REALIST MATERIALISTS

The assumption of Plato and Descartes that reality was based on the existence of innate ideas was challenged by the 17th century writings of John Locke (1632–1704) and Thomas Hobbes (1588–1679). Locke's opposition was primarily based on epistemological concerns, and his position represented an empirical movement* arguing that knowledge is acquired through sense perception. Part of Locke's concern with the body rested on his belief that the senses were the source of knowledge, which led to his natural acceptance of the value of the body, since it was the access to the world.

Though Locke was often critical of the rationalist/dualist notions that placed great emphasis on ideas existing without any reliance on physical data, he often fell into what might be called a dualist interactionist mold. All knowledge, he said, comes from experience, i.e., physical sense data, and impacts on the mind which he called an empty tablet (tabula rasa).† Both simple ideas (sensations) and complex ideas (reflections) fill the mind via the senses. Locke's‡ concern for the body led him to prescribe educational programs that included physical education-type activities, al-

---

*Empiricism is the theory that all knowledge originates in experience and that facts are gathered by the senses.

†Realism is the conception that objects of sense experience or cognition can exist independently of the mind.

‡Locke's thoughts on metaphysics and epistemology are best outlined in *An Essay Concerning Human Understanding,* his thoughts on physical activity are found in *Some Thoughts on Education.*

though his fundamental belief was that the purpose of exercise was to promote physical health.

> And thus I have done with what concerns the Body and Health which reduces into these few and easy observable Rules: Plenty of *open* Air, Exercise, and Sleep, plain Diet, no Wine or strong Drink, and very little or no Physick, not too much warm or strait Clothing, especially the Head and Feet kept cold, and the Feet often us'd to cold Water, and expos'd to wet. (245:20)

He further advocated dancing, fencing, and horsemanship as essential to the education of a gentleman; yet despite the advocacy of the health and well-being of the individual and the nonhierarchical status he accorded the mind and body, the dualism remained. The contingent relationship he accorded the mind and body led to his belief that the primary value in having a healthy body was that it may better serve the mind. "Due Care being had to keep the Body in Strength and Vigour, so that it may be able to obey and execute the Orders of the Mind. . . ." (245:20)

> His ideas on the development of the healthy body as a primary function of education, and his dualistic separation of the mind and body were concepts of great influence in the thinking of physical educators. In fact, the phrase, 'a sound mind in a sound body' became the motto of physical education, where it remained supreme until twentieth-century psychology irrevocably demonstrated the unity of mind and body. (132:75)

A second reaction against idealism and also against any kind of dualism was the realist materialist position of Thomas Hobbes.* Hobbes emphasized the empirical source of knowledge but took the monistic† position of materialism which attempted to explain physical reality in terms of material, i.e., physical, cause-effect relationships. His search for an alternative to the "doctrine of separate essences" was based on what he believed was man's tendency to think of things as a unity and as having a common element. He believed that every aspect of the universe could be reduced to physical bodies which had generative properties; therefore if the mind was not also matter, it did not belong in that universe.

Hobbes, in opposition to dualism, maintained that man had a unified existence:

> . . . when we say that a man is a living body we mean not that the man is one thing, the living body another, and the mind as being a third, but that the man and the living body is the same thing. . . . (169:10)

Hobbes argued that it made no sense to say something can come from nothing—such as innate ideas or Platonic forms—but that there is a causal relationship for all phenomena. This position has also been referred to

---

*Hobbes' position on mind-body is outlined in his works *Elements of Philosophy Concerning Body, Human Nature,* and *Leviathan.*

†Monism is the theory that all reality is of one substance—mind or body. It is the opposite of dualism.

by others as "determinism" and is monistic from the standpoint that the single unifying element in the universe is bodily and that all things are considered matter in motion.

> Whatever effect is produced at any time, the same is produced by a necessary cause. For whatsoever is produced had an entire cause, had all those things which, being supposed, it cannot be understood but that the effect follows; that is, it had a necessary cause. (169:116)

Hobbes explained mental phenomena such as ideas, emotions, and motivations as a form of matter because all of these things result in behavior which is observable and predictable. In the *Leviathan*, he wrote:

> For seeing life is but a motion of limbs, the beginning whereof is in some principle part within: why may we not say, that all automata (engines that move themselves by springs and wheels as doth a watch) have artificial life? For what is the heart, but a spring; and the nerves, but so many strings; and the joints but so many wheels giving motion to the whole body. (169:184)

With regard to imagination, or thought, Hobbes maintained that the body is independent of thought. Everything in the world is an aggregate of corporeal bodies and anything which is not a body is not part of the universe. All knowledge originates in the senses and the cause of sensing is the external body. External sense qualities are just so much motion causing more motion in our bodies.

All things are inevitable for the Hobbes man. The life style is determined, and man acts upon the universe and is acted upon by the universe without choice and as just one of many continuous causal motions. In short, man becomes a machine (a philosophy that many coaches might enjoy knowing would support their views of man). Since Hobbes seems to think the body is supreme, this would, at first glance, seem to have a supportive implication for physical education. However, the very fact that man is a mechanistic and determined being places the body in the position of an object.

Many of Hobbes' ideas about the deterministic nature of man served as the philosophic base for the psychologic position of behaviorism. Hobbes' materialistic position did not place positive or negative value on the body in the same way the dualists did. Therefore, there was no advocacy of physical activity implied in his position. However, his impact on methodology and psychologic approaches to behavior is still felt in the writings and theories of behavioristic psychologist B.F. Skinner, in the motivational schemes that advocate a reward-punishment model and in the teacher-directed teaching strategy that Mosston has called the "command style."

It might be possible to suggest here that much of what has happened in programs of physical education has followed, however unwittingly, some of Hobbes' thinking. Educators can determine for the child his pattern of experiences. For inasmuch as we can establish certain causes or stimuli, these will lead to certain behavioral effects. Physical education has done this in the teaching of skills and in the teaching of people. Skills have been taught in such a way as to eliminate almost all cognitive or affective perception of them. The body has become a machine to be used and measured objectively. People have been taught and coached to respond to X stimuli with a Y response and not to question. Through use of this approach their reactions to movement per se and the movement environment has become deterministic, mechanized, nonvalued, and in many respects, an experience devoid of meaning.

PRAGMATISTS

Seventeenth and eighteenth century metaphysics was a debate consisting of variations on a theme of dualistic and monistic statements that were based in either realism or idealism. Twentieth century positions about the holistic nature of man and his existence took their roots simultaneously but separately in the philosophies of pragmatism and existentialism. While pragmatism* relies heavily on the empiricist's attitude in its belief that experience is the certification of truth, it also promulgates the metaphysical position that man is an embodied† entity. William James, Charles Peirce, and later John Dewey in a more educational format were the primary spokesmen for the pragmatic position. As the first truly American philosophy, pragmatism had far-reaching implications, particularly in the formulation of educational theory.

James (1842–1910) described pragmatism primarily as a method of discovering truth:

> It is primarily a method of settling metaphysical disputes that otherwise might be interminable. Is the world one or many? fated or free? material or spiritual? . . . The pragmatic method in such cases is to try to interpret each notion by tracing its respective practical consequences. (182:45)

Using experience as the test of truth, pragmatic method tended toward anti-intellectualism. This was a radical departure from metaphysical and epistemological theories which relied on logic, rational progressions, and primarily mindful accounts of reality and truth.

> Against rationalism as a pretension and a method, pragmatism is fully armed and militant. . . . The attitudes of looking away from first things, principles, "categories," supposed necessities; and of looking towards last things, fruits, consequences, facts. . . . (182:54–55)

In most respects, Charles Peirce (1839–1914) and others held that pragmatism was not a doctrine of metaphysics and that it did not seek to

---

*Pragmatism is the doctrine that the function of thought is to guide action and that truth is known by testing the practical consequences of a belief.

†Embodiment is the metaphysical theory that the mind, or spirit, is a part of the body and that the mind and body are integrated into one entity.

uncover the nature of reality. Pragmatism is based on a criterion of utility, and pragmatic philosophers protested against the view of absolute truths proposed by the rationalists and idealists of previous schools of thought. However, although the pragmatists did not take a specific metaphysical approach, they did address the mind-body problem. They held that experience as the source of truth is the only reality. The epistemological position that all knowledge had to be based on experience was based on the belief that verifiable knowledge was obtainable through observation and experimental testing. Truth arises from experimental testing, and theories must be tested in practice to discover their consequences. The test, then, is to determine if any practical difference would result from holding one notion as opposed to another.

Both Dewey and James discuss materialism and dualism. James suggested that dualism was a meaningless view because it made little *practical* difference whether the mind and body were separate, whether there was a hierarchy of mind and body, or whether the mind and body were an integrated entity. He viewed materialism as a pessimistic, unrealistic, and meaningless way to live.

John Dewey (1859–1952) suggested that the failure by science and philosophy to resolve the question of the mind-body relationship was a "testimony to the absurdity of the mode of the search." He took a scientific physiologic stand to explain that matter per se has no higher category than that of physical causality and to suggest that the psychical transcends matter.

> The physical process awakens the mind; it incites it to action; the mind, thereupon, spontaneously and by its own laws develops from itself a sensation. We must recognize that we have got to go beyond the principle of physical causation to the principle of self-developing activity. (78:106)

He further maintained that the mind and body are bound together in a homogeneity, i.e., they are embodied, and that the mind is present in all of the body.

> Now this gives one alternative: Either there is absolutely no connection between the body and soul at any point whatever, or else the soul is, through the nerves, present to all the body. This means that the psychical is imminent in the physical. (78:96)

Dewey does not see it as possible for the body to be merely an object reacting to the cause-effect principles outlined by Hobbes, since the soul, or mind, is present everywhere in the body.

> In short, not only is the soul imminent in the body, as teleological, as subordinating and adjusting its various activities to an end, but the body is the stimulus to the soul. (78:106)

Within the metaphysical framework of pragmatism, the body is not objectified, viewed as a machine, nor disparaged. Pragmatism was the first position to view the body as having value in and of itself (existential value) rather than just serving the mind. The idea that all knowledge is based on the experience of a person suggests an integration of mind and body. This testifies to the value of the body as the source of knowledge. From the standpoint that the various movement forms (sport, dance, exercise, play) which comprise physical education may be unique experiences adding to the human knowledge base, their inclusion in formal education appears mandated. As physical educators, we often maintain that the experiencing of movement and of our bodies in movement is unique, significant, and meaningful. The experiential concern of pragmatism would, in a broad and applied fashion, be supportive of these views.

Dewey noted that: "Insofar as a physical activity has to be *learned*, it is not merely physical but is mental, intellectual in quality." (77:68) Gerber evaluates Dewey's position:

> This concept of the 'whole child' being involved in learning brought a new philosophical respectability to physical education. From Dewey's theory it was reasoned that physical education had a legitimate role in education. The idea developed amongst physical educators, notably Jesse Feiring Williams, that if academic teachers educated the whole child, not just the mind, then the same held true for physical educators. As a direct result emphasis in physical education shifted from caring for the body's health and strength to teaching for the promotion of total educational values. (132:109)

EXISTENTIALISTS AND PHENOMENOLOGISTS

Neither existentialism nor phenomenology can be considered to be a philosophic system in the same way as idealism or realism. In many respects both of these views represent revolts against routinized philosophic systems and crystallized, absolute theories and beliefs. Existentialism* is perhaps best characterized as a series of statements about the nature of man. It represents a very diverse group of writers, including Christians and atheists, that have been called "prophets of love," and "prophets of doom." Existentialists, despite their diversity, call for a reflection on the "lived" or ongoing experience. Hence, they often employ phenomenology,† which, like pragmatism, is essentially a method for coming to know truth and reality.

The major contrast to many of the previous positions is that existentialism views man as a subject rather than an object and considers the human being as an end in himself rather than a means to an end. The existential position suggests that man is not subject to systems but that

---

*Existentialism is the twentieth century position focusing on the analysis of existence, the subjectivity and irrationality of man, and his relationship to the world.

†Phenomenology is the study of human consciousness and self-awareness in an attempt to acquire knowledge and understand existence.

he is free to choose based on his own free will. It also argues strongly about the irrational nature of man and suggests that many things, particularly feelings, do not fit predetermined patterns. Although feelings, ideas, and behavior can be explained up to a certain point, logical cause-effect must, in the end, give way to certain "leaps of faith." Jean-Paul Sartre (1905–1980) explains the subjective nature of man:

> . . . first of all, man exists, turns up, appears on the scene, and, only afterwards, defined himself . . . . Man is nothing but what he makes of himself. Such is the first principle of existentialism. (362:45) If existence really does precede essence, there is no explaining things away by reference to a fixed and given human nature. In other words, there is no determinism, man is free, man is freedom. (362:21)

Metaphysically, the body is viewed as being the access to the world, the instrument of communication with the world. There are two perspectives by which the body can be viewed—as object and as subject. When others view or experience our bodies or as the individual views and analyzes his own body, then the body is an object; but when a person experiences his/her own body, it becomes the center of his/her experience and becomes a subject. Body as subject and experience as subjective take on a privacy and an irrationality that are often difficult to translate into absolute theories, truths, or values. There is a belief that experience takes on meaning and qualities which cannot be explained by sensory data or by pure application of reason.

A very subtle assumption that the mind and the body are a functional unit is made by the existentialists. The dualistic notions which disparaged the body are dismissed as irrelevant to the kind of introspective examination necessary for resolution of the existential quest: Who am I? What am I? What is the meaning of my life? Since the quest is meaning and self-understanding, then the phenomenological method is applied in an attempt to achieve answers. There is a belief among some existentialists and some phenomenologists that experience is knowledge, that the body is not an instrument of the mind but is a person's access to the world. You are your body and your body is your "being-in-the-world."

> On the other hand, the body prereflectively understood as the *lived body* is not something which I *have*; rather it signifies who I *am*. *I am my body* or I exist as body. The lived body refers to my personal manner of existing, and the meanings attached to this manner of existing, in a world in which I experience presence. (370:157)

Sartre's distinction between the body as object and the body as subject represents the existential position in trying to solve the mind-body problem. He argues that when we view the body as object, "as a certain *thing* having its own laws and capable of being defined from outside," it is difficult to connect this body/thing with a consciousness that is very personal and has an "inner intuitiveness." When the body as an object is viewed by an audience, the integration of mind and body is difficult.

However, when the body is experienced, or lived, by the individual personally, it takes on a subjective dimension, a status Sartre calls "being-for-itself:"

> We must in succession examine the body as being-for-itself and then as being for others. We must keep constantly in mind that since these two aspects of body are on different and incommunicable levels of being, they cannot be reduced one to another. (362:164)

The body in its subjective state is integrated with consciousness in what are called prereflective and reflective activities of the mind. In the objective mode, I *have* a body, I train it, I use it, and in this regard "it" can be viewed as separate from me. But this same body in the subjective mode means that I *am* my body and that my consciousness is embodied, or integrated, in this subjectivity.

In the context of this idea of body subject and the belief that the body is the access to the world, man's physical being takes on a value for its own sake. It is no longer viewed as the servant of the mind but rather as an integral part of a person's existence, or being. The experiences of one's body are the experiences of one's self. The existential focus which places a priority on self-awareness, experience, freedom, and choice creates a climate for viewing the body with esteem and as the source of knowledge and self-understanding. The concept of a holistic being translates into educational beliefs that the education of the whole person is important, and that through sport experiences, the individual can achieve a sense of self. Through the body which takes on a significance and subjective uniqueness for the individual, Kleinman suggests that physical activity can "enable one, ultimately, to create on his own, an experience through movement which culminates in meaningful, purposeful realization of self." (205:356) Sport and other movement forms become one more medium for the acquisition of our knowledge about truth, reality, beauty, justice, and morality. The body achieves a status of supreme importance in contrast to its earliest status as second class under dualistic philosophies.

ZEN BUDDHISM

In Western cultures it was not until the middle of the twentieth century that philosophers lost interest in the metaphysical duels focusing on the mind-body problem. The Zen sect is what Westerners might call "mysticism," since many of its "doctrines" center on religious experiences. As one of the many sects of Buddhism, the Zen approach most emphatically insists on one's inner spiritual enlightenment. Suzuki's (404:12) description of Zen suggests that "subjectivism and individualism are strongly set against traditional authority and objective relevation." In this sense the Zen approach is very much like existentialism.

Dating back to sixth century Japan and also having roots in China, Zen is described by Suzuki as "as special teaching outside the Scriptures." It is akin to pragmatism and phenomenology in its reliance on experience rather than on rational thought as a guide to reality.

> Zen upholds, as every true religion must, the direct experience of Reality. It aspires to drink from the fountain of life itself instead of merely listening to remarks about it. However believing we may be, we cannot cherish real faith until we experience it in our own lives. . . . (404:50–51)

The Zen approach has been alien to Westerners partly because of its reliance on experience but also because it is not a systematic set of beliefs that can be logically and easily followed but a way of life. There are no rational metaphysics and no absolute dogma. Instead, the focus is on a method by which the individual may achieve religious enlightenment and self-realization. While Zen has no thought system of its own and refuses to commit itself to any specified pattern of thinking, it does employ a unique method of body-mind training.

Part of the Zen method involves meditation and focusing the mind on the body:

> To facilitate his experience of this fundamental truth, the Zen novice is instructed to focus his mind constantly at the bottom of his hara (area between navel and pelvis) and to radiate all mental and bodily activities from that region. With the mind-body's equilibrium centered in the hara, gradually a seat of consciousness, a focus of vital energy, is established there which influences the entire organism. (189:15)

In much the same way as the existential phenomenologists view the body as subject, the Zen position represents an embodied entity. No formal metaphysical position is expounded, but the method for seeking self-realization implies an integration of body and mind, described as a "flowing of forces." Just as with the existentialist, the body is viewed as the access to the world, the source of experience. The mind and the body are not viewed as separate but as complementary, and in many respects the "lived experience" is seen as the "gestalt" where the whole of the man's existence is greater than the sum of its parts. A recurring theme exists in this Eastern "philosophy": within unity there is polarity, yet interlocking harmony. This idea carries over into the beliefs about the relationship of the mind and the body. Lama Govinda writes:

> While according to western conceptions, the brain is the exclusive seat of consciousness, yogic experiences show us that our brain-consciousness is only *one* among a number of possible forms of consciousness and that these, according to their function and nature, can be localized or centered in various organs of the body. These "organs" which collect, transform and distribute the forces flowing through them are called centers of force. . . . These are the points in which psychic forces and bodily functions merge into each other or penetrate each other. They are the focal points in which cosmic and psychic energies crystallize into bodily qualities, and in which bodily qualities are dissolved or transmuted again into psychic forces. (233:135)

The body is given great attention in the Zen orientation because it is the source of experience and subsequent self-realization. It is also important because the body can provide the discipline for a transformation of character. Self-mastery and courage are goals of Zen training, and these are achieved through a balance of physical, emotional, and intellectual energies.

> With the body and mind consolidated, focused, and energized, the emotions respond with increased sensitivity and purity, and volition exerts itself with greater strength of purpose. No longer are we dominated by intellect at the expense of feeling nor driven by the emotions unchecked by reason or will. (189:16)

IMPLICATIONS FOR PHYSICAL EDUCATION

It should be apparent from this brief overview of classical philosophic positions that great diversity has existed along the time-line from Plato to the present. There are, however, two models of man that emerge from all of these writings. One clearly states that human nature is primarily a function of intellectual activity, and the other argues that man's nature is more holistic than dualistic. Whatever variation of these positions there has been, these two fundamental views emerge. A number of physical educators have adapted one or the other of these models to serve as the basis for what the role of physical education should be. Most simply stated they have been either "education of" the physical or "education through" the physical.

The concept of "education of" or "education for" the physical has as its primary purpose the promotion of organic health and development of physical skills. Most of the early leadership in the implementation of school programs of sport and physical education was provided by physicians interested in health objectives. Physical "training," as it was called at the beginning, consisted of a program of gymnastics and calisthenics and placed a great priority on the fitness of youth. This fitness was viewed as essential from two standpoints: one from a nationalistic point of view and the other from a dualistic perspective. Steinhaus succinctly sums up the dualistic attitude that even recent physical educators have had about the body: "All forms of education may develop the mind and spirit of man but only physical education can develop the body." (390:19) While in some ways this statement is accurate, it fails to accept the realization that much learning occurs phenomenologically *through* the body, even in the classroom.

A more holistic view of man was taken by those who advocated the concept of "education through" the physical. This belief saw physical activity as a means to the total education of the individual rather than as a separate end in itself. The "new physical education," as it was called, found its advocacy through such writers as Clark Hetherington and Jesse Feiring Williams. Their insistence that physical education was more than just physical recognized, however unwittingly, the holistic model of an embodied man. Physical education was advocated as an integral phase of the educational process and was an end in itself in educating the whole person.

Earle Zeigler (449) and others have been outstanding in their abilities to look at a philosophic position with such idealism and draw implications for teacher/administrator behavior and for program development. Much of the traditional teaching in educational philosophy has also used this "systems approach"; yet sometimes it is difficult to say that a coach who is a pragmatist will behave in certain ways. No one is a pure pragmatist, idealist, realist, or existentialist, and our decisions are contaminated by a number of personal, situational, and pragmatic variables. So, perhaps it is best to decide more basically if we believe that the mind is the essential aspect of existence which the body will, in turn, serve or if we believe that the mind and body operate *interdependently* as a unity in our lives.

These two traditionally opposing models of man have implications for our personal and professional lives. The selection of a view leads us to ask other questions. For instance, is man predictable or essentially unpredictable? Is he free or determined? Is he a being given over to logic or irrationality? Does man live in an objective world to serve as just another object transmitting information or does he live in a subjective world as the generator of something new surrounded by a private world of feelings, emotions, and questions? Answers to these kinds of questions then dictate certain beliefs about behavior and about what should be taught and learned. Our metaphysical view about the nature of man leads us to choose between being a behaviorist or a humanist, between a command style or a problem-solving style, between valuing physical education enough to require it, give it grades and credit or attaching "frill" status to it. Either individuals will trust their bodies or they will not. They will put their trust either in analysis or awareness, in logic or in experience. Or, they will come to understand that these dichotomies may, in reality, be both complementary and valid.

DISCUSSION QUESTIONS

1. What are the influences of dualism in the kinds of programs of physical education or sport in which you have participated?
2. In what subtle and overt ways do "academic" programs or activities enjoy superior standing?
3. On what functions and skills does our capitalistic society place great emphasis? What are the expectations society has of an "educated" person? Does society demand or expect that young people will be physically healthy or skilled in the use of their bodies?
4. Does society hold outstanding athletes and scholars at the same level of esteem? Do people view the same training necessary to

become a teacher of physical education as they do a teacher of mathematics? Do people believe that coaches and athletes are as intellectually competent as an engineer or a physician, for example? What attitudes or beliefs underlie any differences you may have experienced?

DIRECTED READING

Descartes, R.: The real distinction between mind and body. *In* Sport and the Body, 2nd ed., edited by E.W. Gerber and W.J. Morgan. Philadelphia, Lea & Febiger, 1979, pp. 151–154.

Kleinman, S.: Will the real Plato please stand up? Quest, *14*:73–75, 1970.

Leonard, G.: Aikido and the mind of the West. *In* The Ultimate Athlete. New York, Viking Press, 1975, pp. 47–58.

Plato: The separation of body and soul. *In* Sport and the Body, 2nd ed., edited by E.W. Gerber and W.J. Morgan. Philadelphia, Lea & Febiger, 1979, pp. 148–150.

Smith, P.: Sport is a Western Yoga. Psychol. Today, 9:48–57, 1975.

Chapter 3

EPISTEMOLOGICAL CONSIDERATIONS

Inasmuch as philosophy is essentially a process to acquire knowledge about such things as reality, truth, beauty, or the nature of right and wrong, a method or series of methods, becomes important. However, before examining method, it should be noted that there have been a number of attempts to classify the *types* of knowledge that exist. In particular, such noted philosophers as Polanyi, Royce, and Phenix have written about both the types and sources of knowledge. Theorists concerned with sport have used these classifications to examine the ways in which a player can come to "know" as a result of sport participation.

In addition, knowledge has a number of sources not all of which require thinking or the traditional cognitive processes that usually form the central focus of learning in educational institutions. Once the types and sources of knowledge are known, it becomes possible for the sport philosopher to apply a variety of methods that will yield specific knowledges related to the sport experience. Webster's *New Collegiate Dictionary* defines knowledge as "the fact or condition of knowing something with familiarity gained through experience or association." In a philosophic orientation it is possible to define knowledge as "the act of personal possession of a verified meaning germane to some segment of reality." Knowledge can be passive in the sense that when a fact is acquired, it remains a fact. Game statistics, rules, or the fact that the Los Angeles Dodgers won the 1981 World Series are examples of passive knowledge. Yet knowledge also can be viewed as an ongoing process in that our ability to make constant associations among facts and experiences can yield new knowledge(s). Offensive or defensive strategies, tactics, or approaches to the tasks in sport often reflect knowledge in its more active capacity.

Knowledge also has a personal and subjective characteristic in that it becomes part of us in ways that are often unique to us. Different people perceive the same event very differently, depending on their backgrounds and perceptual biases. Subsequently what one person comes to "know" may be different than what a second person comes to "know" despite their both having heard the same "facts" or having seen the same event. Since everyone wants to believe that what he knows is correct, knowledge in the philosophic sense needs to be verified to the degree that correctness can be assured. The search for the significance and the importance of the knowledge also can verify and lend validity to what we think we know.

TYPES AND CLASSIFICATION OF KNOWLEDGE

Royce (350:11–19) in his early work, *Encapsulated Man*, identified what he labeled "paths" to knowledge. He identified four psychologic processes by which man came to know reality (Table 3–1). While realizing that there are often barriers to be overcome to insure valid understanding of reality, he outlined the criterion of truth that could be used in each system. Royce also warned against trusting only one system in arriving at truth. Instead he advocated what others called "epistemic correlation," i.e., coming to know something from a variety of sources rather than just relying on thinking alone or on experience alone.

The most common process used to gain knowledge and the one most trusted by scientists is thinking. It relies heavily on the use of rational and logical methods to yield facts and concrete, objective information. Rationalism, as may be noted from Chapter 2, also has a long history in philosophic approaches to epistemology. Feeling, on the other hand, often has little to do with being rational. Intuition relies on previous experience and associations which may be indirect and not necessarily rational. This does not necessarily mean intuition is an unreliable means of coming to know reality, but it is less explainable in logical terms. The "I have a feeling" that this is right or that this will work is a demonstration of insight. Physical sensing (seeing, hearing, touching, tasting, and smelling) provides the basis for what is known as empirical data. Sensing relies on the ability to perceive accurately the world around us. The process of believing uses authority as the basis for coming to know. Authority can be viewed as expert opinion, beliefs in the teachings of parents, coaches, teachers or political/religious doctrine. The validity of this type of knowledge is based on whether we are being told the truth by the source of authority.

Table 3–1.   Paths to Knowledge

	Psychologic Process	System	Criterion of Truth	
Man	→ Thinking →	Rationalism →	Logical–Illogical →	Reality
	→ Feeling →	Intuition →	Insight–No Insight →	
	→ Sensing →	Empiricism →	Perception–Misperception →	
	→ Believing →	Authoritarianism →	Ideology–Delusion →	

A second classification of knowledge was outlined by Phenix (321) in his *Realms of Meaning*. He identified six types of knowledge.

1. *Symbolics* includes language and mathematics and the symbolic representations involved in these disciplines.
2. *Empirics* includes the physical sciences, biology, psychology, and the social sciences. The reliance on the sensing modalities and the observation of animal and human behavior in its individual and collective forms is the basis for knowledge in this area.
3. *Esthetics* includes music, literature, the visual arts, and the arts of movement. A focus on beauty and knowledge based on intuition, as well as the uses of space, time, and flow, represents this type of knowledge.
4. *Synnoetics* has as its basis personal knowledge and is grounded in subjective experience, personal introspection, and analytic attempts at self-understanding.
5. *Ethics* deals with acquisition of moral knowledge and attempts to define and understand right and wrong in both standards and behavior.
6. *Synoptics* is the knowledge related to history, religion, and philosophy and serves to provide perspective, background, and a frame of reference for understanding the world.

SOURCES OF KNOWLEDGE

Table 3–2 is a diagram that outlines the three sources of knowledge: prereflective, personal, and explicit.

Table 3–2. Paradigm of Knowledge Sources

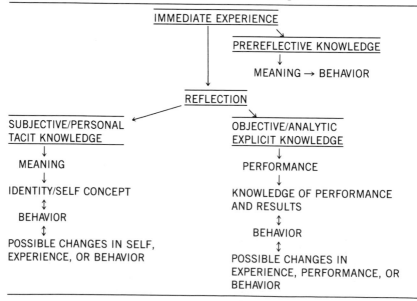

All knowledge starts with some kind of experience. The experience may be highly intellectual and symbolic, such as combining figures in a mathematics or chemistry formula, or it may be experientially based, like throwing a ball. From this immediate experience it is possible to achieve knowledge from one or from as many as three sources. Each source provides a different kind of information about the experience which, if combined, serves as a complementary knowledge base providing us with the fullest understanding of our experience.

Prereflective Knowledge

The notion of prereflective knowledge has a relatively short history in Western philosophy and methods. Its longest tradition lies in Eastern philosophy and is grounded in metaphysical attitudes related to the oneness of mind and body. Basically, prereflective knowledge provides information without reflective thinking. The body itself becomes the source of knowledge. For example, if you walk outside and the temperature is 100°F, you "know" it is hot before you even think about, or reflect on, the heat that is impacting on your body. Another kind of prereflective knowledge occurs when certain sports movements become "automatic." If you are a skilled tennis player, you do not think about where your feet go or how to place your fingers on the racquet. Execution of the tennis swing is prereflective in the sense that your body "knows" how to swing and you are free to "think" about other aspects of the game. In fact, says Polanyi (328:31), "the skillful use of a tennis racquet can be paralyzed by watching our racquet instead of attending to the ball and the court in front of us." He also describes this source of knowledge as the "unreasoned conclusions of our senses." (328:17) Prereflective knowledge is a highly subjective knowledge source that an individual's body experiences. The "knowing" may be unique from what others may experience and come to know. Yet knowing it is hot, one can attach certain meanings to the heat and behave in certain ways without even thinking. Getting dressed in an air-conditioned building and preparing to go out and run, a person may feel great. But upon stepping outside into the heat and humidity, enthusiasm for moving may wilt in direct relationship to the information received about the ambient air on a prereflective level. The reduction in enthusiasm or the sluggishness of any subsequent running pattern may not even come to a cognitive or reflective level, but, nonetheless, behavior has been affected by the information received on a prereflective level.

Objective/Analytic/Explicit Knowledge

In seeking the answers to questions of truth, science and the scientist attempt to deal in facts and relationships—facts that are objective and as value-free as possible. Use of analytic and rational techniques to arrive at cause-effect relationships is the primary concern of this kind of knowledge. Scientific knowledge presupposes a mechanical world and is oriented toward giving information about the properties of space and time. In sport performances, concerns with physics and mechanical analysis to improve technique and to detect error can lead to increases in distance and/or height, greater consistency in performance, and improved performance efficiency.

The objectivity and explicitness of scientific knowledge makes it conceptual in nature, concrete and easy to communicate. The reflection on the immediate experience stems primarily from observation. Sometimes this observation is by an individual, e.g., coach or teacher or spectator, who is not involved in the experience. At other times performers may become audience to their own acts, either by viewing a replay or by reflecting directly on either the kinesthetics or performance aspects of the experience. This kind of reflection is not concerned with affective feelings or the "why" of the experience. It seeks to understand *what* happened and *how* it happened. It also seeks to analyze the experience part by part in an objective manner primarily to improve technique or strategic elements.

Another approach to experience which lends itself to analytic knowledge is that of perspective achieved by the spectator. It is possible to "know" sport in some certain ways without ever having played the sport. Observation yields not only knowledge of performance for both the player and the spectator but also provides understandings of strategy, rules, equipment, and technique for those whose direct experience of a sport may be nonexistent. Many "armchair quarterbacks" are extremely "knowledgeable" about their sport without ever having played the game. Yet, to "know" sport only as an observer or to analyze only its performance aspects is to fail to achieve a full understanding of the sport experience. While the observer may have rational knowledge, the sensuous and intuitive understandings that come from the subjectivity of *doing* sport are missing. Moustakas (290) suggests that the "lived-experience" cannot be *explained* sufficiently. "The experience is real only when it is lived; as soon as it is talked about or defined, the living moment is lost." (290:1) He goes on to argue that "the reality of experience and the personal creations of the individual can never be known in analysis or abstraction, can never be known by precise measurement, but only through a meaningful integration of immediate experience. The unique and idiosyncratic qualities of experience cannot be observed, defined, and classified but must be *lived* to be really known." (290:132) Involvement in sport cannot be explained fully by scientific and analytic means. However, any performance aspects certainly can be improved with these kinds of knowledges, and the performer can come to have a better understanding of personal technique, game strategy, and even ethical behavior. This is an important source of knowledge which when taken as a complement to other sources of knowledge will provide the most complete understanding of sport participation.

Subjective/Personal/Tacit Knowledge

Scientists, as well as philosophers, have stressed that in considering the truth of statements and perceptions or in understanding the reality of experience, it is essential to consider the *context* of the experience. To get at the facts or meanings of a particular situation, consideration of the human element that makes one person's experience what it is and separate or different from that of others becomes a necessity. The "truth" that the philosopher seeks is often related to the significance of the act rather than to the objective facts or essence of the act. And, while this context often may be subjective and personal, an examination of "why" people engage in sport can be objective by reflecting on personal behaviors and motives in much the same way as one would reflect on performance variables.

Philosophy concerns itself with subjective facts; subjective in the sense that meaning is highly personal but also factual in the sense that certain behaviors exist and can be examined. Personal knowledge is often difficult to communicate and is sometimes highly abstract and feeling-based. For example, it is possible for the player to "know" that the momentum of the game may have shifted, but it is a *feeling* which is difficult to explain. While philosophic knowledge in its existential form is not always concerned with cause-effect relationships, it is concerned with effects, or ends. The verification for this kind of knowledge stems from direct experience. Where the quantitative aspects of sport can be known cognitively and scientifically, the qualitative aspects often must be experienced. The personal knowledge of one's self or others in sport must be known in the immediacy, or process, of that experience. Some of this knowledge has its source in intuition and some in empiricism. In running, for example, unless you have run a long distance, it is difficult to "know" about such qualitative experiences as "second wind," "a steady state," or "hitting the wall." It may be possible to observe these as a spectator or in an exercise physiology laboratory, but to really know these dimensions of the sport, they must be experienced.

The meaning that the sport holds for an individual is often difficult, if not impossible, to know as an outsider. Why do people play or not play? What brings them back to the event—some in an obsessive manner? Only by experience and a subjective reflection on that experience is it possible for the *player* to understand the satisfaction and fulfillment or the sense and feelings of defeat or victory or just participating that come from playing. The personal source of knowledge that leads to an understanding of the "flow or power," "the good hurt," "a sweet shot," the finesse of perfect execution, and of self can lead to establishing any number of meaning-based or value-oriented objectives for sport and physical education.

Polanyi maintains that tacit or personal knowledge may be the dominant principle of all knowledge. "Tacit knowing appears to be a doing of our own, lacking the public, objective character of explicit knowledge." (328:12–13) He insists that all explicit scientific knowledge rests on a foundation of tacit or personal knowledge in that the *kind* of facts which a scientist discovers depends on how he as a person with a given set of experiences has chosen to look at reality (327:29–33). In other words, what we choose to study objectively, as well as how we go about studying it, depends on previous feelings and our subjective experiences and biases.

Taken together, the prereflective, analytic, and experiential provide optimal knowledge about sport. The concerns of some philosophers will necessitate employment of methods that very much resemble the scientific method. This is the same perspective utilized by the observer of the sporting event. These objective philosophic methods will yield knowledge *about* sport. We will be able to know what sport is, what it could be, and what it should be. Employment of analytic techniques grounded in logic and a rational reflection will provide the "outside" dimension. Other philosophers will be concerned with the more subjective aspects, not so much with what *is* sport about but rather with what does it *mean* to be *in* sport experience. These methods will rely more heavily on intuitive and descriptive techniques.

METHODS OF KNOWING

Harper et al. (154:42–47) identify a number of different types of thinking that are involved in *doing* philosophy. These include: mental wandering, intuitive thinking, creative thinking, problem solving, contemplation, mediation, comprehension, recollection, gratification, and rationalization. Not all of these thinking processes lead to good philosophy. Sometimes mental wandering, for example, may be helpful in stimulating some interesting ideas, but philosophic research requires a more rigorous methodological approach. Serious and advanced research in philosophy requires a focus of thinking. Morland (289:308) defines the philosophic method as "the rigorous application of the principles and processes of logic, within carefully defined limits, to the analysis of nonempirical [qualitative] problems."

The ability to reason accurately is important regardless of whether the problem is a quantitative or a qualitative one. Historically, Socratic method (dialectic) is the oldest form of philosophic method and reasoning. The writings of Plato are heavily grounded in dialogue, and the reasoning process is comprised of five elements:

1. There is a skeptical ignorance of truth. All parties assume a position of ignorance and doubt anything they may think they know. They attempt to start at the beginning and suspend all biases they may have.
2. Conversational dialogue begins in order to establish a series of questions and answers which, in turn, lead to further questions. This leads to a clearer formulation of the central problem and a separating out of side issues.
3. Definition and conceptualization attempt to define correctly terms and problems so that all parties are discussing the same thing.
4. Inductive reasoning which moves from parts of the problem or issue to a whole answer is then employed.
5. Deductive reasoning is then employed to test the definitions and answers by examining the implications and consequences of the answers.

The major methods of reasoning evolved from this dialectic and were developed further by other philosophers, Aristotle in particular. The deductive method is used to draw conclusions from a series of premises and to make inferences from general principles. Metheny's article, "This Thing Called Sport," (275) uses deductive method by setting out what we know to be the broad notion of sport and deducing or extracting the particular characteristics of sport. This is the method frequently employed by scientists in that it is a step-by-step movement from things that are generally known to be true to more specific conclusions. This deductive form of reasoning, in which two premises or statements are made from which a logical conclusion is drawn, is known as a "syllogism." The danger in this deductive process is that one of the premises may be false, thereby invalidating conclusions. A false syllogism may be as follows: John is a boy: John is tall; therefore all boys are tall. The problem here is not in the actual premises but in the manner in which they are combined. For while it may be true that John is a tall boy (an accurate conclusion), it is inaccurate to assume from the given information that just because John is tall, all boys are tall. Another example is to say: Varsity sports build character; football is a varsity sport; therefore, football builds character. The problem with the conclusion in this particular case is that while football may, in fact, be a varsity sport, the major premise that varsity sports build character makes an assumption that is inaccurate or based on propaganda rather than fact. It is important in looking at statements or conclusions drawn from general premises that the premises are in themselves accurate.

Another type of reasoning is inductive in nature. In this instance, the logical processes move from specific to general, from part(s) to whole, and from individual to more universal conclusions. Personal experience frequently is used as the basis for more generalizable fact. Graves (140) uses inductive reasoning to develop a general definition of sport by examining those individual activities that are generally accepted as sport and then generalizing from the nature of these particulars. The danger in this kind of logic is that too small a sample may serve as the basis for generalization and we begin to think that the whole world thinks like and acts like our small segment of the world. Inductive reasoning is valuable, however, in combining many specifics and making some general observations that are more valid than they would otherwise be. In using the inductive or the deductive process, it is important to review an argument or statement for the possibility of cause-effect errors. For example, it is frequently stated that physical education programs foster physical fitness. If this statement is examined, the error is evident in that it may not necessarily follow that fitness is a product of physical education programs. The development of fitness requires physiologic overload, and if the physical education program consists of activities such as golf and archery that do not produce such overload or if inadequate time is allowed in the program, fitness may not be fostered despite the presence of a program. Often what we would *like* to believe breaks down under more careful analysis. The past tendencies to romanticize and to exaggerate the positive contribution of sport may have been well-intended but have often been based on false premises, inaccurate assumptions, uncritical analysis, and over-generalizing from specifics.

A more contemporary form of deductive reasoning was the pragmatic experimentalism often employed by the philosopher John Dewey. Also known as the "if-then," dialectic, it is comprised of four steps. The first is to clearly identify or specify the problem. The next step is to suggest solutions: "if we do A," "if we do B," and so on. The third step is to deduct probable outcomes or consequences of the proposed solutions: "If we do A, then X or Y or Z may occur." The test of this logic is practical through observation and further reflection.

In attempting to establish facts, particularly in ethical questions, judgments that are emotional or based on interest are frequently passed off as fact. This is faulty reasoning and leads to what is known as the "open-ended argument." If we say, for instance, that sport is good because it fosters fun, fitness, and skill development, this is a faulty line of reasoning. "Good" is not interchangeable with fun, fitness, or skill. It is not a *factual* statement. It is a statement of value or personal opinion. To make it factual and logically correct, it would be necessary to define "good" and "fun" as being synonymous or interchangeable terms in the same way that "John is a brother" and "John is a male sibling" may be used interchangeably. The substitution of value-based or opinion statements for fact has the potential to cloud issues and to decrease our understanding of situations.

MODES OF INQUIRY

The decade of the 1970s brought the greatest degree of sophistication to research in sport philosophy. Fraleigh (111, 118) and Osterhoudt (301, 303) provided an overview of research approaches that served as the first major indication of the diverse potential that existed for the study of sport. Cobb (64) and Metheny (273) urged the separation of fact from value but in the end adhered to modifications of the scientific method for the examination of philosophic questions.

The prolific writings of Zeigler (449, 450, 453) beginning in the 1950s provided the first major use of philosophic method to examine persistent problems in physical education. Known as the *implications approach*, this method frequently provided a good historical overview of problems. The first step in the implications approach was to select a philosophic system from either the parent discipline of philosophy or from educational philosophy to serve as the research content. For example, pragmatism or existentialism might be used. The structure and the basic principles of that system were then delineated, and the basic tenets were examined. In existentialism, for instance, there is a belief that man is responsible for directing his own destiny and is therefore responsible for his own acts and the consequences of those acts.

From the examination of this and other tenets from existentialism, parallel concepts and constructs would be developed for sport or physical education. Then data from such disciplines as psychology, sociology, and biology, as well as personal sport experiences, would be used to validate, disprove, or prove, that the parallels actually existed between the philosophic tenet and some aspect of sport. Essentially the implications approach results in a scientific analysis of a base philosophy with implications, applications, and transitions made to explain a particular aspect of sport.

The initial efforts of Ellfeldt and Metheny (84) to establish a theory of meaning represents the first major attempt at *theory-building*. The formalizing and explanation of this method was accomplished by Fraleigh (118). Like the implications approach, theory-building uses a source philosophy, e.g., pragmatism or idealism, which is described or explained at the outset. The source philosophy can also be a specific philosophic theory such as Dewey's theory of art. The vocabulary and definitions to be used in the theory are then developed. "As a method of research, theory-building attempts to isolate a particular kind of phenomenon" (118), such as the meaning of movement or sport as an aesthetic experience. The source philosophy is then related to the phenomenon of interest in sport, and a theory about some aspect of sport is formulated in an attempt to explain the sport phenomenon. However, simple comparison and saying that something is true is not sufficient evidence to develop a theory about some aspect of sport. Verification is necessary. Fraleigh (118) identifies four means of verifying the theory:

1. Examine the logical relations of the terms in the theory.
2. Validate the terms in the theory in accordance with the structure of the source philosophy.
3. Examine the consistency of the theory with data from other sources.

4. Determine the power of the theory to explain all instances with the area of particular interest in sport.

Fraleigh also delineated the method of *structural analysis,* which is similar to the implications approach. In addition, he outlined the verification needed for accurate implications to occur. First, there should be empirical and scientific evidence for the implications that are drawn between the philosophic system and the elements of sport to which the implications are directed. Secondly, there should be what he calls "deductive consistency" between the antecedents in the source philosophy and the implications or consequences in sport.

In addition to Fraleigh, Osterhoudt (301, 303) has been the most visible and organized in the development of research methods in the philosophy of sport. Using Pearson's (319) "Inquiry into Inquiry" as a guide, he developed the research taxonomy outlined in Table 3–3.

Depending on the desired information, all of these analyses start with known facts and valid philosophic theories or tenets. Use of deductive and inductive reasoning to make connections between the known con-

Table 3–3. A Taxonomy for Research in the Philosophy of Sport

I. CONSTRUCT ANALYSIS
   A. The analysis of one or more constructs for their implications for a discipline.
   B. The analysis of several constructs, noting the similarities and differences among them.
   The products of construct analysis are the implications of the thought of major philosophic figures for physical education and sport.

II. SYSTEM ANALYSIS
   A. The analysis of one or more systems for implications for a discipline or issue.
   B. The analysis or predominant and systematic philosophic views concerning physical education and sport among an identified group of persons.
   C. The analysis of an exhortation to formulate a coherent personal philosophy of physical education and sport.
   The products of a system analysis are the implications of major philosophic systems for physical education and sport.

III. CONCEPT ANALYSIS
   A. The analysis of a single concept in several systems or constructs.
   B. The analysis of a single concept in one system or construct.
   C. The analysis of several concepts in one system or construct.
   D. The analysis of several concepts in several systems or constructs.
   E. The analysis of the historical change in a concept through a period, a construct, or system, or several constructs or systems.
   F. The analysis of the predominant philosophic views concerning issues in physical education and sport among selected individuals, groups of persons, or institutions.
   G. The analysis of concept construction.
   The products of concept analysis are related to the metaphysical, ethical, epistemic, aesthetic, social, and political status of sport and physical education.

From Osterhoudt, R.G.: A taxonomy for research concerning the philosophy of physical education and sport. Quest, *20*:89, 1973.

ceptions in philosophy and a particular aspect of sport is a common technique. In all analyses, careful attention is given to defining terms and striving for consistency in the use of terms.

In a *construct analysis*, we may be concerned, for example, with looking at the philosophy of John Dewey (a pragmatist) and drawing implications for the conduct of coaches in sport. If Dewey believes that correct teaching methodology is more a matter of "what works" than some absolute kinds of behaviors, we may logically translate this to have appropriate implications for coaching. If, however, Dewey's concept of teaching is based on a noncompetitive model or if his idea of sport is weekend fishing while we view coaching as competitive and sport as an intense preparation such as in varsity athletics, the philosophy of Dewey may not be applicable. There must be a certainty that the source philosophy and the applications we make from it are logical, consistent, and use the same terminology. Construct analysis, however, would go beyond just one aspect of a particular philosophy and includes ". . . the *total position* built by a philosopher or theorist." (319:7) Attempts to apply *all* of Plato or *all* of Aristotle to sport have generally not been undertaken, as this involves many complex and interlocking questions and concepts that have limited relevance for the study of sport. Zeigler's work (451), particularly with Dewey and pragmatism, has most closely achieved the method of construct analysis. Osterhoudt's work (302) with the ideas of the philosopher Hegel also has been fairly comprehensive as a construct analysis.

System analysis has been used by writers in physical education for a number of years. The earliest writing was superficial, however, and often reflected a lack of depth of understanding in the source philosophy. Writers in "foundations" areas often would state: "If you were a pragmatist, this is how you would teach, this is how you would do curriculum, this is how you apply measurement and evaluation." Later writings by sport philosophers have reflected greater understanding of the source philosophy and less propensity to make gross generalizations that sound like: "This is what Zen tells the coach."

Concept analysis, which Pearson tells us is ". . . an idea contained within a construct, system, discipline or theory" (319:7), is a narrower approach to understanding some aspect of sport from a philosophic perspective. With concept analysis it is more possible to look at specific issues, ethical concerns, matters relating to meaning, or concerns with artistic possibilities because we can look at *parts* of existentialism or *some* of the writings of Plato to conduct the inquiry related to sport.

The most recent method to be used by sport philosophers is phenomenology. "The phenomenologist accepts, as subject matter of his inquiry, all data of experience. Colors and sound are data; so are impressions of distance and duration; so are feelings of attraction and repulsion; so are yearnings and fears, ecstasies and disillusionments . . ." (94:51) One of the most common criticisms raised against the analytic methods that comprise the system, concept, or conceptual analyses is that the "lived-experience" of sport gets lost in attempts to objectify it. As Kleinman (206:3) has argued:

> The pursuit of objectivity, which has reduced subject to object and experience to a series of categories, treated as operating independently of each other, cannot hope to account for a subject's . . . behavior.

While the various analytic methods used in philosophy and in science can explain what sport is about, that is, what is the nature of sport, what are its potentials, and what should it be like, these methods cannot explain the *significance* of the sport experience. These data related to subjectivity are what the methods of phenomenology attempt to address. "Significant moments in movement activity come from our experiencing them. These are the moments which provide the basis for the worth of activity and which constitute the motivating and driving force which causes us to return time and again seeking new, yet old engagements." (206:11)

Kretchmar states that "sport seems to be a complex phenomenon. No *one* factor captures the whole significance of this experience." (214:1) Similarly, the whole significance of the "lived" sport experience cannot be captured by either analysis alone or phenomenology alone. Two types of phenomenology have been used by sport philosophers. The first has its roots in the method of phenomenologist Edmund Husserl and attempts to identify the *essence* of the sport experience that may be common to many or all participants. Harper (153:4–5) indicates that this kind of description will yield some absolute truths about the essence of an experience. For example, if we were to examine the experience of running, the factors that are true or essential for everyone who runs might be: movement from place to place, increased respiration rate, increased heart rate, perspiration, and so on. It would then be possible to say as a result of this examination of running, via a phenomenological method, that the essence of running (running is) is as follows and then list a series of absolutes. This kind of analysis tries to get at the common core of experience by describing the main factors and ignoring aspects that are contingent on or not directly related to the essence of the experience. Stone (394:10–17) has begun this kind of analysis in an attempt to find answers to the question: "What is it that the individual finds, or appears to find, interesting or compelling or fulfilling about this act in which he/she involves him/herself?"

A second kind of phenomenology which is concerned more with description than analysis may be classified as *experiential description*. This method of phenomenology attempts to reveal the subjective nature of behavior. Instead of drawing universal truths or essences about the sport experience, this descriptive method seeks truth in individual and personal sport experiences. There is a belief that the individual or unique context in which an experience may occur is as important as the universal essence that may comprise the experience. In fact, this phenomenological method allows that context and essence may be inseparable. For example, a person may run a race, and the *essence* of running the race may be the same for everyone. However, if one person runs for, or experiences, aesthetic feelings, another meets achievement needs, others experience "second-wind," achieve a "steady-state," and yet others "flow," "hit-the-wall," experience "joy," "pain," or "reverie," then the context of the experience takes on a special significance for each participant. The context cannot be reduced to essences but may be the source of individual knowledge and meaning for the participant. An examination of many contexts may provide the phenomenologist with insights and understandings about the subjective nature of sport despite the lack of generalizability of results to all participants. As Kretchmar would advocate:

> But despite the multifarious, culturally relative, idiosyncratic, and verbally obscured nature of my experiences, the experiences do remain as a resource for a phenomenological analysis. Instead of attempting to force or reduce all of these activities into a single category, thereby producing an obscure and confused genius, . . . I would simply "look" at the experience . . . . If there is indeed common ground to all, so be it. If there are two, three, or ten different kinds of activity included in these experiences, again, so be it. I've learned more about my world, sport, and my activity in that world. (218:129–130)

DISCUSSION QUESTIONS

1. Select a sport in which you have a good background of experience and observation. In terms of this sport, what kinds of knowledges can be acquired from observation either as a participant-observer or as a spectator? What kinds of knowledges are gained from direct participation? Is it possible that some things are best known through observation or best known through experience? Explore these means of gaining knowledge.
2. Using the Royce and Phenix categories, try to identify what kinds of knowledge sport can provide the participant or the spectator in each category.
3. Examine a sport experience using the analytic phenomenological method where the experience is reduced to its "essences."
4. Examine a sport experience using the descriptive phenomenological method which accents the context of the experience.

DIRECTED READING

Kleinman, S.: Is sport experience? Quest, *19:* 93–96, 1973.
Osterhoudt, R.G.: A taxonomy for research concerning the philosophy of physical education and sport. Quest, *20:*87–91, 1973.
Pearson, K.: Some comments on philosophic inquiry into sport as a meaningful human experience. J. Philos. Sport, *1:*132–136, 1974.
Thomas, C.E.: Science and philosophy: peaceful co-existence. Quest, *20:*99–104, 1973.

Chapter 4

PLAY

In looking at the wide variety of physical pursuits that are called sport, we can identify two major features that distinguish sport from other movement forms and have strong drawing power. One feature is that sport has its basis in play and that, while sport may not always be considered play, it has the potential to be play. Sport also has many of the same values thought to be obtained as a result of "playing." The second dominant feature of sport is that it is agonistic or involves the contesting of an interest. In a paper by Kretchmar which examines the possibility of sport as play, the issue about whether it is possible to play and to compete simultaneously is raised:

> It is often thought that play and sport are highly, if not totally, incompatible. The competitive projects of sport stand at odds with the freedom, spontaneity and lack of seriousness thought to be characteristic of play. The extreme goal orientation of sport, including the drive to win, the quest for honor and the thirst for excellence, seems to beg a work not a play orientation. It is more correct to say, so the argument runs, that one *works* sport, not plays sport. (219:113)

Ellis (88:140) also maintains that "to the degree that competition is sustained by extrinsic pressures, it is not play." However, both Kretchmar and Ellis, among others, maintain both from an ontological perspective and in terms of the emphasis placed on either means or ends, it is possible for sport to be considered as play.

Kretchmar (219) argued that play is a spontaneus expression of self. Then after analyzing the basic relationships that exist in sport and play (freedom, intrinsicality, unique space and time elements, and opposition), he pointed out that these relationships are not found in work. There is, says Kretchmar, an intrinsically motivated bond between opponents in play but not in work. It is possible for a player in a sport setting to express himself *with* the opposition rather than having an opponent hinder what might be playful expression. Ellis maintains that it is possible to consider sport as play as long as certain conditions are met. In an athletic orientation where the emphasis is placed heavily on winning and the process of playing is not a sufficient enough reward, the play element may be lost.

A competition must not have a predictable outcome if it is to remain arousing for all. In situations where the outcome is of importance, the most playlike situation occurs when the probability of winning is equal for all competitors. When the process itself is not rewarding then the procedures must be sustained by the end product; feelings of power, trophies or money for the winners and social obligation to continue by the losers. These are extrinsic to the process. (88:140)

As will be noted later in the chapter, play is its own reward, that is, it is intrinsically motivating. When the process of sport remains intrinsic rather than relying on extrinsic rewards to justify participation, it can be considered play despite the competitive element. Much of our sport/play is highly structured and is often controlled by people outside the playing situation. In this sense, the players lose control of their own play process. To the degree that the player loses control, the play element is also diminished. A third factor to be considered is the emphasis on consequences. While the outcome of sport is important, if it becomes the overriding concern, play is lost. Strong emphasis on outcome rarely allows the individual to suspend the realities of the world; so when the goals are primary, the situation may be better described as work rather than play. For sport to be play, Ellis (88:125) maintains that the answer to the following questions must be "yes": Does the player (rather than outside managers) control the sport situation? Is the behavior of the player motivated by intrinsic rather than extrinsic rewards? Is it possible to *suspend* reality rather than *focus on* the reality of means and outcomes?

Play has been viewed as an activity by some writers and as an attitude, state of mind, or stance by others. For several decades play has been of interest to historians, psychologists, sociologists, anthropologists, and philosophers. Huizinga (174:1) has advanced the theory that the apparent play of many species of animals serves as evidence that play preceded culture and, therefore, serves as the basis for culture. Play is seen as generating many benefits and values for human existence. From a philosophic perspective Levy perhaps makes the most direct statement of the potential value of play:

Play, then, is necessary to affirm our lives. It is through experiencing play that we answer the puzzle of our existence. To be free, and therefore to know play (know oneself), means to realize simultaneously the supreme importance and utter significance of our existence. To play means to accept the paradox of pursuing what is at once essential and inconsequential. (240:1)

SPORT AND PLAY

Defining play in general terms has taken many directions. Sapora and Mitchell (360:114) have capsulated the most common definitions of play:

Lazarus—Play is an activity which is itself free, aimless, amusing, or diverting.

Dewey—Activities not consciously performed for the sake of any result beyond themselves.

Gulick—What we do because we want to do it.

Stern—Play is voluntary self-sufficient activity.

Patrick—Those human activities which are free and spontaneous and which are pursued for their own sake. Interest in them is self-sustaining and they are not continued under any internal or external compulsion.

Defining play as an activity has almost always reverted back to Huizinga's classic definition of play as:

> a voluntary activity or occupation executed within certain fixed limits of time and place, according to rules freely accepted but absolutely binding, having its aim in itself and accompanied by a feeling of tension, joy and the consciousness that it is different than ordinary life. (174:28)

In Chapter 1, this definition was analyzed as it related to the nature of sport. Play has also been defined by outlining its characteristics. Caillois' list (54:9–10) is perhaps best known:

1. Free: it is voluntarily entered into.
2. Separate: the temporal and spatial limits are defined and fixed in advance.
3. Uncertain: the results and course of action are not predetermined.
4. Economically unproductive: neither goods nor wealth is produced.
5. Regulated: it has conventions that suspend ordinary laws and establish new laws which alone count.
6. Fictive: it is accompanied by a make-believe, a free unreality.

Schmitz (368:27–32) adds to this list by suggesting that play and sport are comprised of elements of spontaneous celebration, imagination, pretense, creativity, contesting, tension, and dramatic resolution. "The essence of play comes into existence through the decision to play." (368:27) It is this decision to play or the voluntary aspect of play and sport that allows for a great deal of personal freedom. Essentially play is free and without predetermined standards of performance or excellence. Despite the competitive nature of sport, Schmitz maintains that sport is free and shares with play "certain of its features: the sense of immediacy, exhilaration, rule-directed behavior, and the indeterminacy of outcome." (368:30)

Completing the list of characteristics commonly viewed as play, Meier identifies two components of what he calls the "play stance":

> First, play is of necessity, a voluntary endeavor which cannot be forced, externally demanded, obligated, or imposed by necessity, coercion, or any form of duty. Indeed, during moments of play, man is fully his own master. Second, play is an autotelic activity. That is, play is an intrinsic, non-instrumental, self-contained enterprise . . . and is participated in for its own sake. Play is not a means to external ends or purposes; it does not further survival, sustenance, pragmatic or materialistic interests. It is process rather than product oriented . . . the reward is in the act. In summary, play is . . . an activity voluntarily undertaken for intrinsic purposes. Participation in any venture, including a game or sport . . . may therefore be legitimately termed a play occurrence. (264:25)

Given the characteristics delineated by Caillois, Schmitz, and Meier, it is possible to see the sport experience as play—sometimes, but not always.

CATEGORIZING PLAY

Another means of explaining play behavior has been to classify the various types of play. In Chapter 1, Caillois' four types of play/games were outlined as they related to the nature of sport. These included the agon, alea, mimicry, and ilinx. The greatest proportion of sport activities falls within Caillois' category of agon. It is here that the competitive element is primary and that the spirit of play is met in the rivalry of the opposition.

> The point of the game is for each player to have his superiority in a given area recognized. That is why the practice of the agon presupposes sustained attention, appropriate training, assiduous application, and the desire to win. It implies discipline and perseverance. It leaves the champion to his own devices, to evoke the best possible game of which he is capable, and it obliges him to play within the fixed limits, and according to the rules applied equally to all. . . . (54:15)

McIntosh (257) also developed a classification scheme for sport and athletic activities. His list, while similar to that of Caillois, stems from an analysis of the behaviors that are required to play. McIntosh identifies four categories as follows:

1. Better than Activities: These are sports or games closely approximating the agon where the primary focus is the demonstration of superiority. The social psychological need met in these kinds of activities is dominance.
2. Contact/Combative Activities. These activities are often aligned with the agonistic "better than" sports but meet the need to demonstrate power through sanctioned physical aggression.
3. Challenge Activities: Most of these activities are of a self-testing nature and are often in non-rivalry contests. These meet the need to demonstrate competence.
4. Expressive and Communicative Activities: These closely approximate the mimicry category of Caillois and tend to include children's games, dance, floor exercise, synchronized swimming, and diving rather than the more traditional agonistic competitions.

CLASSICAL THEORIES OF PLAY

The play of man, whether it is spontaneous or structured, understood, or irrational, has enough appeal for the player to become not only involved in but committed to the activity in one or all of its many categories. In addition to that appeal, a variety of theories indicate that there is a diversity of instrumental values which are not only educational but therapeutic, physical, socio-emotional, psychologic, and intellectual.

Ellis in *Why People Play* has outlined thirteen classical, recent, and modern theories of play.* The five classical theories—surplus energy, instinct, preparation, recapitulation, and relaxation—are outlined in Table 4–1.

Surplus Energy Theory

Two of the earliest attempts to explain play date back to 1875 and to the writings of Spencer (386) and Schiller (367). The theory that play is the result of surplus energy which is not necessary for basic survival was a commonly held view throughout the nineteenth century. "The animal works when some want is the motive for his activity, and play when the superabundance of energy forms this motive." (142:2) The theory basically suggests that man has a finite amount of energy, some of which is required to meet the daily needs of living. The surplus energy is then logically diverted into play activities.

This theory has also accounted for play as a means of "letting off steam" and allowing the organism to achieve a state of homeostatic balance. Sociologists have noted that, as the American society developed and technology increased, the amount of energy necessary for daily living decreased, permitting not only more time but also more energy for play. The concept of "recess" may well be grounded in the surplus energy theory, since children are let out of the classroom to play and use up some of the surplus energy that makes them restless or inattentive in the classroom. The instrumental value of play in this context takes on dualistic overtones when academic work is viewed as most important and physical activity in the form of play is seen as a means to foster optimal learning. Levy (240:80) notes that the use of gymnasiums and playgrounds has been advocated as a means of channeling so-called surplus energy into socially acceptable and useful behavior. From the standpoint that play is seen as "useful" in fostering optimal work and study behavior, it may be viewed as positive; yet within the context of this theory play is not necessarily valued as an end in itself, i.e., as being intrinsically valuable.

Criticisms of the surplus energy theory include:

1. Play is not necessarily aimless and random. Some play is highly goal-directed and structured.
2. People, especially children, will play even when fatigued, i.e., when they have little energy.
3. From a physiological standpoint, energy does not get "stored up." There is no known process whereby unexpended energy "backs up" and creates a pressure demanding release. (24:528)

---

*Levy's book *Play Behavior* (1978) also provides an excellent and in-depth analysis of play theories.

Table 4–1. Classical Theories of Play

NAME	PLAY IS CAUSED:	THIS EXPLANATION ASSUMES THAT:	IT CAN BE CRITICIZED BECAUSE:
Surplus Energy: I	by the existence of energy surplus to the needs of survival	1. energy is produced at a constant rate 2. if stored, storage is limited 3. excess must be expended 4. its expenditure is made on overt behavior which is by definition play	1. children play when fatigued or to the point of fatigue, so a surplus is not necessary for play 2. the process of evolution should have tailored the energy available to the energy required
Surplus Energy: II	by increased tendency to respond after a period of response deprivation	1. all response systems of the body have a tendency to respond 2. the response threshold is lowered by a period of disuse 3. after periods of disuse, eventually all available responses should reach a low enough threshold to be discharged either by some stimulus events or spontaneously	1. some responses available to the persons are never used
Instinct	by the inheritance of unlearned capacities to emit playful acts	1. the determinants of our behavior are inherited in the same way that we inherit the genetic code which determines our structure 2. some of those determinants cause play	1. it ignores the obvious capacity of the person to learn new responses that we classify as play 2. the facile naming of an instinct for each class of observed behavior is to do no more than to say, "because there is play, there must be a cause which we will call an Instinct"

Theory	Play is explained	Assumptions	Weaknesses
Preparation	by the efforts of the player to prepare for later life	1. play is emitted only by persons preparing for new ways of responding 2. the player is instinctively prepared for responses that will be critical later 3. the instincts governing this are inherited imperfectly and youth is the period during which these imperfectly inherited mechanisms are perfected	1. play occurs most frequently in animals that live in rapidly changing circumstances 2. it requires that the player inherit the capacity to predict which responses will be critical later. This requires the inheritance of information about the future 3. people do not stop playing as adults, when presumably they are acceptably prepared
Recapitulation	by the player recapitulating the history of the development of the species during its development	1. the critical behaviors occurring during the evolution of man are encoded for inheritance 2. a person emits some approximation to all these behaviors during his development 3. since these behaviors are currently irrelevant they are play 4. the stages in our evolution will be followed in the individual's development	1. there is no linear progression in our play development that seems to mirror the development of a species. At one point, late boyhood and adolescence, there may be similarity between sports and games and the components of hunting, chasing, fighting, etc., but before and after there seems little relation 2. it does not explain play activities dependent on our advanced technology
Relaxation	by the need for an individual to emit responses other than those used in work to allow recuperation	1. players work 2. play involves the emission of responses different from those of work 3. the emission of different responses eliminates the noxious byproducts of work	1. it does not explain the use in play of activities also used in work 2. it does not explain the play of children—unless they are clearly working some part of their day

From Ellis, M.J.: Why People Play. Englewood Cliffs, NJ, Prentice-Hall, Inc., 1973, pp. 46—47.

Instinct Theory

Thinking during the late nineteenth century also produced a theory that play is caused by an instinctive need to play. At a time when "instinct psychology" was a primary force in explaining the behavior of infants and young children who had no "instruction" in play, a belief developed that there was an instinctual need for play that was rooted in biology. The argument over whether behavior was genetically based or learned through socialization also began to rage among social scientists. The genetic code that universally produces such instinctual behavior as play and aggression has had twentieth century advocates in Robert Ardrey's *The Territorial Imperative* and Desmond Morris' *Naked Ape.*

Instinct theory can be criticized because it ignores the impact of the environment and socialization on learning *to* play and does not recognize the different kinds of play. Many of the beliefs about the instincts of man are based on observations of animals. Such observations tend to ignore human psychologic needs and symbolic expressions that influence behavior in humans but not in animals.

Preparation Theory

Stemming from his view that play behavior was instinctive, Karl Groos advocated a belief that play prepared people for later life. Play allows the animal to perfect his instinctive skills to the point that later, when they become critical, they will be effective. (142:40) The stage of "playful experimentation" that Groos advocated was a period in which the human learned to master the "senses of survival." Influenced by Darwin, Groos believed that "play was the opportunity for the child to perfect an 'insufficient hereditary endowment' in preparation for 'coming tasks of life'!" (240:81–82)

The theory of "playful experimentation" has served as a basis for ideas about the perceptual-motor functioning in the child. It has also served as the source for propaganda about the values of sport and physical education. Beliefs about "toughening people up" and teaching them what it takes (good or bad) to win, as well as many coping behaviors, have been advocated as instrumental values because sport, usually athletics, will prepare you for "real" life or later life. The "survival of the fittest" theory of play is alive and well in the late twentieth century where, on the one hand, it may be possible to teach positive values related to later life, but the activities related to the teaching of hostility, cheating, and winning also have been predominant themes.

The criticism of this position lies in the fact that adults do not stop their playing even when they are "prepared" for the lives they are living. As society changes, the survival techniques for a child born in 1983 may not be known for the life that child may live 25 years from then. It would be difficult to know what the child should do now in terms of play behavior to prepare. Ellis (88:42) claims that "adults who have played appropriately may be more successful in meeting the selective pressures of the environment, but to claim that play exists as preparation reverses the processes and is unacceptable."

Recapitulation Theory

Hall (145) believed that the child was an evolutionary link between present-day man and all the cultural stages that preceded him. The playful responses of the child incorporate the skills of past generations. It was a belief that "ontogeny recapitulates phylogeny." "Through play, man recapitulates the behavioral traits that made survival possible for his ancestors, that is, climbing, swinging, throwing, catching, running, yelling, and so forth." (240:85) The attraction of this theory, maintains Ellis (88:43), is that some thinkers of the early twentieth century tried to explain the popularity of some games based on ancestral predicates. "Those games depending on hard, straight throwing, rapid running, and accurate, hard-hitting with a club are prominent. They tell of the early pre-human ancestral activity when life was dependent on these activities." (144:63)

The major criticism for the belief that play behavior mirrors the behavioral evolution of the species is that, like the instinct theory, it ignores the impact of the environment on the developing child. The immediate environment and the role model provided by significant others serve to provide major themes for the play and games of children. Ellis further notes that "it is not possible to perceive an orderly and linear progression in play that recapitulates more than the occasional survival activities of prehistoric man." (88:44)

Relaxation Theory

Another early twentieth century theory was based on the writings of Patrick (317). Patrick saw the role of play as a period of recuperation from work. It was also believed that inactive rest was not sufficient for recuperation from work but that play and sports had restorative powers. The fact that work and modern technology placed great stress on cognitive functioning necessitated playful release. Play was contrasted with work in a fun versus serious, intrinsic versus extrinsic, and process versus product model. Many of the contemporary ideas that recreation is an important aspect of life because it allows for recuperation have their bases in early relaxation theory. Again, however, it must be noted that the important aspect of life is the work role and play is seen as allowing the person to recuperate so that work may again be resumed. Play has a value, but it is instrumental to accomplishing more important life tasks. Play in and of itself is still not viewed as valuable when viewed in the role of only providing relaxation so one can resume productive work behaviors.

The problem with the relaxation theory is that it does not explain why children, who do not have to work, engage in play. Levy (240:91) also points out that because not all play has a physical base the use of play to recuperate the mental stresses of work does not always hold true. Video games and board games are perhaps the most recent examples of "play" which are not physically based in terms of gross motor movement.

RECENT THEORIES OF PLAY

The second category of play theories that Ellis (88:78–79) delineates is found in Table 4–2. "These theories," he says, "are concerned with the actual form of the play behavior and attempt to link the antecedent and subsequent events via causes and effects." (88:49)

Generalization and Compensation Theories

Generalization and compensation are linked together as complementary theories. On the one hand, the generalization theory suggests that people find certain aspects of their work highly satisfying. They are then inclined to take these satisfying work behaviors and find further outlets for them in their leisure or play pursuits. This position suggests that both work and play experiences are selected on the basis of their abilities to satisfy needs. However, not all work or behaviors associated with work are pleasurable. Nor does work satisfy all psychic needs. The compensation theory suggests that play pursuits are selected, based on meeting needs that work does not satisfy. Both of these theories assume basic hedonistic motivations—to seek pleasure and to avoid pain.

The major problem with these two positions is that while they may provide insight into the behavior of adults who work, they do not explain the play behaviors of children. Also, people play even when their work is totally satisfying or totally unpleasant, making the generalization or compensation behaviors to play either unnecessary (work is enough) or inadequate (play could not be enough to meet needs).

Catharsis Theory

Much of the interest in both play and competition has been related either directly or indirectly to the expression of aggression. Views of catharsis generally had to do with the purging, or relief, of pent-up emotions, particularly hostility, frustration, and aggression. Socially sanctioned and harmless expressions of competitive behavior and the attendant hostilities have been sought by social scientists. Many prominent researchers including Menninger (268), Lorenz (247), and Ardrey (11) have advocated competitive games as an acceptable means of venting aggression and hostility. This theory found advocates in physical education and recreation who proclaimed sport and play to be a means to "work off" hostilities. Instead of smashing someone out of frustration, smashing a tennis ball or tackling someone was seen as best alleviating these disorganizing emotions.

Most data collected by social scientists, particularly Berkowitz (31), to test this hypothesis have not validated the catharsis belief. In fact, the nature of the competitive situation often leads to increased frustration and subsequent outright or displaced aggression. Berkowitz (31) indicates that aggression breeds aggression and rather than reducing frustration and hostility by substituting sport and play for "real life" situations, levels of aggression may increase as a result of participation, especially if the contest is viewed as important and the player loses.

Psychoanalytic Theory

Psychoanalytic theories have been concerned primarily with the play of children in nonsport activities and from a therapeutic standpoint. Levy indicates that within the psychoanalytic perspective, "play provides the opportunity to fulfill two major needs of man: (1) the need to be grown up and (2) the need to assume an active role." (240:100) In this theory the child is seen as being motivated by the "pleasure principle" and seeking gratification in play. "However, the psychoanalytic theory goes beyond the pleasure principle to explain the play of children that is related to real experiences that are not pleasant." (88:58)

Play is viewed as separate from reality, but from a therapeutic standpoint, play is a place for the "acting out" of real life situations. The acting out may involve role playing, role reversal, or the repeating of unpleasant "real life" experiences. Such "acting out" is then the basis for therapy as attempts are made to reduce seriousness, gain a perspective on real work or real life through play experiences, assimilate negative experiences, or purge negative feelings. "The child distinguishes play from reality by creating a world of his own, in which he can order and alter events in such a way as to derive only pleasure." (3:34)

General application of these theories is limited from the standpoint that many of the "play" situations have been contrived for emotionally disturbed people. While it may be that "mimicry" is "acted out" or fantasies among children and adults are "played out" in sport and play, the experiences are not necessarily the repeating or role playing of negative feelings. Psychoanalytic theory in its application to normal behavior is limited.

Table 4–2. Recent Theories of Play

NAME	PLAY IS CAUSED:	THIS EXPLANATION ASSUMES THAT:	IT CAN BE CRITICIZED BECAUSE:
Generalization	by the players using in their play experiences that have been rewarding at work	1. there are at least two separable categories of behavior 2. the players transfer to play or leisure, behaviors that are rewarded in another setting 3. to be useful we understand what rewards individuals at work	1. it seems to exclude play of preschool children 2. it assumes that at least some aspects of work are rewarding
Compensation	by players using their play to satisfy psychic needs not satisfied in or generated by the working behaviors	1. there are at least two separable categories of behavior 2. the player avoids in play or leisure behaviors that are unsatisfying in the work setting experiences that meet his psychic needs 3. to be useful we understand the mismatch of needs and satisfactions in the work setting (or vice versa)	1. it seems to exclude play of preschool children 2. it assumes that work is damaging or does not satisfy some needs
Catharsis	in part by the need to express disorganizing emotions in a harmless way by transferring them to socially sanctioned activity. This concept has been limited almost entirely to questions of aggression, and will be so here	1. frustration of an intention engenders hostility towards the frustrator 2. this frustration or hostility can be redirected to another activity 3. this hostility must be expressed to reduce psychic and physiological stress	1. it is a partial explanation for only the compensatory behavior engendered by hostility 2. the data show conclusively that sanctioning aggression increases it 3. the planning of activities to provide outlets for aggression constitutes its sanctioning

Psychoanalytic I	1. stimulating unpleasant experiences in another setting reduces the unpleasantness of their residual effects	in part by the players repeating in a playful form strongly unpleasant experiences, thereby reducing their seriousness and allowing their assimilation
Psychoanalytic II	1. achieving mastery, even in a simulating experience, allows the elimination of the products of unpleasant experience by passing similar experiences on to other beings or objects	in part by the player during play reversing his role as the passive recipient of strong unpleasant experience, and actively mastering another recipient in a similar way, thus purging the unpleasant effects	Both I and II ignore play that is not presumed to be motivated by the need to eliminate the products of strongly unpleasant experiences.
Developmental	1. play involves the intellect 2. as a result of play, the intellect increases in complexity 3. this process in the human can be separated into stages 4. children pass through these stages in order	by the way in which a child's mind develops. Thus play is caused by the growth of the child's intellect and is conditioned by it. Play occurs when the child can impose on reality his own conceptions and constraints	1. it doesn't account for play when and if the intellect ceases to develop
Learning	1. the child acts to increase the probability of pleasant events 2. the child acts to decrease the probability of unpleasant events 3. the environment is a complex of pleasant and unpleasant effects 4. the environment selects and energizes the play behaviors of its tenants	by the normal processes that produce learning	1. it doesn't account for behavior in situations where there are no apparent consequences. (However this theory would maintain that there are no such settings.) 2. it doesn't account for the original contributions to behaviors made by an individual's genetic inheritance

From Ellis, M.J.: Why People Play. Englewood Cliffs, NJ, Prentice-Hall, Inc., 1973, pp. 78–79.

Developmental Theory

Based on the thinking of Piaget,* developmental theory does not address itself to answering the question of why play occurs. Rather, it suggests that play takes place in the child's mind and then manifests itself in physical behavior. As the child's mind develops, then the play becomes more structured and complex. As comprehension of reality is mastered, the child interprets it and then uses past experience and cognitive abilities to impose constraints and to structure or restructure the environment. For Piaget, just as there are stages of cognitive development, there are also stages of play. The stage of play on a continuum from solitary to competitive has much to do with the existing level and complexity of cognitive functioning. Piaget (323:168) points out that games that have rules, i.e., structured "kid games" and sports, mark the decline of spontaneous and unstructured children's games and the transition to adult play which reflects the impact of socialization.

One of the major problems with Piaget's theory is the lack of research evidence provided by him or others to verify his linear concept of developmental play. Also, if play is so integrally linked to the development of the intellect, there is no explanation of why play continues to develop among children whose intellect ceases to develop "normally."

Learning Theory

This theory suggests that play, like many other behaviors, is learned as a result of experiences and through the interplay of positive and negative reinforcers. Based on the hedonistic principle of seeking pleasure/reward and avoiding pain/punishment, the learning of play is a function of the culture and significant others, with strong indications that operant conditioning is present. Sutton-Smith (403) noted from his research that the culture and the way in which children are reared has a great deal to do with *what* they learn to play and *how* they play. "In societies valuing achievement and performance, games of physical skills seemed to reflect this skill directly." (88:73)

There is, in this theory, some difficulty in establishing consistent cause-effect relationships between motive and play. Play frequently occurs with no apparent motive or positive-negative payoff. While the environment certainly impacts on the motive to play, it does not seem to explain "internal" drives.

MODERN THEORIES OF PLAY

Most play theories have stemmed from an attempt by social scientists to explain the cause of play from the standpoint of behavior. In this respect

---

*Levy provides a full exposition and critique of Piaget's developmental theory of play in *Play Behavior,* pp. 109–123.

play has been seen as having not only a cause but a use, or instrumental function. The concept of play has frequently included children's play, low organized games, and mimicry but has dealt only indirectly with games of the agon. The classical theories—surplus energy, instinct, preparation, recapitulation, and relaxation—have in common the idea that there must be a biologic reason for man to emit playful responses. These biologic reasons can be seen as having instrumental value in that they allowed the species to return to a homeostatic balance or produced benefits that would allow the individual to return to optimal work behaviors. In this respect play was not viewed as being an end in itself or having a value of its own.

The second wave of theories—generalization, compensation, catharsis, psychoanalytic, development, and learning—also promoted organismic equilibrium. The psychologic health and maintenance of the species was a primary focus. But in this regard it was the cognitive development or psychologic well being that was the main concern. No direct interest was given to the player's physical well-being nor was the person viewed as an embodied, or holistic, entity. The two most contemporary theories of play (outlined in Table 4–3) begin to view the player in a much more holistic way and also lay the groundwork for play as an existential possibility, that is, as intrinsically valuable in and of itself.

Play as Arousal-Seeking

Play as arousal and as knowledge seeking have a basis in problem solving. The motivation to play is found in the need to elevate interest or to provide stimulation. The seeking of knowledge (epistemic behavior) lies at the root of this need for arousal.

> There is a simple equivalence between the motives for stimulus-seeking and knowledge-seeking behavior. Stimulus-seeking behavior means more than merely seeking exposure to any stimuli. The stimuli must have arousal potential. They must be to some extent novel or not congruent with established systems. They must contain information in the sense that their perception reduces uncertainty. Knowledge-seeking or epistemic behavior has the same characteristic in that it results in the reduction of conflicts, mismatches, and uncertainties. They share the same motive. (88:99)

Zuckerman's (455) work in sensation seeking and on the various techniques of measuring risk-taking behavior seems to indicate that while man does seek security he also has varying degrees of the need and propensity to take chances. People seek a variety of situations where arousal will occur. Drugs, gambling, alcohol, sex, and rock music represent recent and common social phenomena where such arousal may occur. However, within the context of sport, a wide range of risk activities can be found. The decade of the 1970s saw an increasing number of people participating in risk-taking/thrill-seeking sports owing to the availability of instruction and the inexpensiveness of equipment. Many sports occurring in the

Table 4–3. Modern Theories of Play

NAME	PLAY IS CAUSED:	THIS EXPLANATION ASSUMES THAT:	IT CAN BE CRITICIZED BECAUSE:
Play as Arousal-Seeking	*by the need to generate interactions with the environment or self that elevate arousal (level of interest or stimulation) towards the optimal for the individual*	1. there is a need for optimal arousal 2. change in arousal towards optimal is pleasant 3. the organism learns the behaviors that result in that feeling and vice versa 4. stimuli vary in their capacity to arouse 5. stimuli that arouse are those involving novelty, complexity, and/or dissonance, i.e., information 6. the organism will be forced to emit changing behavior and maintain engagement with arousing stimuli	1. it is very general but it handles questions of work and play equally well. In fact it questions the validity of separating work from play
Competence/Effectance	*by a need to produce effects in the environment. Such effects demonstrate competence and result in feelings of effectance*	1. demonstration of competence leads to feelings of effectance 2. effectance is pleasant 3. effectance increases the probability of tests of competence	1. for the organism to constantly test whether it can still competently produce an effect seems to require uncertainty as to the outcome. Uncertainty or information seem to be the very attributes of stimuli that are arousing 2. it can be argued that competence/effectance behavior is a kind of arousal-seeking

From Ellis, M.J.: Why People Play. Englewood Cliffs, NJ, Prentice-Hall, Inc., 1973, p. 111.

natural outdoors and in noncompetitive settings provide the opportunity for arousal but are also tempered by the need to self-test and to control the risks.

Houston (172) suggests that there is an adventurousness in this play which provides a sense of thrill in experiencing danger, exhilaration, confidence, control and self-satisfaction. Voluntarily "the stress seeker struggles under heavy baggage and against severe hardships to 'stretch his capacity' to do what few others can do—his capacity to bear the fear of falling and endure thirst, sunburn, frostbite, blisters, fatigue." (172) He accepts these hardships as part of the contest. Speaking especially of the lonely, risky sports, Alvarez contends that "intentional, planned risk demands all the qualities most valuable in life: intelligence, skill, intuition, subtlety, control." (8:205) Man, in short, seeks arousal and risks as a testing ground, as a means of finding himself in the world, of extracting the figure from the ground, of being unique among the commonplace.

While this is one of the first theories that has concerned itself with sport, as well as with other kinds of play, it is not without its criticism. As a relatively new theoretical position in the context of many new kinds of sports activities, there are few field research data to validate the theory or its claims. As "a type of activity that includes information search, skill training, and repetitive practice, motivated by lack of information" (70:6) the possibility for a holistic view of play exists. It remains, however, for "real life" field data to validate or invalidate the theory.

Competence Theory

Linked with the need for arousal and the knowledge-seeking aspects of the arousal theory is the purpose that play behavior serves to demonstrate a capacity to control and master the environment. White (442) called this the competence/effectance motivation. He argued that exploration and epistemic behavior were not sufficient explanations for behavior which continued after the novelty of a new situation wore off. Mastery became a motive for the player to engage in and continue play behavior. Mastery then led to feelings of effectiveness, and these feelings, in turn, led to more attempts to find situations to master.

Ellis suggests that this theory seems to be an extension of arousal theory in its development of a familiarity with the environment through play. The need to produce effects, the effectance motive, and to subsequently master the environment is, in a sense, a kind of arousal or stimulus seeking. The results gained by producing effects and mastering the environment are "preserved by learning. . . . they build up an increased competence in dealing with the environment. The child's play can thus be viewed as serious business, though to him it is merely something that is interesting and fun to do." (442:321)

EXISTENTIAL FUNCTIONS

There is, and has been, a difficulty in explaining play behavior, and in general the propensity that people have to play in all stages of life and in all cultures. The resistance play seems to have in being analyzed as an intrinsic phenomenon led to a variety of instrumental justifications. These accounts and explanations of play had the effect of turning attention away from play itself to some external values it may have had. People play. They like to play and seek out play settings. It seems play was viewed as being important but could not be adequately explained. Could anything that brought so much pleasure be anything but frivolous. In North American and Western European societies where the work ethic, grounded in strong religious beliefs, was prevalent the adage "play is the work of the devil" became a part of North American ethical make-up.

Theories attempted to show that there was biologic and psychologic value in play, that relaxation and escape are essential, and that education and character formation are by-products of play. However, to view play *only* in terms of observed effects without focusing on its intrinsic and holistic nature not only limits an understanding of play but returns it to a status as "second-class" activity to be engaged in only when more important activities in life are completed.

In the *Power of Play*, Caplan and Caplan (59:xii–xvii) delineate the functions of child's play as follows:

"Playtime aids growth. . . .
Play is a voluntary activity. . . .
Play offers a child freedom of action. . . .
Play provides an imaginary world a child can master. . . .
Play has elements of adventure in it. . . .
Play provides a base for language building. . . .
Play has unique power for building interpersonal relations. . . .
Play offers opportunities for mastery of the physical self. . . .
Play furthers interest and concentration. . . .
Play is the way children investigate the material world. . . .
Play is a way of learning adult roles. . . .
Play refines a child's judgment. . . ."

From the standpoint of what the potential and power of play can be as an end in itself, it is the ultimate form of education. "Go out and play" should not be viewed as a banishment of the child but as a circumstance that treats the person as an embodied being. If play had been more like work and less like fun, perhaps the need to justify play would be unnecessary.

INTRINSIC CHARACTERISTICS

"Intrinsic motivation is the drive to become involved in an activity originating from within the person or the activity: the reward is generated by the transaction itself." (240:6)

In his advocation that play was the basis for culture, Huizinga laid the groundwork for later notions that play was a meaningful form of human behavior. Novak in his "Preface" to *The Joy of Sports* states:

> The basic reality of all human life is play, games, sport; these are the realities for which the basic metaphors for all that is important in the rest of life are drawn. Work, politics, history are the illusory, misleading, false world. Being, beauty, truth, excellence, transcendence—these words, grown in the soil of play, wither in the sand of work. Art, prayer, worship, love, civilization, these thrive in the field of play. (298:xii)

One of the features commonly alluded to in many writings about play is that it is intrinsically motivated or enjoyed for its own sake. Harris (155) attempts to build a case for the belief that play and enjoyment are interchangeable concepts stemming from the fact that play is intrinsically motivated. She identifies three motivational mechanisms underlying the intrinsic nature of play:

1. Importance of the human need to perceive an optimal level of novelty or complexity in the environment.
2. The second set of perceptions which may result in intrinsic motivation is the perception of personal competence. . . . it is important for a person to receive information about his competence.
3. The third group of perceptions related to intrinsic motivation is a total, all-encompassing focusing of attention. (155:61)

From a more philosophic perspective, attentional focus can be likened to the transcending nature of play. This may be seen as the Zen-like coming into "oneness" of man and activity. As Csikszentmihalyi (69) points out, one knows what actions to take without having to think about them (pre-reflective behavior). And, there is a total devotion to the activity without concern for self or the appropriateness of doing the activity in the first place.

Harris goes on to suggest that enjoyment "appears to be a major motivation to play." (155:71) She identifies the characteristics of enjoyment (search for novelty, total focusing, and finding the midpoint between the psychologic states of boredom and anxiety) as foundational to the intrinsic motive to play. The key to intrinsically motivated play is that the player has control over the situation and that the process, i.e., the playing, is the central feature of the behavior. Deveraux (75) studied two types of play, informal sandlot baseball games and more structured Little League play. In the informal setting, play was its own reward and adult intervention was minimal or nonexistent. The games were played, scores were kept, and from this standpoint it was an agonistic sport situation. In the Little League setting, Deveraux found that the many extrinsic rewards and outside intervention tended to diminish the play element. Underwood (424) argues in the same vein as Deveraux that we have managed to take the fun out of the game and to destroy the values of play by placing great emphasis on the goals of games rather than on the process of playing them. Kleiber summarizes this potential for the destruction of the play element:

> In such activities the consequences—typically approval and disapproval; sometimes money and other rewards—are provided by coaches and parents rather than by teammates and the game itself. The intensely dire seriousness of the activity precludes the potential of gradual assimilation. Although it may be great fun to win there is usually little enjoyment in the process and losing can be devastating under these circumstances. The awareness of adult evaluation and other extrinsic consequences changes the context of the activity to the extent that it is hard to call it play in any sense. (202:70)

PLAY AS A STANCE

When play is considered as an activity, it is easy to begin to attach objective and concrete characteristics to it. For example, we say it is voluntary, that it is bounded by spatial and temporal limits, and so on. The difficulty with viewing play *only* as an activity is that it does not explain the reasons that people choose either to play or not to play; nor does it explain why some activities which might be considered serious or worklike, including sports and athletics, are "played" by many participants. Considering these things, then, it seems that play is also an attitude, a psychologic state, or what sport philosophers have called "a stance."

The pursuit of play and the play "stance" have not been openly advocated or promoted in North America or any society which became technologically oriented, grounded in the work ethic, or based on economic competition and the capitalistic motive. "Because play, in effect, produces nothing, neither material goods nor works of service, it is often described as basically empty, sterile, misspent or lost time, rather than as time well-applied." (264:27) Meier (264) points out that play has often produced feelings of guilt in a society that so highly values work. He notes that people even work at their leisure and seem incapable of getting away from the clock and time constraints to "do nothing at all." Many avoid leisure and play and choose to spend their would-be free time doing work either in the form of second jobs or overtime. There is a comfort and social justification in work that does not seem to be found in play. Consequently, the attitude toward play as a sanctioned activity has been negative.

Social scientists and philosophers nevertheless have agreed over the decades that play has a tremendous drawing power, and people play even if they often feel guilty about it or make excuses to play. Aside from the external attitude toward play as frivolous and irrelevant, the play attitude, or stance, itself seems to stand in clear opposition to such negative social attitudes about not playing.

Roochnik introduces the concept of play stance when he says:

> Play is a mode of being. It is a way of comforting oneself, a way of approaching and extending oneself to the world . . . it can become a stance. A stance is

> very much like an attitude. An attitude is a way of thinking about things; it is a mental disposition and orientation toward the world. . . . But a stance is more deeply rooted than an attitude; it permeates all aspects of human being. . . . A stance goes beyond the intellect to the body and the spirit, and becomes a mode of being-toward-the-world. (349:39)

Roochnik, like others with an existential orientation, indicates that play is a holistic involvement of the player, a full commitment of body and spirit. As a result of this total involvement, play takes on meaning for the player, and the play itself carries its own meaning and its own reward.

Whatever is gained in play by way of meaning or reward has more to do with the "stance toward a given activity than with the behavioral details of the activity itself." (179:90) Hyland gives the example of two people exhibiting the same kind of behavior—hitting a tennis ball across the net to another person. While this may be the same behavior, only one of them may be "playing," since intention and temperaments determine the attitude, or stance, that the players are taking. (179:90)

> When we play, we seem to have a certain orientation toward those with whom we play, toward our play equipment if there be such, toward time, space, indeed toward the world, which is distinctive. It is . . . different from our mode of comportment when we consider ourselves not to be playing. This orientation, mode of comportment, or way of being, I call the stance of play. (179:88)

The stance that one takes toward an activity is important. For if you choose to play, then it is possible to gain from play the meanings and rewards that are available to the player. It is possible that the interplay between what play can potentially become and what it actually becomes will take place. Without the play stance, those meanings and rewards remain potential but never become actualized. Hyland suggests that there are two characteristics of the play stance that create the mechanism for people to achieve, or actualize, the potentials that play holds for them. Play calls upon the player to "have a heightened sense of openness" toward the surroundings. The second characteristic is what he calls responsiveness or being able to react to the situation as it is revealed as a result of the awareness or openness.

Since play necessitates the total commitment of the player, Hyland suggests that the appeal of play may be in this totality of involvement in an activity:

> ". . . play is one of those phenomena where we again and again achieve that sense of totality, that intimation of completeness . . . grounded in the very stance of play itself which I have called responsive openness." (179:90)

The play stance allows man to become, in a way, available to himself for understanding the world, others, and himself. It heightens awareness and requires that the player respond. Such awareness and response can then serve as the basis for a variety of knowledges. In later chapters the potential meanings and knowledges available as result of our sport and play involvements will be examined.

DISCUSSION QUESTIONS

1. What elements of play are found to some degree in any movement form?
2. What factors intervene in a play situation to turn it into work?
3. What advantages and disadvantages are available to the participant in unstructured play situations compared to the more structured activities of some sports and athletics?
4. How have the *instrumental* values attributed to play led people away from the real essence of play as a value in and of itself?
5. What are the values of play (regardless of the movement form in which it occurs) that should be promoted in programs of physical education and *educational* sport/athletics?

DIRECTED READING

Caillois, R.: The classification of games. *In* Sport and the Body, 2nd ed., edited by E.W. Gerber and W.J. Morgan. Philadelphia, Lea & Febiger, 1979, pp. 30–37.

Huizinga, J.: The nature of play. *In* Sport and the Body, 2nd ed., edited by E.W. Gerber and W.J. Morgan. Philadelphia, Lea & Febiger, 1979, pp. 18–21.

Meier, K.: An affair of flutes: an appreciation of play. Journal of the Philos. Sport, 7:24–45, 1980.

Schmitz, K.L.: Sport and play: suspension of the ordinary. *In* Sport and the Body, 2nd ed., edited by E.W. Gerber and W.J. Morgan. Philadelphia, Lea & Febiger, 1979, pp. 22–29.

Underwood, J.: Taking the fun out of the game. Sports Illus., *43*:86–90, 1975.

Chapter 5

COMPETITION

SPORT AS CONTEST

Like play behavior, competitive endeavors have drawn social scientists and philosophers to examine the causes and effects of man's agonistic nature. Sociologists and anthropologists have been consistent in their insistence that games reflect the society in which those games are played. For example, capitalism is built on the competitive model, and the children in a capitalistic society are socialized at an early age to learn to compete. Many long-standing discussions have focused on the role of winning or the emphasis on winning which has created ethical problems. These ethical concerns will be treated in Chapter 10. Before it is possible to study competitive behavior objectively and intelligently, examine ethical problems, or study the potential of sport as a means of coming to know self and others, an understanding of the *concept* of competition is necessary.

Common Elements

All of the play, or games, that we identify as sport have a contest element. The agon, i.e., contest, is a key element in games, although it is possible for the contest to end before the game is over. For example, when one team is being "blown out" in the late stages of a game, the uncertainty of the game is gone and the winner is certain. Yet the game will continue until the allotted number of minutes are played and the gun goes off, ending the game. It is not an uncommon sight to see home team fans get up and leave early during a game when the outcome has been determined. They head for the parking lots or postgame refreshment spots, leaving only the "die-hards," or "true fans" to watch the end of the game.

The element of unpredictability or an even chance to win or be successful is essential to all kinds of competition. Otherwise, it would not classify as contest, agon, or competition. Winning, or success, is the object of the game. In this sense, winning per se is not a moral question. No one sets out in competition to lose, or else they are not truly playing according to the letter or the spirit of the game. The extreme emphasis placed on winning from the standpoint that such an emphasis may create a perversion of means often creates a moral problem. It is possible to be an "underdog," but upsets are common in sport and the outcome at the outset of the contest is in doubt. Playing to win at the beginning is an objective of all sport, although the objective for a given player may change once the *contest* is over but while the *game* is still going on. For example, if it becomes obvious during the course of a game that you are being so outplayed that it is becoming a rout, the outcome has been determined. You are going to lose. At this point, another kind of competitive objective may help retain the contest element. You may say to yourself or a coach may say, "OK, we can't win, but let's try to get five more points or one more touchdown." So, a contest within the contest is created. A winning player may set up the same kind of contest when a defense, for example, decides to try to keep the other team from scoring to preserve a shutout.

Another essential element in competition is the "other" in some form. There is someone or something to go against or against which to measure success. Depending on the sport or the kind of competition, the "other" can be a person, self, a river or mountain, time, previous performances, or a score or person in absentia such as in telegraphic meets. A related commonality is that an outcome is evident. There will be a winner(s) or loser(s), or you will either succeed or fail in the objectives that were established for the contest.

Cultural Bases

The social context is a major consideration in the study of competition. While there are some biologically based theories about the roots of competitive behavior, these have, like many of the play theories, failed to explain the competitive phenomenon as it is found in late twentieth century sport endeavors. Desmond Morris, in the *The Naked Ape*, for example, claimed that man, like other animals, was instinctively competitive and needed activities such as sport. Sport alleviated the competitive "urge" in a positive way and aided in the alleviation of warlike tendencies. The survival instinct and the need to get and maintain territory have also been cited as being competitively based.* No human data have been gathered to support these hypotheses, and war continues in most cultures despite the presence or absence of organized sport.

---

*In particular the writings of Robert Ardrey, *The Territorial Imperative* and Evelyn Brown, "An Ethological Theory of Play," *JOHPER* are directed at the concepts of sport and territory.

For the most part, the culture determines what is worthy of competing for and who should compete. In North American society sport is one activity that is viewed as worthy. In other societies sports and games are viewed as either similarly important, less important, or as fitting into a more casual framework. Believing for a long time that sports taught leadership, discipline, hard work, and the ability to be "cool under fire," all of which were necessary to survive the competition of "real life," we have considered sport a valued means of teaching competitive behavior. Children are taught to compete, but they are also socialized into knowing that it is important to win and that winners are somehow better off than losers. People whom we call "significant others" (parents, siblings, peers, teachers, coaches), evaluate winning and losing and teach us the importance of winning and the good or value of efforts directed at success. Playing a good game can be valued as an end in itself and rewarded, or it can be valued and rewarded only if it includes a winning effort.

Children are socialized at an early age into knowing what things are important to strive for: good grades, a good education, a good job, power, status, prestige, a lot of friends, a nice house. They are then taught that in this society, one has to "go out and get it." The means for having the "good life" is by learning to compete successfully and coming out ahead is an important part of living. This is an economic orientation to competition and one which is a strong agent in North American and capitalistic societies. Yet other forms of competition are fostered which promote challenge and self-testing.

William Sadler and Charles Reich have each identified a scheme that places competition within a social context and also identifies more than one kind of competitive orientation. Although Reich has been criticized as being somewhat romantic in his conclusions, his 1970 work, *The Greening of America* provides both an historical and cultural overview of competitive interests in America. He identified three types of consciousness that have and do exist in this country and their implications for competition. Consciousness I (Con I) is based on power, self-interest and competition that seeks dominance and personal goals. It was the consciousness of such nineteenth century capitalists as Ford, Vanderbilt, and Rockefeller.

> . . . There was another side to the American character—the harsh side of self-interest, competitiveness, suspicion of others. Each individual would go it alone, refusing to trust his neighbors, seeing another man's advantage as his loss, seeing the world as a rat race with no rewards to losers. Underlying this assumption that human nature is fundamentally bad, and that a struggle against his fellow man is man's natural condition. 'There'll always be aggression and a struggle for power, and there'll always be a pecking order,' says Consciousness I. (337:23–24)

This outlook, based on strong economic interests, has led to a view of competition as the "survival of the fittest." It still prevails in direct forms of competition which will be discussed later in the chapter and is reflected in the belief in the "self-made man" and the view that sport provides upward social mobility.

Central to Consciousness II is the acceptance of the superiority of institutions, organizations, and society. The individual is seen as not able to "get anywhere" alone but must learn to "fit in." He becomes an "organization man," "a team player."

> In Consciousness II, that created by the Corporate State, the same outlook prevails: Behind a facade of optimism, Con II has a profoundly pessimistic view of man. It sees man in Hobbesian terms; human beings are by nature aggressive, competitive, power-seeking; uncivilized man is a jungle beast. (337:70)

Power and the end product characterize Con I and Con II. The rewards are extrinsic, and so, for the most part, is the motivation to compete. In Con II, the submission of individual identity to the institution is a key distinction from the focus on "going it alone." Contemporary athletics with its emphasis on the coach as authority and the giving up of individuality to be a "team player" reflects much of the Con II corporate orientation to competition. Again, direct competition is the primary mode.

As a reaction to direct, product-oriented competition, Consciousness III has liberation as its fundamental premise.

> It (Con III) comes into being the moment the individual frees himself from the automatic acceptance of the imperatives of society. Consciousness III does not believe in the agonistic or competitive doctrine of life. Competition, within the limits of a sport like tennis or swimming, is accepted for its own pleasure. (337:225)

The Con III attitude more closely resembles what has been identified earlier in Chapter 4 as play. Competition is seen as indirect and self-testing in nature. Con III very much represented the counterculture that spawned the civil rights and war activists and the "hippies" of the late 1960s and 1970s. Individual sports and outdoor pursuits gained their greatest popularity during this period as an alternative to organized, structured, and corporate kinds of direct competition. Perhaps the motto of the New Games Foundation best expresses the competitive orientation of Con III: "Play Hard, Play Fair, Nobody Hurt."

Sadler (353:180) advocated a contextual approach to the concept of competition in which he identified "four cultural constellations to be characterized by their conceptions of normative activity." The most primitive context is what he called the "being" culture and may be found among Native Americans of the United States and Canada and Spanish Americans in the Southwestern United States. It is a "let it be" perspective where the status quo and the family are predominant. "The forces of nature are seen to dominate the lived space of this world; consequently, the proper role for man is submission to them. In this perspective, man exists *under* nature. The people of a "being" culture tend to be fatalistic.

Man is dominated by forces of the past and by his environment. There is no reason to change one's situation. Whatever will be, will be." (353:181) The self is not seen as an independent unit which strives to get ahead or toward any kind of personal self-expression. As Sadler notes:

> . . . within this type of value orientation competition does not have a logical place. When we find evidence of competition, it may be regarded as a deviant form of activity; or, it could signify a source of tension and confusion. (353:182)

The second cultural orientation is the "becoming" culture. In many respects, this orientation resembles Con III and has its basis in the humanistic theory of such writers as Rogers and Maslow. Personal life is measured in terms of self-development and the present is more important than the past—the "now generation." Sadler sees man's proper relationship to nature in this cultural orientation as one of cooperation. (353:183) In fact, cooperation characterizes much of this cultural context.

> Cooperation is emphasized rather than submission and obedience. The goal of life is conceived as the fullest realization of human and natural powers. Individuals and cities should strive for the achievement of excellence. . . . Insofar as competition is consonant with a becoming value or orientation, it is viewed as an activity *with* rather than against. . . . The aim of competitive activity here is to interact so that participants actualize their fullest potentialities; it is not meant to deprive someone else of something valuable. (353:184)

The third cultural constellation is the "doing" culture which characterizes much of North American and capitalistic societies. There is a future orientation and man is seen to be in control of nature. Productive, useful, hard work is seen as inherently valuable. "This type of culture is production oriented and utilitarian. Its heroes are the producers. The view of self in this perspective is characteristically individualistic." (353:185) It is a context of "movers and shakers" and "life in the fast lane" with extrinsic success as the ultimate objective. A doer values winning and the refusal to quit. This is in contrast to the becoming culture where competition serves as a means to self-actualization.

> In the doing orientation, one competes to accomplish results which may be extrinsic to the actual competitive process. Competitiveness then may be encouraged in the most unlikely areas, such as learning, working, and attracting friends. It is possible that all meaningful doing is eventually interpreted in competitive terms. (353:185)

The fourth orientation is the "having" culture, often found in modern industrial states. The orientation shifts from production to consumption. The immediate future is the focus for acquiring things. It reflects the attitudes of a materialistic, throwaway society that has mastered nature but felt no responsibility for restoring the resources it has used. Sadler remarks that "there is a marked increased self-centeredness and relativeness. It's good if you like it. Living well is interpreted in terms of feeling good." (353:186) Within the "having" orientation, "one competes against another to have something valuable in greater measure than he already has." (353:187) A spectator orientation develops related to competition in that sport is seen as a form of entertainment. The professionalization and commercialization of athletics is a prevailing view.

> Even the competitor sees his activity as oriented toward more having, for wealth is the primary means toward greater consumption. Competitors and the competitive activities become commodities to be consumed with a lifestyle that is oriented towards having more and more. (353:187)

Both Sadler's and Reich's categories can be seen theoretically as pure types, but in actuality there is a mixing of attitudes in practice. The main point here is to realize that when addressing the concept of competition, it does not exist as a single concept that means the same thing to everyone. Nor does a given society exhibit just one attitude about what competition is or what it should be.

TYPES OF COMPETITION

The commonalities of competition—an "other," uncertainty of outcome, contest, and the inevitability of success or failure—are not sufficient to define competition. There is considerable dialogue in the philosophy of sport literature related to the definition of sport which was outlined in Chapter 1 but which is also related to the definition of competition. Two major types of competition will be examined here: direct forms and indirect forms.

Keating (191:265) in looking at the distinction between sport and athletics goes back to the etymological base of the words *sport* and *athletics*. The root of the word *sport* means literally "to carry away from work" and has evolved into a contemporary definition that includes such descriptions as "diversion," "recreation," and "pastime." (191:265) This conception of sport strongly suggests the play element is a factor and that the process and the struggle may be major characteristics in the competitive process. On the other hand, the word athlete derived from Greek roots means "to contend for a prize." (191:265) The contest and the end product become the primary concerns. This distinction between the process and product of competition will serve here as a major distinction between the two types of competition.

Agon and Rivalry

Perhaps the most common conception in sport and athletics is its agonistic nature. From the Greek *agonia*, a contest or a struggle for victory in games, Morford explains the original concept of the Greek agon:

> The agon embodied the concepts of struggle, toil, hardship, risk, and the nike. This latter was the qualitative victory embodied by the triumph of the

cause, of the struggle within oneself and against one's competitors, even unto death. To merely overcome was not enough, for one must internally deserve the victory if there was to be a true agon. (288:84)

He laments the loss of the true agon ideal in sport when he says:

For victory which used to be the winning of, or the struggle for, the prize has now become merely the prize or the reward, an external outcome which becomes the new symbol of success. (288:85)

The focus on the prize or on the winning of the contest as the primary concern of competition has led to a definition by Keating that reflects a strong economic orientation:

Competition is an attempt, according to agreed-upon rules, to get or keep any valuable thing either to the exclusion of others or in greater measure than others. (192:159)

This is the orientation of the "doing" and "having" culture constellations that Sadler has outlined. It is also in keeping with what is generally considered athletics.

A number of features characterize the contemporary agon. It is a "better than" motivation, a desire to seek dominance or to establish superiority over a direct rival. There is an effort to control or master the opponent and there is no feeling of responsibility for the loser. Luschen (253) has characterized this kind of rivalry as zero-sum competition. One individual emerges as a winner and one, or more, individual(s) emerge as losers, i.e., $+1$ (winner) $+ -1$ (loser) $= 0$. Thus, the outcome from competition results in a value of zero. The standards set for winning (one best score, one best time) reward the fastest, the strongest, and so on. There are always as many or more losers than winners. Ten thousand people may run a marathon, but there will be one overall winner and 9999 losers, except for those who win in their divisions; yet what is sought in the rivalry is that 1 in 10,000 chance to win and to be superior.

The rival and the rewards are external to the individuals. This is not the kind of competition where playing well is a sufficient enough reward if the outcome of the contest does not also include the prize of winning. Personal excellence is secondary to externally established standards of excellence and achievement. Superiority in the contest is more important than performance. In many respects involvement in this kind of competition meets the psychologic need that many people have to demonstrate dominance and to see themselves as competent. Rivalry meets achievement needs in very quantifiable and objective terms. While superiority may be the most desired outcome, it is possible that both team and individual excellence also may be achieved, and often both personal performance is outstanding and the outcome of winning is achieved.

Three conditions are generally prerequisite to the achievement of superiority and/or excellence. First of all, skill is important. It is unrealistic to make winning the primary goal in the contest if one has poor skills.

Competition calls for uncertainty of outcome and "playing too far over one's head," and expecting to win can only lead to disappointment. So, sufficient enough skill to have a chance at winning is necessary. Keating (191:265) maintains that the kind of competitive activity "which has for its end victory in the contest . . . is characterized by a spirit of dedication, sacrifice, and intensity." The work ethic prevails in preparation for the contest and factors such as discipline, perseverance, and courage are highly regarded in the preparation for victory.

This work ethic rests on a second condition—attitude. Much of the distinction between the contemporary agon and more "playlike" sporting pursuits rests on how the player views the opponent and how important the outcome is perceived. Cooperation is at a minimum in this kind of competition, and the opponent is seen as a barrier to be controlled and overcome. Often perceived as the enemy that home fans boo during the introduction, there is little thought of the opponent as the "loyal opposition."

The third condition of the agon reflects the Con II idea of subjugating individuality to the needs of the team in order to be successful. This orientation also includes abdicating a variety of personal preferences and the decision-making process to authority figures. The motto "There is no 'I' in the word *team*" perhaps sums up this condition. Team success is paramount, and self-determination and individual concerns become secondary to this objective.

Vince Lombardi's dictum, "Winning is not the most important thing; it is the only thing," sums up the focus of the contemporary agon. However, as Lipsyte points out:

> Lombardi was always celebrated in the extreme. His saintly dedication to winning was hailed as a beacon on the path toward America's renewal. His diabolical dedication to winning was denounced as an example of creeping fascism. (243:52)

The controversy about the value of placing such an emphasis on winning will be examined in a later chapter. Valentine's (425:61) perspective, "Lombardi on Winning," suggests that the *desire* to win seems central to our sport experience.

> Lombardi considered his dictum to be literally true as regards the ethics and attitudes of the sporting establishment and of the society in which we live. I will then argue that Lombardi did not consider his dictum to be literally true if taken as a principle to which athletes ought to adhere. . . . Losing was a sign that athletes . . . had not realized their full potential.
> Implicit in Lombardi's views on winning, there is a theory of self-realization . . . . and this theory is to be preferred over the Greek view that the true importance of winning lies in having most closely embodied an objective idea of perfection. [Or,] . . . in having most closely achieved the perfection of which humans are capable in a given contest. (425:61)

The role of winning in sport and athletics takes on many dimensions, but in the contemporary agon it is the primary focus of the participant.

The Arete

In contrast to the focus on the end product in the agon, the arete has as its central focus the process of competition—the struggle, playing well. The underlying Grantland Rice adage, "It isn't that you win or lose but how you play the game," partially explains this orientation. In addition, there is the belief that concentration on playing well will lead to the best effort possible. And, the best effort is all an individual can ask of self or others. It is hoped that the best effort would also lead to triumph. There is a desire to win because success is seen as the object of any competitive contest. However, the "good game" is also an integral part of this competitive orientation. The pursuit of excellence rather than of superiority is the more dominant theme. "Know thyself" and prove thyself are the competitive attitudes which reflect Sadler's context of the "becoming" culture and Reich's Consciousness III.

Morford explained that the agon originally included these ideas but that it was lost when man was enslaved by need to seek only the prize.

> The earliest attempts to explain agon takes us back to the Homeric Greeks where sport . . . emerged from a life ethic that embodied man's struggle within life for personal excellence. Throughout life, man sought the opportunity for victory through the struggle provided by the contest or battle to achieve arete—the Greeks' conscious ideal of perfection. (288:84)

Weiss (437) argues that one of the major attractions that sport has is that it demonstrates the optimal excellence of the body and allows the participant to pursue it.

> Excellence excites and awes. It pleases and it challenges . . . a superb performance interests us even more because it reveals to us the magnitude of what then can be done. Illustrating perfection, it gives us a measure for whatever else we do. (437:3)

The challenge of excellence, the desire to become what one is capable of becoming, forms the source of the need to compete. If, in the process, superiority is established, then the true and ancient agon is accomplished. If, however, the contest is lost but the challenge is met, then there is honor and nobility in having genuinely and authentically competed. The "good fight" is seen as bearing its own rewards. In the last decade the desire to achieve personal excellence rather than to go *against* another person has manifest itself in the popularity of outdoor pursuits—mountain climbing, skiing, whitewater canoeing, hang gliding. "Winning" in these endeavors takes on a strong consciousness of the struggle. As mountain climber Sir Edmund Hillary succinctly states:

Whom have we conquered? None but ourselves. Have we won a kingdom? No—and yes. We have achieved the ultimate satisfaction, fulfilled a destiny. To struggle and to understand, never this last without the other. (172:58)

This kind of competition retains much of the spirit of play in that the player maintains control of the goals which are set, as well as the process of attaining those goals. Cooperation is often part of the striving and the rewards are intrinsic—to meet the challenge rather than to conquer. Perhaps the best descriptor for this kind of competition is "encounter." Rather than having the characteristics of a rivalry, it is an encounter of self-testing, a display of ability, and the optimal development of self. In many respects it is a means of expressing what one is *becoming*.

The challenge takes many forms. For some it remains very agonistic, and the other team or person becomes the opponent against which the self is tested. There is a hope that the opponent will play well so that an accurate assessment of just how good we are can be made. A "worthy opponent" is sought out. For others the challenge is in mastering, at least for the moment, some feature of the natural environment—mountains, rivers, air currents. And yet for others, the challenge is what is known as the "historical self." To improve over a previous performance or to maintain what has previously been accomplished becomes the goal of the competition; or, it can be against a norm as a kind of social comparison. For example, most people my age can accomplish X at a given time or at a given speed; therefore the competition becomes meeting the challenge by matching the norm. In all of these instances competence rather than dominance is the prevailing competitive attitude.

The end results of any competitive efforts have become a very important consideration in this culture while the means to achieve positive results are often viewed as irrelevant or pragmatic. As Morford notes:

Without the opportunity of an internal satisfaction or joy in experiencing the triumph of his struggle, he turns instead to seek the benefits of the outcome of his performance. Thus, he seeks to be rewarded for his performance rather than being honored for it. . . . (288:86)

The belief in the beauty of the struggle and the honor in competition coming from "doing it well" and "doing it right" does not preclude the desire for superiority. It does, however, view the means as being just as important as the ends. Only the scores get recorded, but what the score *stands for* is important in this competitive orientation even if only the players know what the score means in terms of achieving or failing to achieve personal excellence. It is difficult in this society to accept "good effort" as the primary gratification for having "taken part" in the contest. Failure is not generally accepted as a positive effort. Yet the achievement of self-realization as a result of the "good fight" in meeting a challenge is intrinsically rewarding for many. Bannister suggests that even for the spectator, a good effort is worth watching. "Failure is as exciting to watch

as success, providing the effort is absolutely genuine and complete."
(22:212) Since there are many more losers than winners, there must be
more to sport than establishing superiority. George Leonard (238) argues
that we can start looking for the "larger potentialities that already exist
in the realm of sports and games. . . . How we play the game may turn
out to be more important than we imagine, for it signifies nothing less
than our way of being in the world."

DISCUSSION QUESTIONS

1. As a sport participant, how do you define success?
2. What best describes your approach to competition: demonstration
   of competence, mastery of technique, dominance over opponent,
   self-testing, meeting challenges? How do the games you play allow
   you to compete to meet these needs? Can you see yourself changing
   your focus now or in the future?
3. Which is more important to you if you had to choose only one of
   the following: to win and play poorly or to lose and play well? Defend
   your position.
4. What is a contest and when can it be considered over? When does
   competition or a contest lose the play element? Is it ever acceptable
   to quit or prematurely stop a game if the contest element is missing?
   Defend your answer.

DIRECTED READING

Broekhoff, J.: Sport and ethics in the context of culture. *In* The Philosophy of Sport, edited
   by R.G. Osterhoudt. Springfield, IL, Charles C Thomas, 1973, pp. 219–229.
Morford, W.R.: Is sport the struggle or the triumph? *Quest, 19*:83–86, 1973.
Sadler, W.: A contextual approach to an understanding of competition. *In* The Philosophy
   of Sport, edited by R.G. Osterhoudt. Springfield, IL, Charles C Thomas, 1973, pp.
   176–191.

"What is play indeed if not an activity of which man is the first origin, for which man himself sets the rules, and which has no consequences except according to rules posited. . . . He himself sets the values and the rules for his acts. . . . His goal, which he aims at through sports and games, is to attain himself as a certain being, precisely the being, which is in question to his being."

Sartre

"Competition, as a striving or questioning together towards excellence, insofar as it most adequately fulfills its possibilities, does so as a mode of friendship."

Hyland

Chapter 6

SPORT AND MEANING

Over the past quarter century, most philosophic discussions of meaning, except those found in existential literature or in the writings of such thinkers as Michael Polanyi, have centered on the study of symbols. Recently linguistic analysis, which focuses on the "meanings" of words or concepts, has gained steadily in popularity. While this kind of analysis has provided considerable insight into the nature of the world and the symbols, i.e., words, which we use to communicate about the world, linguistic analysis has on the other hand moved away from the concept of meaning as a source of personal knowledge. Polanyi and Prosch (327:22–46) in *Meaning* have argued that personal knowledge and personal meaning have practical, subjective, and tacit dimensions that are unique to an individual and cannot always be reduced analytically or symbolically. It is this dimension, Polanyi and those with more existential leanings argue, which provides the basis for the meaning of life and for the way in which we respond to our world.

The search for meaning can be seen in two distinct ways. First, in subtle and overt ways, man seeks to identify his own uniqueness, a self-hood, and to measure himself against himself and against the world in the hope of coming to know "who I am." Since we are not only conscious beings but conscious of our consciousness, we think about what we do and what we have done. We think about and question what we think. This leads to action and to the choices we eventually make relative to our participation in the world. Man takes action in ways that are consistent with "who" he thinks he is. The quest for self-understanding or for achieving the meanings that help explain "who I am" requires a certain degree of introspection. Moustakas (291:4) maintains that "to experience the deepest truth concerning oneself and others, it is necessary to retreat within, to engage in a process of open inquiry and meditation that will reveal oneself to oneself. Dialogue with oneself precedes clarity of awareness, a sense of direction, and action."

A second search for meaning involves finding a purpose to life or death, answering the question: "why?" Man seeks out what the existentialists call "projects" or activities in which he tries to find both purpose and justification for his life. "Why am I here?" and "What for?" pose very complex questions for every individual. And, while the struggle for subsistence is the primary preoccupation of man and often an arduous task, the search for meaning is perhaps even more difficult. Yet, we know the search for meaning has touched all human endeavor and has spawned many of man's most beautiful creations: his myths, his religions, his works of art, his philosophic systems, his scientific theories, and his games. Many living creatures seek both pleasure and power, but man alone cares about or seeks meaning. The "projects" of man, including sport, give some indication that we have not only recognized but organized our quests for self-understanding and purpose.

The presence of sport permeates our technologic and analytic society in its spectatorial and participatory forms to the extent that few are left untouched either directly or indirectly by the existence of sport. Despite its pervasiveness, dualistic attitudes persist which place the value of sport participation a distant second to work, intellectual activities, and artistic accomplishment. Despite these societal tendencies to ignore or discount sport or related physical activities, people persist in seeking out participation. Philosophers and social scientists have pointed to varying degrees of alienation Americans face in their attempts to find and attach meaning to their lives. They also note with increasing degrees of certainty that people seek out participation in activities that are meaningful, self-enhancing, and positive complements to their daily and routine activities. This *voluntary* search has led people to religion, a variety of art forms, and to sport. The key notion here is that the involvement is voluntary. The voluntary dimension of sport has been delineated in earlier chapters. By nature people do not engage in activities voluntarily if those activities are meaningless or if there is no return on the time and energy invested. From these premises, then, let us examine the potential of sport to provide meaning in response to the human needs for self-understanding and a sense of purpose in life.

POTENTIAL FOR SELF-UNDERSTANDING

Sartre and Sadler argue strongly that the existential nature of sport and play allows the participant to search for purpose and self-understanding. Sartre maintains:

> What is play indeed if not an activity of which man is the first origin, for which man himself sets the rules, and which has no consequences except according to rules posited. . . . He himself sets the values and the rules for his acts. . . . It might appear that when man is playing, bent on discovering himself as free in his every action, he certainly could not be concerned with *possessing* a being in the world. His goal, which he aims at through sports and games, is to attain himself as a certain being, precisely the being, which is in question to his being. (365:86)

Man looks for himself, for his nature, for clarity about who he is in many endeavors. Sartre has suggested sport as one of those endeavors. The nonutilitarian aspect of sport and play which allows them to be set apart from the everyday world offers a unique opportunity for meaning. The nonutilitarian nature of sport not only sets sport apart from the "real world" but gives an indication that it is of little use. Metheny (271) has called sport "absurd," pointless, useless, of little value as a functional activity. She has compared sport to the task of Sisyphus from the standpoint that after all the effort exerted in the sport endeavor, nothing is lasting or ever really accomplished. "Nothing has been changed by the performer's attempt. . . ." (271:59) Like Sisyphus whom the Greek gods condemned to roll a rock up a hill in full knowledge that it would always roll back down to the valley, sport leaves no trace of mortal efforts.

> The athlete's javelin flies through space and falls to the ground; the distance is measured, and the javelin is brought back to the starting point or stored away unchanged. . . . His ball is tossed into a bottomless basket, only to fall to the ground. (271:59)

Metheny goes on to elaborate on the absurd and useless character of sport. However, she claims it is *because* of its absurd nature that sport can be a meaningful experience.

Man is removed from external factors when he enters sport, and sport becomes a world of his own creation within the rules. He leaves behind pressures of school, work, family, finances, and interpersonal relationships which often impact on actions in other life projects. But in sport, if there is sufficient enough commitment to the sport task, albeit a futile and absurd one, these pressures are set aside to focus on the accomplishment of the goals of sport. Man is free to become what he is capable of becoming which may not be possible in everyday life.

> Within the complex conditions of life, we are seldom, if ever, free to focus all our attention on one well-defined task and bring all our energies to bear on one whole-hearted attempt to perform the task effectively. . . . In contrast the rules of sport provide us with a man-made world in which this freedom is fully guaranteed. These rules eliminate the demands of necessity by defining an unnecessary task. (271:63)

Metheny further indicates that in sport the materials, approach, evaluation, and methods are established by the rules of the game and that our motives are free from social or political ramifications existing outside the sport setting. (271:63) The structure of sport and the freedom to act within its framework, combined with the fact that the involvement is voluntary to begin with, provide the performer with a unique opportunity to achieve some understanding about himself. Sadler notes that these boundaries of sport provide a fundamental source of personal meaning and allow for an encounter with others. "As people play together we have a paradigm of interpersonal freedom creating its own meaning and its own forms of communication." (357:116)

Harper (147) also argues that sport allows a freedom to act authentically because, despite the involvement of others, the individual is alone in sport. It is possible for the player to be alone with himself to transcend the expectations of others, to identify his own subjectivity and uniqueness, and to meet himself in authentic encounter.

> Whether he is hurling a javelin, soaring off a ski-jump, performing a double back flip off a diving board or screaming toward earth in a free fall skydive, man is alone. He is beyond the world of public determinations; of official identities; of functions; of self-deceptions and everydayness. And in the solitary state of oneness, man can meet himself. (147:127)

As the philosopher Martin Buber (46) has noted, there is nothing in man (the I) nor in the world (the Thou) except the relation between them. Sport, like a book, or a script, or a score, or a canvas is inert until defined or interpreted by the acts of man. Sport is not limited; man brings his own limitations and structures sport in his own image. Sport is, essentially, amoral and does not generate values; man brings his values to sport and makes it as worthy as he is. The player is largely responsible for defining his own sport world and for accepting the rule structure. With skill, desire, and intensity the athlete fashions a separate, "absurd," sport world, a world created in his own image with the potential of revealing that image to him.

> Sooner or later in sport, the serious striver after excellence will meet a situation that is almost too big for him to master. Such situations occur in ordinary life and can often be dodged. We can play hide and seek with reality, avoiding facing the truth about ourselves but in sport we can't do this. . . . As a result, sport leads to the most remarkable self-discovery, of limitations as well as abilities. The discovery is partly physical . . . but mainly the discovery is mental. In time we learn how far from being self-sufficient we are, we realize the value of cooperation and assistance from others. But unless we start out alone, we never learn the answers others can best answer and those we must answer for ourselves. (271:66)

POTENTIAL FOR ACHIEVING A SENSE OF PURPOSE

Existential philosophy, literature, and psychoanalysis are replete with the concepts and problems of commitment, choice, and freedom. The literature is instructive when we consider sport as a separate, nonutilitarian stage for the inevitable human searches for commitment to a cause, fulfillment of potential, a sense of purpose, or even the sense of immortality and acceptance by others. While it may be possible to explain these motives in the context of some hierarchy of psychologic needs, it, nonetheless, remains that sport can be one medium for the acting out or the playing out of man's search for self, for the fulfillment of goals, or for a purpose.

One of the modern prophets for goal setting was playwright Henrik Ibsen, and his dramas frequently attempted to show us how essential it is to have a life project that gives meaning to life. In the life of the literary character Peer Gynt we find no purpose, no search for a purpose, no life project, no submission to higher tasks, no ideals, no striving for self-improvement, no altruistic endeavor. At every moment of his experience, Peer Gynt is disposable, available for any adventure promising momentary fun, ready to give it up for another whim; yet toward the end of his life he regrets his aimlessness and realizes that a life without a guiding project is meaningless: "Beautiful earth," he cries out, "forgive me for having trodden thee all to no purpose." (Act 5, Sc. x) Ibsen's writings are representative of many writers and artists who depict man's search for meaning and his subsequent successes and failures.

Similarly, Sartre (362) has emphasized the moral necessity for man to commit himself to something by choosing a project and assuming the responsibilities for choices, successes, and failures. Ortega preaches about the ethical ideal of men who live under the bondage of self-imposed tasks and imperatives, who devote their lives to higher ideals, and he insists that this dedication can give meaning to their existence. Fraleigh speaks to this in relationship to sport when he says:

> . . . And it is in entering such a world sport that man may know himself symbolically as a powerful agent in being since, in that world, he literally uses externally controlling necessities . . . to serve his own purposes. (117:114)

What is life about? Why am I here? What purposes do I serve? How do I fit in? If this is success, is that all there is? People seek out reasons and a purpose for the things they do. They wonder if there is a "grand design" in life; if there is a God or some Being greater than themselves controlling their destiny. When we don't understand our world or if we seem to have no control over what happens to us, a sense of helplessness often takes over. People generally like to feel that they are in control of their lives and that their life efforts "make a difference." As a result, they often seek out projects that allow them purposeful activity and allow them to see themselves as being in control of their own destiny. Thoreau has remarked that "the majority of men lead lives of quiet desperation." An individual strives to leave a legacy, or as Bannister asks: "Breathes there a man with a soul so dead that he has lost the urge to impress on the world some indelible mark of his personality." (21:67)

Sport provides an opportunity for an individual not only to "leave his mark," at least for the moment, but also to assume control over his own destiny. Despite the absurdity of sport, players enter into it often believing their performance is unique and will somehow be remembered. There are any number of risks in sport: physical death, injury, social defeat, loss of status, or damaged ego; yet by placing oneself in a risk situation where the individual must assume complete responsibility for the outcome, it may be possible to overcome the social conditions that lead to feelings of purposelessness, helplessness, and alienation. As Alvarez has pointed out, "intentional and planned risk demands all the qualities most valuable in life: intelligence, skill, intuition, subtlety, and control." (8:205) Sport provides a place where man can dominate fear and passion, a place where adventure and purpose and commitment can remove a sense of "dread" that may otherwise prevail.

> However trivial the context—who, finally, cares about a piece of rock, or a big wave, or a racing record that will be broken next year?—the element of risk can turn a weekend hobby into a small-scale model for living, a life within a life. (8:205)

The moments of glory, of recognition, of taking part, however fleeting they may be, provide us with the knowledge that we can achieve, we are in control, we are worthy, we are of some "use" in the world.

STAGES OF PARTICIPATION

Sport participation involves a number of different stages: intent, preparation, involvement, commitment, and resolution. Each of these aspects carries a significance of its own. While it is possible to examine each of these stages separately in terms of structure or any meanings the performer may gain, the sport experience involves all five stages. Sometimes the stages occur in a linear fashion and sometimes one or more may overlap.

Intent

"Man engages in sport and athletics in neither a casual nor accidental manner." (204:54) Before sport can become more than just a casual activity among many daily activities, it must somehow be set apart as a goal-directed task. Intent is one factor that separates sport from play; serious sport, or athletics, from pleasure-based sport; and, winning as a goal from playing well as a goal. Much of the subsequent preparation, commitment, and evaluation stems from what is intended by the performer at the outset of the event. A 5-kilometer "fun run" with beer and pretzels and good company as the reward requires considerably different training and evaluation than a mile run as a member of a varsity team. While it is possible that the commitment may be the same, the intent of the performer may set the foundation for the kinds of meanings derived from the sport experience.

The primary focus of any intent related to sport has to do with what the performer plans to accomplish and whether these plans are fulfilled. This plan involves the setting of some goal, the assessment and realization of one's abilities, and establishing a judgment, or evaluation, within the context of these abilities. This does not preclude some alteration of intent once the actual participation begins but would suggest that achievement should be grounded in actual capabilities rather than being a haphazard or pragmatic experience.

Philosopher Martin Heidegger's concept of "authenticity" is instructive in explaining both intent and achievement. The concept of authenticity, which is "the excellence of being what one is, fulfillment of one's particular functions, true self-realization in the sense of self-disclosure and self-fulfillment" (158), is a seeking after the unique "mineness" of a self. Heidegger's concept of authenticity, seemingly, is not intended to have a connotation of ethical rightness or wrongness. Authenticity is stated as nothing more than one of the possible ways of "being-in-the world." (158:43, 129)

An extrapolation of Heideggerian authenticity in the development of an authentic intent prior to and in the achievement of intent during the sport experience is merely to know what one is capable of doing and becoming. One does not become lost in the anonymity or demands of others but remains free from unessential involvements, free to assess capabilities and realize what is accidental and inauthentic. The authentic intent, like the authentic existence, is a positive realization of what I truly am and the positive movement of what I am toward what I am capable of being, a movement toward a unique self and a unique experience in a sport situation.

Buber (46) and Moustakas (290) argue that the highest relationship of man to man or man to experience is direct and spontaneous and that a prior plan, or aim, negates this spontaneity. However, the desire or intent to win does not negate the spontaneity nor the ability to become involved in the experience; nor does the recognition of one's abilities inhibit full and direct participation. Winning, however, is an authentic intent and an authentic achievement only when there is a legitimate and an even chance to win. The upset is authentic only when the underdog truly has the capabilities to win.

Intent does not imply a play-by-play game plan but is the determination of the *most feasible* approach within the individual's limitations. The fineness or grossness of this determination is again dependent on the individual's ability and willingness to assess himself. Complex intents may be found in such experiences as skydiving, sailing, and mountain climbing in which both environmental and personal conditions must be met. The novice will select an easier route or more ideal conditions. Other sports may be relatively simple in intent. Recreational skiing, for example, requires little more than choice of slope and determination of speed, given the snow conditions and one's personal skiing abilities. For some skiers, just getting down the hill in "standard fear position" without injury is an intent appropriate to their skill and training. For others, not only getting down but how fast and/or how well they look while doing it are important criteria in the intent.

Preparation

The preparation, or "getting ready," stage often requires commitment but is, essentially, the willingness to prepare optimally for the sport encounter through training the body, development of the required technical expertise, and sacrifice of time and other pursuits to get ready to play. While this stage occurs prior to the actual sporting event, it is the essential foundation for the sport encounter to carry its full meaning. Although it is possible to engage in sport with minimal preparation, it may be difficult to experience one's full potential in an ill-prepared state. Decathlon winner Bruce Jenner's T-shirt slogan, "Feet Don't Fail Me Now," reflects the desire of the athlete to succeed in the goals set and to trust in the preparation that was undertaken to achieve those goals.

The preparation stage has a primary focus on the body as an object, as another piece of equipment that must be honed and readied for the event. It is also the place where strategy is devised, a "game plan" or "race plan" is established, technique is perfected, and where mental preparations are most evident. In the sense that the player wants to be a worthy opponent, he/she also wants to encounter a worthy opponent. The preparation stage is intended to optimize the possibility of the well-played game.

Buber (46) has described the world as a series of relational events. "All actual life is encounter." Every relationship, or encounter, in life, whether it is between man and man, man and nature, or man and object, is either what he called an I-It relationship or an I-Thou relationship. The I-It relationship is typically a subject-object relationship. The I uses things for some specific reason—to compare, to manipulate, to attain some goal. The "Its" are means to an end. In the realm of It, it is possible to analyze, break down, or see the characteristics of things. It is possible to take a detached view of the self in which the body becomes an object in much the same way as do other "things." In the preparation stage for sport, the I-It relationship perhaps best characterizes the attitude of the I toward the body and toward sport.

There is a significance for many who come to know the body as object, as an It, during the preparation stage in sport. It provides a perspective of what my body is, what it can do, and how well it can do it. LeMay points out that training requires a decision not only that one will train but how well they will train for sport.

> Training ensues only after the decision has been reached that one will, indeed, train. . . . Decision, of course, implies choice and the elimination or exclusion of other possibilities. Training is a chosen activity. . . . He may choose how well he is to play. (235:59)

The choice to train with dedication or with half-heartedness has the potential to reveal to the individual insight not only about his/her approach to sport but about self-directedness, perseverance, and dedication. The statement "I can't, I'm in training" can be spoken with joy or sadness.

Giving up "happy hours" or "junk food" or going to the beach in lieu of training is a conscious decision. So is a combination of junk food, happy hour, and training. Both choices make statements about who we are.

> Consider the notion that training is planned activity. With sport as its focus, its cause, and ultimate rationale, training can still be appropriate or inappropriate, effective or ineffective. . . . It is certainly possible to play a sport badly but still be playing it. By the same token, it is possible to train badly for a particular sport, but still be training for that sport. (235:59)

There is a certain pride or sense of accomplishment that many individuals take in a well-trained body. The body has the potential to become an object of beauty. Since training is, essentially, specialized exercise with a focus, physical fitness is a natural by-product. Some *only* prepare for their sport, practice their "moves," concentrate on the skills and the physical requirements of their position. For these individuals, the "feeling good," "looking good," aspect of training is secondary or not even sought. Yet for others, being "in shape" to play also means being fit and a sense of pride in a well-conditioned and aesthetic body. Again, the choice can potentially take on a significance for the individual.

Another focus in the preparation stage is equipment. Ill-fitting equipment is not only uncomfortable but often an inhibitor to all-out effort and performance in the sport. Perhaps those most fanatical about equipment are those involved in high risk sports such as mountain climbing, auto racing, or downhill skiing. Equipment is checked and re-checked for any flaw until it can be trusted without having to think about it. In any sport the acquaintance with and mastery of the equipment to be used is a critical aspect of the sport experience. Weiss argues that equipment must, in a sense, become part of the body:

> But no matter what the sport, the equipment it requires offers a challenge to man, demanding that he not only accept his body but unite himself with items beyond it. . . . Equipment is initially not within the individual's control. It is instead an integral part of the objective world. There it must first be met and isolated, and then be adjusted to, before it can be made into a continuation of a man. (437:74)

We get the "feel" of our equipment; we tune it, check it, adjust it. "Ideally the athlete arrives at the point [in action] where he hardly notices his equipment." (437:75) A whole terminology and mystique has grown up in a number of sports centered on the equipment. Perhaps the most recent example is the debate about running shoes. For many people a great deal of meaning related to sports resides in the selection, comparison, and preparation of equipment. It is not uncommon, for example, for a skier to spend 2 to 3 hours waxing skis and adjusting bindings before a race. The commitment and involvement in this preparatory act is an integral and important aspect of the sport experience for these individuals; but for any individual, effective preparation, knowledge, and use of equipment is a prerequisite for optimal performance.

Strategy provides perhaps the greatest opportunity for creativity in the sport situation. The devising of new strategies based on the strengths of the individual or team and/or upon the weaknesses of others or the situation demands intelligence, command of the essentials of the contest, intuition, and the ability to analyze and synthesize information. While adjustments are made during the actual sport experience, the initial game plan, race plan, or route provides the participant with a focus and an initial direction. The outcome of any contest depends on a number of factors, but strategy plays an important role. Victory or defeat and any meanings attached to them may stem either directly or indirectly from the initial planning process, or "game plan."

Perhaps the most important aspect of the preparation stage is that of skill development. A commitment to physical training, mastery of equipment, and a sound strategy all have a bearing, but lack of skill will inhibit the kind of total involvement in a sport that may provide the most meaningful kind of experience. In order for the performer to direct his thoughts away from himself and technique toward the "feeling" of the experience or in totality toward the "other," a consistent command of techniques is necessary. Otherwise, how would it be possible in surfing, for example, to "hang ten" or really "take off" if you keep falling off the board? The *full* potential and meaning of the sport experience requires mastery of technique, at least at the level you are playing. Take the case of writer George Plimpton who, in the *Paper Lion*, describes his attempt at playing football with the Detroit Lions. He played with the pros, but it was apparent that he was not a pro. Rather than knowing and having the experience of a pro, he, despite his participation in and articulation of the pro experience, remained outside the real professional football experience. His level of mastery of technique may have been appropriate for total involvement in a sandlot game but for only a pseudoinvolvement in a pro game.

Openness to the possibilities of the sport experience depend on spontaneity and a sense of security. Security stems from a self-assurance that one can do what one intends to do. Fear of failure, lack of confidence in one's skills or equipment, or a lack of training and technical expertise can serve to hamper spontaneity, openness, and the ability to become committed or completely involved in the experience. Many players view the preparation stage as boring and want to get on with the game; others find pleasure and meaning in the refinement of skills, in practicing to achieve mastery, or in "playing" with new possibilities. The body as object, as an "It," during the preparation phase of sport has its possibilities for providing meaning and insight to the performer. It is a stage of sport frequently passed over as a "necessary evil," but it is an essential foundation for later involvement and total commitment to yield not only positive outcomes but a meaningful experience.

Involvement

After the initial preparation for the sporting event comes the actual participation in the event. While the preparation stage could most accurately be characterized as analytic, the involvement stage may be either analytic or prereflective or a combination of both. (See Chapter 3, Sources of Knowledge.) The sport experience may be approached with I-It focus and may continue in this dimension as the player begins to play. However, as the play continues, it takes on more subjective aspects and has the potential to become the relationship that Buber viewed as the I-Thou. The involvement stage is a transition stage between getting ready for the sport event and actually achieving the commitment required for a "oneness" or completeness to occur. It is possible to "take" an interest or participate in any activity but not really "give" of oneself. The mere involvement in sport does not guarantee that meaning will occur for the performer or that the experience will be meaningful for either the performer or the audience.

Sartre (362:368–431) has described three dimensions of the body which occur during the initial involvement of the player in the sport experience. The second and third dimensions of the body delineated by Sartre are akin to Buber's I-It relationship from the standpoint that the body is treated as an object. However, rather than the performer treating the body like an object in preparation for the event, an audience see "it" (the body) as it performs and treats it as another thing among things capable or incapable of completing a successful sport task.

> The second dimension of the body comes into being under the eyes of his fellow-man. . . . his situation is watched by another who remains unperceived. (426:113)

Unknown to the performer, the spectator sees what the performer has forgotten, i.e., those parts of the preparation stage that are no longer conscious to the performer. The audience focuses on the nuances of technique, equipment, changes in strategy, and injury and visually/cognitively treats the body as a thing. "This dissectable thing-body is a derivative of the second dimension." (426:113) The second dimension may not be as common an ocurrence as the third dimension in which the performer *knows* that there is an audience watching the peformance. It is, however, possible that the player can "constitute his body in the second dimension," that is, become his own audience.

> This happens, for instance, when he tends the wound in his leg. The wounded place is examined and touched in *order to* cure it, or: *in order to* be able to continue on his way. (426:113)

The player temporarily takes himself out of any commitment to the totality of the experience to examine the body, considering it a piece of equipment which may have temporarily broken down. It is not uncommon to hear athletes refer to the injured body in terms of *"it* let me down." Somehow the body in the second dimension is seen as outside, or separate from, the self.

The third dimension comes into play during the involvement stage when the performer realizes that there is an audience. In some respects it is the "look" which prevents many athletes from making a total commitment to sport. They become too concerned about what others think and are never "free" to play or to be themselves in a contest. Using a mountain climbing experience, Kleinman explains the look involved in the third dimension:

> For Sartre, this dimension of being is always destructive. It destroys the 'passing beyond.' The climber becomes annoyed, uncomfortable. He feels vulnerable and defenseless. He miscalculates, he stumbles, be becomes ashamed. For Sartre, the look of the other aways results in alienation. Van Den Berg disagrees. There is [on the other hand] the look of understanding, of sympathy, of friendship, of love. (208:178)

The "look" may be one of alienation when the player is inhibited by coaches, fans, critics and is made nervous or anxious enough to "foul it up." In learning something, many people have had the experience of doing the task very well until the teacher or coach watches them perform. At this point, they often become inhibited, cannot get totally into what they are doing, and manage to fail in their performance. Yet there is also what social scientists call "social facilitation" when performance is enhanced by the support of others watching. The "home court" or "home field" advantage is probably a good example of the positive aspect of the third dimension look.

An important aspect of the involvement stage is that the performer begins to move from the I-It relationship that he/she has with the body and initiates a commitment in *doing* a sport. It is possible that from a strictly "fun" standpoint, involvement without commitment carries potential meaning for the player. It may also be possible that the "look" of the other in its giving of approval, status, understanding, and concern may provide valuable meanings for the performer. Yet without commitment, involvement is a "playing *at*" sport rather than a "playing *of*" it. Perhaps unknowingly, coaches have recognized lack of commitment but have often called it "lack of concentration" or "lack of seriousness" on the part of the athlete. And, while it may be possible that concentration and seriousness, or even the "head games" unrelated to the actual sport event, may be factors in not moving from a stage of involvement to a stage of commitment, the impact of the "look" in the second and third dimensions may also be inhibitory.

Commitment

The belief that commitment yields meaning rests on the premise expressed by Plessner: "It is only the behavior, the act, the movement that explains the body." (325:6) The body as subject, as an integrated and embodied entity, is not separate from the experience but becomes the experience. Sartre's first dimension of the body calls for a going beyond the preparation stage:

> He no longer thinks of his shoes to which an hour ago he gave such great attention, he "forgets" the stick that supports him. . . . he 'ignores his body' which he trained. For only by forgetting, in a certain sense, his plans and his body, will be able to devote himself to the laborious task that has to be performed. What there still is, psychologically speaking, is only the mountain: he is absorbed in its structure, his thoughts are completely given to it. (426:107)

This first dimension approaches Buber's I-Thou, the relationship of mutuality. Gerber states Buber's position as follows:

> Unlike Sartre, Buber believed that man is not doomed to live alone and alienated, finding himself only in a confrontation with his own non-Being. In *I* and *Thou* he theorizes that man finds himself, man becomes, man is, only in relation to his Thou. . . . the development of the real man, the essential man, striving for meaningful life, can occur only through the I-Thou relation. (131:129)

Similarly, Sartre's first dimension is a coming together of the athlete and the sport experience, a union which allows the performer the opportunity to fully experience what sport can be and what he/she can be in sport. The performer who voluntarily enters sport and commits his whole being to the sport experience transcends, or goes beyond, outside distractions to a fusion of subject and object that allows the performer to know sport in an authentic, profound, and very individual, special way. It is this kind of "knowing" which has the potential to provide a source of meaning, a sense of purpose, or self-understanding.

The fusion of the performer with the experience represents one kind of commitment. An attendant phenomenon involves the "body-as-subject" experience. Rather than treating the body as an object, or as an "It," as was done in the preparation and involvement stages, man becomes one with his body. In the phenomenological sense not only do I *have* a body, I *am* my body. In this regard the body becomes the access to the world, becomes the source of much knowledge and meaning. Wenkart explains as follows:

> When the body is in action, as in sports, we can look at it as a human existence open toward the world. Man's personal relation to his body can be explained in terms of his positional consciousness. Man can become deeply involved in an external situation but he can keep a certain distance from it. That is why we can say that man not only is his body, but also *has* his body. (439:401)

Feeling becomes a consideration in our "knowing" the world and self. Up to the point where commitment occurs and the player enters the I-Thou or the first dimension, much of the knowledge is cognitive and analytic and an attempt at objectivity. While this important phase of sport yields concrete information, the knowledge and meanings which come from feelings and subjectivity are complementary to the objective data of the I-It and are equally as valid. Since such affective data are dependent on the individualistic "whole man," these feelings, perceptions, and experiences are often private, and meanings are difficult to verbalize and verify by external standards.

In the first dimension man passes over the landscape. Where on the one hand we do not know it is cold or that people are hollering at us, on the body level we do "know" these things. As Van Kaam points out:

> . . . my body is already a meaning-giving existence, even if I am not yet conscious of this meaning-giving activity. My body invests my world with meaning even before I think about this meaning. . . . My body makes the world and the other available to me. . . . My behaving body—which I am— is the locus for the appropriation of sense and meaning. (431:229)

The concept of the body-subject leads to the idea that man can become completely involved in doing. Although body-subjectivity is a relatively recent concept in Western philosophy, the concept of an integrated mind, body, and spirit, or at least the desire for this integration, reaches as far back as ancient Greece. The Delphic spirit, which embraces both the Apollonian and Dionysian concepts of existence (discussed later in this chapter), represents the striving and struggling to reach perfection, and conceives of man as a unity.

> Sikelianas expressed the Delphic spirit of unity as he spoke to the Greek people, saying, "In your midst I place the great statue of Effort, and by it I revive your bodies and your minds." It is through this revival of spirit, mind and body that the total person is created. (130:43)

Resolution

Depending on the intent of the performer at the outset of the sporting event, some assessment or evaluation of whether the intended goals were accomplished is the culmination of the sport experience. In the case of a contest, a resolution that determines success or failure, winning or losing, ends the contest.

Regardless of the individual motive for commitment to the sport world, it is suggested here that the game, like the script or the choice of a life project, provides a medium to play out a variety of searches, be they for knowledge, self-assessment, purpose, or acceptance. Where Sophocles has viewed drama as the "instrument for achieving sublime knowledge," the playwright Arthur Miller (279:1) sets the tone for tragic consequences in many "life projects" resulting from commitment and evaluation. "Tragedy is the consequence of man's total compulsion to evaluate himself justly." "The commonest of men," he says, "take on tragic stature to the extent of their willingness to throw all they have into the contest." While there may be tentativeness that precedes any contest and the uncertainty implicit in the nature of competition, the readied and committed athlete's attitude is characterized by confidence that he will not hesitate. The athlete trusts his training and his body to perform as required during the performance. He "reads the river," believing that the ride through the rapids will be both thrilling and successful. He enters the contest believing that skill, intelligence, and choice will prevail over fate and that the test will be an authentic one.

Ermler (90) has written that both success and failure in sport are forms of a symbolic death because defeat and success bring about the collapse of an athlete's sports world either as a result of the performer's inability to actualize his goal or by the accomplishment of the goal. Success and failure resolve and thereby end the contest. She maintains that this "death" in sport can be viewed one of two ways by the athlete. Either it is a motivation to set new goals, to reassert commitment, or more characteristically it is tragic in that the athlete gives up hope or interest and symbolically dies. We cease to be or feel significant or see significance in our world when we fail, not so much because we are in reality insignificant but because we have come to believe that failure makes us less significant than we are. Similarly, success may also lead to a symbolic death characterized by resting on laurels or an attitude of "is that all there is?" As we are aware from even elementary psychology, perception is selective and reality is second to our perception of it when it comes to behavior or the formation of attitudes. It is not the world but how we see the world that guides our attitudes and behaviors.

In any case, resolution ends the experience. Such resolution is not unlike the third act of a play where we find out "what happens" and often how the characters feel about and react to what has happened. This resolution is almost a necessity, since the desire to win, achieve excellence, or prevail is one of the primary determinants of action. The player defines and shapes the sport experience through his own mental and physical acts and must then accept the consequences of those acts.

Camus' (58) definition of revolt as a "constant confrontation between man and his own obscurity" seems applicable to sport, for just as the ennobling quality of a literary character like Oedipus was his commitment to the impossible and his following of the quest to its final depth, so the athlete will follow the quest to its conclusion equally committed. The irony in either case is that in this confrontation with obscurity Oedipus finds Oedipus, the athlete finds himself. While success or fulfillment of intent has potential in revealing man's capabilities, often it does not have the impact that failure has in self-realization. Failure is more difficult to come to grips with, more easily rationalized. Again, it is not man's confrontation with the fates but his *reaction* to them that demonstrates the authenticity of his being, the trueness of his identity.

When the athlete has truly given all because he wanted to, because it was important and necessary to do it, he has put himself on the line. When he cannot retreat anywhere to hide his ignorance or incompetence in a sport "world" uncomplicated by the outside world, perhaps we have a true test and one of the cleanest confrontations of man, will, and fate. The necessity of choice in the sport contest is not unlike choices in life, except that it is probably more direct, immediate, reactive, and clear. This reactive aspect is perhaps the most self-revealing—no time to be phony; no time to think and cover up. Perhaps it is on this kind of "stage" that the "common man" can come to realize that the sport experience is more than the fates, the consequences of choices, success, or failure. It is also the player's *reaction* to these things and the ability to deal with them that make the real difference in how a person assesses his/her own authenticity and being-in-the-world.

THE NATURE OF EXPERIENCE

Most experience falls into one of two antithetic types. Even John Dewey, who discounted such dualisms as mind-body, subject-object, and means-ends wih regard to experience, maintained a distinction between ordinary experience and *an* experience. Dewey (76:37) maintained that *an* experience has a unity that gives it its name: *that* meal, *that* storm, and possibly, *that* game, *that* jump. In discussing dance, Hawkins (156:34) suggested that dance experiences are usually perceived as gestalts. The separate elements impinge on one another, and the reaction is to the total event or experience. Sport as a movement form is a similar kind of gestalt. "It [movement] does not lend itself to analysis because its unity dictates a viewing and sensing of the work as a whole." (38:65) The gestalt notion that what happens at one point in the organism is never independent or without its influences upon what is taking place at any other point of the organism permeates Dewey's thinking to the extent that he acknowledges a mind-body unity in response and a gestalt-kind of unity of form and substance—what he calls *an* experience.

When sport moves from the involvement stage to the commitment stage, it moves out of the realm of everyday ordinary experience to become *an* experience. The immediacy and unity of subject and object which characterize *an* experience has been noted with regard to the sport experience. Slusher (379:65) writes that the movement experience is now and immediate, not past or future. In discussing bullfighting, Wenkert also writes: "Here the training, mobility, and versatility all converge to achieve a degree of attention that eliminates all extraneous perception and pinpoints one decisive moment." (439:397) Metheny maintains that man is given over to and becomes involved as a totality with sport because ". . . the rules of sport prohibit him from thinking about those meanings while he is involved in the sport experience . . . while he is perform-

ing . . . the task, he must focus all his attention and energies upon it."
(271:68) Beets further suggests that "the sportsman may be looking for
experiences in which he can forget his body, especially the parts of his
body, to find something of a very different nature: a sense of wholeness,
a sense of unity of some kind." (25:75) Flushing a toilet is a common
experience in our ordinary life, yet it provides little significance or meaning. It tells us little about the world that we don't already know and little
about ourselves. On the other hand, an overflowing toilet may be *an*
experience that demands all our skills, intelligence, energy, and attention.
However, the significance and meaning derived from *that* experience
over which we had little control may be minimal compared to those
experiences which we intentionally design and voluntarily commit ourselves to in order to achieve predetermined goals.

Aside from Dewey, the more typical classifications follow Nietzsche's
concepts of Dionysianism and Apollonianism. (296) Brinton has summa-
rized and attached value to this polarity:

> The Dionysian is a Good Thing: It is God's and Nature's primal strength,
> the unending turbulent lust and longing in men which drives them to con-
> quest, to drunkenness, to mystic ecstacy, to love-deaths. (37:39)

The Dionysian is that kind of experience or that part of man's nature
which is given over to spontaneity, affectivity, irrationality, and subjectivity. It is that aspect of personal experience which is often difficult to
communicate. It is the doer rather than the talker in us, the lover, the
fighter, and the passionate nature. For the most part it is a performer's
perspective and an integral part of the "lived experience." In the sport
experience the Dionysian orientation may be most commonly found in
the commitment and resolution stages. The meanings generated from this
kind of experience tend to be feeling-based, may be very subjective in
nature, and may be difficult to put in words. Buytendijk (50:159) explains
that to describe what one feels is to describe the situation in which one
exists. Feelings, he says, are modes to detect the significance of situations.
For example, if you get angry at losing a game of racquetball, the anger
may be an indication of any number of things—how well or poorly you
played, the importance of the match related to personal status or ego, or
not wanting to be beat by a particular person.

The Dionysian nature of play is alluded to by Kretchmar and Harper
when they state that "the lived reality of this union between man and
play defies all attempts to reduce it to a rationally explicable understanding." (220:58) Bannister comments that there is difficulty in explaining
feelings such as joy or failure in sport or their meaning to anyone who
has not experienced the same thing:

> . . . this attempt at explanation is of course inadequate, just like any analysis
> of the thing we enjoy—like the description of a rose to someone who has
> never seen one. (21:11–12)

Brinton's explanation of the contrasting and complementary type of experience suggests it is primarily a rational experience.

> The Apollonian is a Bad Thing—though not unattractive in its proper place: it is man's attempt to stop this unending struggle, to find peace, harmony, balance, to restrain the brute in himself. But the Brute is life and cannot be long restrained. (37:39)

The Apollonian in its rationality serves to analyze in order to provide perspective, to critique, or to reflect analytically. The Apollonian is primarily the spectator perspective, which is characterized by cognitive objectivity, criticism, logic, and what is often called "scientific method." In the intent and preparation stages of sport, it is a common kind of experience for the athlete. In the involvement stage, the critical eye of the audience takes on the Apollonian orientation. It may, from an audience standpoint, follow the performer into the commitment stage but remains outside the "lived" sport experience. The "armchair quarterback" remains outside looking in on the experience. The athlete may again experience sport in some Apollonian aspects through reflective analysis in the resolution stage. Where the Dionysian yields personal and subjective meanings for the performer, the Apollonian may yield more concrete meanings, particularly if performance and results can be quantified or analyzed. Missing a turn is a concrete error which bears a meaning for the next performance in that it may change either intent or preparation. These meanings are objective and relatively easy to communicate. The examination of sources of knowledge in Chapter 3 closely parallels the sources of meaning and significance that may be found in the Dionysian and Apollonian experiences.

DISCUSSION QUESTIONS

DIRECTED READING

Questions and readings related to meaning and sport are at the end of Chapter 7.

Chapter 7

POSSIBLE MEANINGS FOUND IN SPORT

To comprehend the 'inner world' of the performer and to understand the reason why each man, as an individual, chooses to partake in sport activity, is to pursue inquiry into personal forms of meaningful and significant existence. (379:220)

There is always difficulty in outlining the meanings found in sport or in attempting to identify the reasons that people participate in sport. Since each person brings a unique self to a different or unique sport situation, the combination is bound to produce a variety of motivations and intents. What one person seeks or finds in sport may be of little or no interest to another. The "drawing power" of sport and a person's willingness to pursue sport in the first place or return to it over and over again is both situation specific and specific to the individual. While the search for self and for a purpose in life may be found in a variety of meanings, one meaningful experience does not explain sport involvement for all people.

Stone* (394:10) defines meaning as ". . . a relationship, or pattern of relationships, found by the perceiver between the stimulus pattern (object/event/situation) and some idea, feeling, or action (referent) either within the perceiver's experience or which is now created by the perceiver." The same event can be perceived and/or experienced by a number of different people, and while the ideas, feelings, and actions related to the event may be the same, the meanings which are derived may be different. For example, roughly 45 players may participate on the winning Super Bowl team in any given year. They may experience joy and a sense of achievement to which they attach meaning, but for each of those 45 players who have experienced the same event the meaning may differ. In addition, immediate observers and more distant observers who par-

---

*Stone has provided an excellent overview of the concept of meaning in her article, "Human Movement Forms as Meaning Structures: A Prolegomenon," Quest, 23, January 1975, pp. 10–14.

ticipate in the event may also experience joy and achievement. The meanings that the coaches attach to the achievement are likely to be different from those of the players and of the fans.

Stone also categorizes the kinds of meanings that may be found in the sport experience:

> Meanings *within the act* are intrinsic meanings in that they are the experience of the act itself. They are sub-divided into (a) functional relatedness, in that they serve to continue the act; and (b) experience-enhancing relatedness, in that they give rise to personal insights, pleasure, satisfaction. . . .
>
> Meanings *for or about the act* are extrinsic meanings in that they satisfy the act's role as a means to some other end such as economic gain or the achievement of some result seen as socially or politically desirable . (394:13)

The complexity of meaning as it may be experienced or observed in sport is evident in the many attempts to talk about why we play. Personal attempts to explain what sport means or why we play often break down, and people who do not play often cannot be made to understand what the attraction is for either players or fans.

Before examining possible specific meanings that sport may provide the participant, a brief general consideration will be given to what an involvement in sport may lead an individual to equate about self, a possible being-in-the-world, or the meaning of existence. Artistic endeavors are highly valued by this culture, as they are viewed as a means for creatively exploring and expressing the structural and substantive dimensions of meaning and existence. Although the concept of art will be discussed more fully in Chapter 9, let us look briefly at the contribution of art and draw some relationships from media which are generally held to be meaningful to sport and movement.

One looks at a work of art not merely to identify or discover an object as object, but rather to see the object in a particular way. The poet or musician tells us what it means to hear; the painter, what it means to see; and the novelist, that it is possible, for example, to live believing that every existing thing is born without reason, prolongs itself out of weakness, and dies by chance. These artists reveal in part what it means to be. Thus, one might say Beethoven's *Ninth Symphony* is not about joy, it is joy; the committed listening to that work is a participation in the mode of being joyful.

Why do we read great literature, go to see the characterizations of great drama, and identify with the music of the masters? Perhaps because we think they tell us of the world or about parts of the world we have not had the chance to experience. Perhaps we think they expose us to the full range of human behavior and emotion, which will provide us with insights about others and ourselves. It may be the tree against which we measure ourselves and our lives. What is compassion, love, hatred, joy, anger, tragedy? Is it really possible that a Willie Loman, a Scarlett O'Hara or a Walter Mitty resides in each of us? Am I far from being Camus' "stranger" or Hesse's Siddhartha? Is it really possible that the emotional spectrum reflected in the demonic anger of a Liszt, the passionate involvement of a Brahms, or the precise orderliness of a Haydn is available to me? Is the sadness of the song really in me? We are drawn to the bizarre, the absurd, the impossible, the beautiful, the ugly, the ridiculous, and the sublime; or else Fellini, Bergman, and Woody Allen would not fill the same screens. Why? Perhaps because we wonder about the potentials of humanity, the depths of depravity, the heights of glory. We wonder about them and keep looking for those parts of us that show up on stages, canvases, and screens and in the books, concert halls, and lyrics that are part of our everyday lives. We look for signs that we are unique and yet like everyone else. What are the ways that I am potentially available to myself?

But there is something lacking in our search for self in artistic pursuits. Perhaps it is total commitment. We remain experientially separated, despite our most persistent attentiveness, from the ongoing artistic or aesthetic process. While it may be possible that observationally we can understand the intuitive essence of love, hate, tragedy, defeat, and victory, we can come to understand self only through a more complete involvement. It is at this point that the philosopher Friedrich Nietzsche (296) is instructive. One of the conclusions he reached in his brief treatise, *The Birth of Tragedy,* was that the intellect alone could not provide sufficient comprehension of existence. Although his position is not an appeal to irrationality or emotionalism at the expense of thought, he argues strongly for the passionate involvement of the total man in his search for self. The central message of his later work, *Thus Spake Zarathustra,* is clear: if one wishes to transcend the mundane to get at the very source and power, to one's worth and value, one must exist in certain ways, go beyond himself without appealing to anything other than himself, and have the courage to recognize that man, because he can thoughtfully reflect on himself, can, in fact, understand what and who he is. With regard to sport, man, in his mind and through his reflections, becomes audience to his own act in much the same way that he becomes audience to the novel, the drama, and the musical score. And while some might argue this is a confusion of the observational and experiential modes of understanding, the intent is self-awareness and the information, though received from different sources, is complementary.

From Nietzsche and the philosophers and psychologists who have followed him, two things seem exceedingly clear with regard to man's potential and need to look introspectively. First, the dimensions of self-awareness cannot be the consequence of mere intellectual conceptualization. Man must place himself in a wide variety of experiences that resist the temptation to remain safe or to venture little of the self. Sport and physical education would seem to have the potential to be one of those kinds of "venturing" experiences. One of the apparent distinctions between physical and intellectual endeavors is that once you commit yourself to a physical activity—even something as simple as walking across the room—there is little hidden from public assessment. It is possible to hide ignorance by remaining silent, but it is not possible to hide the fact of the body, its movements, its successes, its failures. To choose to play is a venturing of self: either you hit the ball or you miss; you are fast enough or you are not; you are strong enough or you are not; you are graceful or you are awkward; you are willing to take the risk or you are not. You are what you are in sport and it is difficult, if not impossible, to mistake what is revealed.

THE PURSUIT OF EXCELLENCE

Most democratic societies ascribe to a belief in equal opportunity for their citizens to pursue their optimal potentials. Basically, this means an equal chance to compete within the rules to achieve a particular goal. But, as Gardner points out, despite the belief in equal opportunity, "We know that men are not equal in their native gifts nor in their motivations; and it follows they will not be equal in their achievements." (126:12) There are many kinds of excellence; some are recognized and rewarded, and other kinds are obscure. Similarly, the definitions of excellence are varied. In some instances, it can be objectively measured by comparing one person, product, or performance, with another. In other instances, excellence rests on more personal criteria grounded in becoming the person one could be. For many who seek out the sport experience, achieving excellence—even for just one performance—carries a great deal of lasting significance. For others, there is meaning in the *striving* to achieve a form of excellence.

While the striving for excellence may be a common endeavor, the achievement of excellence is an exception. One of the most impressive things about watching a great athletic performance, be it of a Bruce Jenner or a Nadia Comaneci, is that it demonstrates so much about ourselves that we never may have realized, for through the athlete's excellence and the demonstration of body potentials, we can come to understand as an observer what it means to have a body and legs which, for example, can achieve optimal balance in movement. It is through our own experiences in dance, football, gymnastics, skiing, surfing, or skate boarding that we come to know balance, not only in our own unique ways but also in the sense of knowing we share with others the universality of a phenomenon called "balance." I am unique and I am "everyman." One may strive for *comparative* excellence, but few achieve it; yet for many spectators and performers there is significance in seeing or in *trying* to achieve an excellent performance that is judged by external or comparative standards. Achievement of *personal* standards of excellence, which on a comparative basis may not be considered excellent, may still provide a dimension of meaning. A 60-minute time in a 10-kilometer race may be a personal standard of excellence that when compared with the performance of others cannot be viewed as excellent.

Weiss points out that spectators see the athlete as the personification of a physical excellence that they may not desire to achieve for themselves.

> Few men work at becoming all they can be. Fewer still try to do this by achieving a disciplined mastery of their bodies. . . . In the athlete all can catch a glimpse of what one might be were one also to operate at the limit of bodily capacity. (437:14)

The involvement of the spectator is a vicarious achievement. "At the same time we feel as though we ourselves had personally achieved something." (437:14)

The striving of the athlete for a measure of excellence takes two forms. The first may be to attain some degree of perfection by breaking or setting a record. In a sense, this is a "better than" attitude, but it is not so much a need or desire to dominate as it is to be the best, to represent the ultimate in performance at a given time and in a given place in history. The other dimension is a more intrinsic comparison between what was and what is—the challenge of the historical self or the striving to better or maintain a previous performance. Weiss sums up succinctly:

> The excellence that the athlete wants to attain is an excellence greater than that obtained before. He wants to do better than he did; he would like to do better than anyone ever did. . . . This is a truth that will surely hold as long as men compete with one another. (437:14)

Those interested in sport are frequently consumed with a passion for records, and media announcers are given over to the transmission of even the most trivial of records in a given sport. There is also a fascination with the "great moments in sport." The record or the "great moment" may be one of excellence in technique or in achieving a personal best. It may be witnessed by millions of people or it may be a solitary and lonely occurrence. It may be a universally acclaimed form of excellence or it may be a personal achievement. White states that:

> . . . the purpose of an athletic action intended for excellence is to actualize a humanly physical possibility as if it were an actual possibility for all individuals. The duffer who finally breaks 100 has experienced a personal "great moment in sport," even if he is the lone man to share in his triumph. (441:212)

The achievement of excellence or, at least, the striving for it in sport is the culmination of training, preparation, and commitment. It is wholly, or in part, the fulfillment of intent, for to post one's best performance and perhaps to break a previously existing world record simultaneously yet finish in second place is still a form of excellence. It may not be superiority, but it can be an excellent performance and a meaningful experience.

DOMINANCE AND SUPERIORITY

For some people who play, excellence without superiority lacks meaning and fulfillment. The intent is to be dominant and winning is the prize valued. It is the resolution which carries meaning. While a focus on winning is often decried by humanistic philosophers, the desire to win and to make winning the most meaningful aspect of the sport experience is not necessarily wrong. The object of sport as a contest is to win, to be better than the opponent, to conquer the mountain, to master the waves. Given a choice, is there any sport participant who would rather lose than win? It is perhaps safe to say that most would prefer a combination of an excellent performance and superiority in the contest. However, they are not the same things. Some would prefer to sacrifice excellence as long as they win. Others would argue it is a hollow or incomplete victory if excellence is not part of the intent.

Yet winning carries with it many positive feelings. There is the obvious social status that comes with being superior, particularly in a society that values success in any competitive endeavor. In 1981 when the Tampa Bay Buccaneers went to Dallas for a football play-off game, the fans of Tampa planned a massive reception (win or lose) the evening of the game for the returning Bucs. When they were humiliated 38–0 by Dallas, the reception was called off by the team management before the game was even over. A poor effort with a one point win or a good effort in a close defeat would have justified such a rally, but a poor effort coupled with such a resounding defeat left nothing to cheer about or celebrate.

There is a feeling of power and control that comes with success. Winners are afforded privileges that others often must work hard to receive. Everyone likes to identify with a winner. The Dallas Cowboys and the New York Yankees, long considered "America's teams," became the darlings of the media and of sports fans without a "home team" because they were consistent winners. Since excellence was often part of the winning tradition, their narrow wins or poor efforts in winning or losing were excused. Winners are never "bums," no matter how poorly they play. For many who play, the trappings of a winner are extremely important. The belief that superiority in the contest leads to upward social or economic mobility, provides an entree to desired social circles, or brings popularity, visibility, or security gives a meaningful and significant aspect to the sport experience.

Right or wrong, a great deal of ego involvement is connected with the outcome of a contest. Whether in a casual game of racquetball or in a professional sport, feelings of self-worth are often tied up in winning or losing. Somehow not being good enough at racquetball is transferred to not being good enough as a person. Being able to control or dominate an opponent is also a strong positive or negative feeling that is intricately woven into some individuals' personal identities. Even for many who achieve excellence, "going for the Gold" is the only meaningful end, and the silver medal might as well be a "booby prize." Sport, with so many more losers than winners, does provide a unique opportunity to redeem either a poor effort or a losing effort. If the preparation, intent, and commitment can be sustained, there is always another day, the next game, or next season to be a winner.

Vince Lombardi once described a champion as an individual like Bart Starr. "That is, to me, the mark of a champion—the kind who plays just as well whether you are losing or whether you are winning." (74:125) Yet Valentine tells us there is little glory or pride or self-esteem left for the loser when the crowd and a society make winning so much more pleasant than losing and rewarding the winners while ignoring or forgetting the losers.

> Whether it is a prize-fighter sinking to his knees after he has given his all, a runner being caught at the tape after she has run to the point of total exhaustion, or a football player who has dug down into himself with the last ounce of strength only to be overpowered by an opponent, [some] views on winning justify us roaring on the victor while ignoring the absoluteness of the effort of the vanquished. (425:65)

DEFINING PERSONAL LIMITS

Involved in what has also been called "self-testing" are some aspects of the pursuit of excellence and superiority. The opponent in this case is usually past or future self, a previous performance or one which is being aimed at in the future. The achievement is not so much one of dominance or superiority in the "better than" sense but of establishing goals and meeting the challenge of accomplishing those goals. The performance may not meet any external standard of excellence and may even fall short of personal standards of excellence. For example, there is a ski-run in Alta, Utah called "High Rustler," which is an advanced slope. It is possible, however, for a less than advanced skier to attempt the run. No records would be set, no comparative style considerations would merit the run of a novice as excellent. Despite falling, fear, and probably poor technique it would be possible for the novice skier to "make it" down the hill. Deciding to "make it" may be the ultimate in a personal limit. Despite the lack of speed, style, technique, and any other aesthetic consideration, just making it down the mountain and proving only to oneself that it is possible may make the contest with the mountain a highly meaningful encounter.

For many individuals the sport experience becomes a "proving ground" for the self-paced and self-directed setting and meeting of challenges. Such contests may be conducted oblivious to crowds and without a formal opponent. The meanings often are found in the mastery of fear, passion, or self-doubt. As a demonstration of persistence, sacrifice, and willingness to prepare and put oneself "on the line," the feedback is important only to the individual. It is a demonstration of competence which is intrinsically motivated. For many who engage in the more nonathletic forms of sport, the attitude that "I just wanted to see if I could do it" is a prevailing motivation. The thousands of retirees in the Sun Belt who often join strangers in social or recreational rounds of golf yet count every stroke and record every penalty on the score card reflect the need to demonstrate continued competence and to self-check personal limits.

TAKING CHANCES

Closely aligned with the need to meet challenges and define personal limits is the motivation to seek out risks. The last two decades have produced a marked increase in the number of sports that lend themselves to risk taking, thrills, and adventure seeking. Seeking an escape from urban and impersonal environments that lack natural beauty, people have moved their leisure and sport pursuits out of the "concrete canyons" of the cities to wilderness or more natural outdoor settings. While many of the more noncompetitive activities such as camping, hiking, or cycling involve little social or physical risk, among the most popular activities are those that involve a high degree of risk. As Siedentop notes:

> Public reactions tend to vacillate between admiration and criticism for the many who now regularly participate in high risk activities, such as hang gliding, sky diving, scuba diving, and mountain climbing. Often, what is risked is life itself. . . . yet the sense of rugged individualism in American life and our heritage in the pioneer spirit also call forth our admiration for those so willing to risk all. . . . (375:189)

Wilderness and outdoor pursuits fit within the educational concept that came to be known in the 1970's as "experiential education." Prompted by a belief that "action education" or learning by doing is valuable, the Outward Bound and Project Adventure models became popular educational concepts. The development of self-awareness, self-understanding, and character are the central goals, and physical fitness, safety and skill development are fostered. In the use of "risk" activities, stress, self-testing, and self-reliance are key factors in the sport experience. Drengson summarizes the educational and learning potentials of experiential education:

> . . . learners come to know themselves and also the natural world through immediate experience and by means of total immersion in a context that demands action rather than speculation or theorizing. There are elements of risk here but all development involves risk. . . . It requires the capacity to respond intelligently with all of one's emotional, physical, intellectual, and spiritual energies. (80:115)

Perhaps not coincidentally, the advent of risk-taking and adventure-seeking sport activities occurred during a period where the Con III counterculture attitudes ran very strongly against organized and agonistic athletics. The 1970's, with an emphasis on individuality and humanistic approaches to education, seemed to be the the the right time for "solo" activities rather than team efforts. Self-testing challenge rather than dominance was the primary focus. Seeking to "do their own thing" in a technologic society where anxiety, alienation, and disruption were strong social influences, many people sought risk and adventure in sport with the hope of feeling "in control" of their own destinies.

In contrast to the tendency in a modern industrial society to eliminate risk and make everything safer is the urge to seek out excitement, thrill, and adventure in high-risk sports. Those who seek adventure in the truest sense of sport are not reckless or foolish. The risks are calculated and the thrills are, in a sense, planned. Alvarez sums up the significance of taking chances:

> More important still were the other resources we had had to call on—the obscure doggedness that prevented us from simply giving up. . . .
> And that finally, is what the risky games are all about. They are like a sharp close-up of your own life, in which all of the essentials are concentrated and defined. You deliberately set up a situation which, in order to survive, you must respond to as fully as you know how. The situation itself may be utterly artificial—on a mountain there is always an easier way to the top—but the element of risk makes it terribly serious. The fascination for me is keeping the risk in complete control. Flirting with danger for kicks bores me; it is a form of exhibitionism, a vulgarity to one's self. . . . You must take complete responsibility for your own life. . . . in doing something difficult, something that extends your concentration and effort and resourcefulness without ever losing control. (8:205)

EXPRESSION

Expression in sport can take many forms. The use of language symbols for what the athlete intended, what was accomplished, what it means, or how the experience felt is the most common means of expressing what happened or is on-going in the sport experience. Roberts, in his examination of expression in sport argues that *what* sport expresses may vary with time and place and who is doing the expressing but that *how* sport expresses whatever it expresses remains the same. (343:39) While his main concern was discussing *how* sport expresses, Roberts did note the kinds of things it was possible for sport to express, or exemplify.

> In order for sport to exemplify or express, or both, it or any of its aspects must be . . . capable of possessing certain properties . . . of being denoted by certain labels. . . . Sport, in its phenomenal form, is just as capable as anything in our world of being denoted by applicable predicates. . . . Sport and its aspects can be and are denoted by a myriad of predicates. (343:47) Some of the more popular are: speed, power, grace, agility, coordination, strength, endurance, flexibility, accuracy, symmetry, balance, rhythm, vitality, efficiency, success, failure, fortitude, dedication, excellence, preparation, hope, victory, defeat, and so on. (343:54)

Verbal expressions about the feelings and thoughts about the things on the list Roberts has outlined do rely on the symbols of language, and what joy in victory may mean in words to one winner may not mean the same to other winners or to the spectator who observed the victory. "It felt great!" expresses a general sentiment of satisfaction but lacks precision in that we do not all know what "great" really means. Other expressions such as strength, balance, and agility are almost exclusively physical expressions. To experience or observe a display of superb strength is to become aware of the possibilities of strength and to feel or to see what strength is capable of achieving. But again, the expression retains a certain ambiguity, for what the performer intentionally or unintentionally expresses may not be what the audience sees. What one person sees as strength, another may not.

For the performer or the spectator it is possible to suggest that sport provides a means for expressive outlets despite ambiguities or a lack of agreement about what is being expressed at any given time. The most obvious of expressions are those that are overt and emotional. Sometimes they are intentionally sought after; sometimes these emotions "just happen" as a result of participation. Phillips points out that: "immersion in a sport experience produces an intense emotion: one feels 'tremendous,' 'great,' 'way out,' 'whole,' or 'complete'." (322:97) The player may strive for these things, may seek out sport to experience a sense of wholeness. It is also possible that we come to know ourselves as being capable of anger, hostility, or fear, and it is possible to see how those feelings are expressed in action. How do you actually express the joy that is sought in victory? One only needs to look at the variability in expression among highly visible professional players and coaches: Mark Gasteneau in contrast to Reggie McKenzie, John Madden in contrast to Tom Landry. Nevertheless, they all come to a common frontier: the reckless and the studious, the fighters and the dancers. There is a variability in style and expression in how the contest is approached by players and how they react to its progress and outcome.

The possibility that fear will surface and show itself in performance or that hostility, hate, joy, or love may be expressed in ways you may or may not have previously experienced, carries a variety of significance and meanings for the performers. In sport the extensiveness and variability of human emotional response is manifest in ways that are often either surprising or predictable. Sometimes they are appropriate or facilitative; sometimes they are not. Sometimes they are likable; sometimes they are despicable. Often they are meaningful as outward expressions of what is happening "inside" the experience. While this kind of emotional discharge has been dismissed as having no potential to be art, it does retain its potential as a mirror of human feelings and behaviors.

Expressions of mastery, challenge, excellence, and dominance have been treated earlier in the chapter. In addition to these expressions which focus on the ends, or outcome, of the sport experience, are two process-oriented forms of expression. One is style and the other is creativity. Everyone who plays has a certain style in the way they perform. Some of this style may be ritualistic in nature, such as bouncing the ball three times before serving, or it may be particular quirks or a flair that goes along with the technique. Style, to a degree, gives a performance individuality, and to the extent that it does not interfere with good mechanics, it becomes an accepted part of technique or performance. Individual style often sets a person apart from others who do the same thing. In many instances, style is irrelevant as long as "the job gets done" or the outcome is positive. In other sport settings, style or flair is important. In figure skating and synchronized swimming, two scores are awarded—one for technique and one for style. As a form of expression, style takes on meaning for the performer to the extent that a person wants to look good. Even novice recreational skiers, golfers, or surfers want to "look good" while performing and often try to add flair or style within the boundaries of their skill levels.

Creativity takes two forms in a sport setting. In technique, the mastery of basics and innovative movements are commonplace. Often they are known only to the individual performer and/or a coach who "discover" a better way. At other times, creativity is highly visible in world-class competition, and the new techniques become widely adopted and developed further. The "Fosbury flop" in the high jump and the floor exercise and uneven parallel bar moves of Nadia Comaneci are recent examples. Inherent in such studied efforts at creativity is a satisfaction both in finding a better way to do something and in a realization of competence and mastery. Sensing that such innovation may lead to success is often an exhilarating feeling.

A second kind of creativity manifests itself in the development of strategy. Some of this is evident in the planned stages of preparation and may evolve from studying an opponent's weaknesses. The "shotgun" formation and a myriad of "flea flickers" are recent additions to a long history of plays and formations in football. Volleyball has just begun to use multiple option offenses which include fakes and screens. Such intricate strategies were unheard of in the American game before 1970. The nature of creativity allows for a degree of experimentation and playfulness. Sometimes a new "move" or a new play is a complete bomb. Other times it may be a game winner. It is a risk that adds a dimension of fun, uncertainty, and excitement to the game. Much of the pleasure from "pick-up" games stems from the free-lance nature of the play; yet even in structured sport, or athletics, the opportunity for creative expression exists and adds a dimension of meaning for the player. For the fan who watches the holder for a short field goal pick up the ball and sprint for a touchdown, innovation is exciting. The opportunity for creative expression in sport, as in other avenues of life, is grounded in risk-taking payoffs. For many, meaning lies in taking calculated risks where one's own mental and physical abilities will make a difference in the odds and the outcome.

ALTERED STATES AND MYSTICAL UNIONS

> There is no waiting, no goal, no doing. Yet nothing is left undone. In these delightful moments, the thrower is not separate from the thrown. We blend in a single motion. (239:53)

A great deal has been written over the past decade about what has been broadly termed "altered states of consciousness." Theorists have called such moments "flow," "peak-experiences," "oneness," "inner games," and "perfect moments." Athletes have described such experiences as "highs." While these kinds of experiences or "moments" are not commonplace and cannot be planned for, sought after, or guaranteed in the sport experience, they do occur, and when they do, they are highly significant for those who experience them. We often attribute such experiences to individual activities—running, tennis, skiing— yet in many ways even a team player acts alone while part of the group. For as Kleinman points out:

> Although all participants . . . may be performing exactly the same movements, the individual, if he is truly engaged in the act, knows nothing of the others. He is completely absorbed in his landscape. He is acting only as *he* can act. He is deriving meaning and significance only in the way *he* is capable. (208:178)

Stone delineates two types of consciousness:

> These speak of such altered states of consciousness and prescience and transcendence with attendant ecstasy, but there remains the dualistic state of "I" and the "other," that is, the report is expressed in terms of subject and object. In experiences of mystical union, the dualistic state disappears and one emerges from the experience knowing something one did not know before. (395:103)

Typical of the I-Thou relationship is the belief in the union of subject and object which, while dualistic at the outset, comes together to achieve a "oneness" of experience. Runners have said, "I become the running." The literature has provided many accounts of athletes' feelings about being in union and harmony, not only with the activity but of transcending the ordinary self. Ravizza reports two such recent accounts:

> I am at one with everything. There is no distinction between myself, the bicycle, track, speed, or anything. It is effortless. I am everything at this time and everything is me. (333:98)

> "It was no longer the hill and I, but both of us, it was perfect." (333:114)

Maslow's (262) original concept of the "peak-experience" was grounded in motivation and personality study, but the actual characteristics of the peak-experiences are found in all experiences that are called "altered states" or "transcending" experiences in sport. Although occurring in a spatial-temporal setting, these "peak experiences" are characterized by a disorientation in space and time during which the sport participant becomes oblivious to surroundings and the passage of time. There is an intensity, a sense of wholeness and completeness as if "one small part of the world is perceived as for the moment all of the world." (262:88) There is a sense of nowness, a freedom from past and future and a "here-and-now" character that makes the experience very immediate. The individual feels more integrated, more a total being, with a feeling of being at the peak of his powers. (262:104–105)

Csikszentmihalyi has written most recently about the concept of "flow" which sums up many of the ideas embodied in the literature about altered states of consciousness. He suggests that flow may occur in many life situations but that "games are obvious flow activities and play is the flow experience *par* excellence." (69:36–37)

> . . . We shall refer to this particular dynamic state—the holistic sensation that people feel when they act with total involvement—as "flow." In the flow state, action follows upon action according to an internal logic that seems to need no conscious intervention by the actor. He experiences it as a unified flowing from one moment to the next, in which he is in control of his actions, and in which there is little distinction between self and environment, between stimulus and response, or between past, present, and future. (69:36)

Too frequently "altered state of consciousness" has come to mean an association with mind-altering agents—alcohol, drugs, hypnosis, and in some respects, flow or a peak-experience is mind-altering. The "highs" reported by athletes rival the "highs" reported in other mind-altering adventures. One of the keys to an altered state of consciousness in sport is that frequently it leads to a "higher state of consciousness," to an awareness. "Awareness is consciousness together with a realization of what is happening within it, or of what is going on within ourselves . . ." (334:50) While awareness is not a thinking *about* movement or the experience, it is an integrated perspective. (334:69) The significance of this kind of awareness can allow participants to more fully understand the meaning of their involvement in sport and to enhance their performance through an understanding of their own internal body states. (334:70)

According to Gallwey (124), the essence of the "Inner Game" learning process is increasing awareness. In a culture where the emphasis has been on achievement in sport, little importance has been given to body awareness. Gallwey argues that body awareness is directly related to body achievement and he points to Eastern philosophies and approaches to movement for their advocacy of awareness. "Achievement," he says, "is an inevitable and natural by-product of awareness." (125:89) He advocates a balance between our desire to achieve with its goal-directed emphasis and attention to the body awareness achieved in "altered state" sport experiences.

> Pure awareness with little will to achieve, lacks direction, but the will to achieve with too little awareness is strained and lacks the requisite refinement to achieve the highest levels of excellence. (125:89)

The coming together of running and the runner, basketball and the basketball player facilitates an increased bodily awareness. Once the crowds, the coaches, criticism, and the environment are "passed over," and cognitive considerations of technique and strategy can be minimized or eliminated, it is possible for "flow," oneness, or the peak-experience to occur. While there is no guarantee that it will, if and when it does, reports are that it is a highly meaningful experience and one that heightens both physical and personal awareness.

Stone's description of a true mystical experience goes beyond what she claims are "altered but still dualistic states." (395:103) The true mystical union becomes a meditative state where thought and action become inseparable whether in sport or in other daily activities. Such a state of "satori" may be difficult to achieve in sport, since Stone claims that "any activity involving the use of the external 'target' (object of concentration) is *not* conducive to attaining "kensho" [mystical union]. . . ." (395:104) Many Eastern philosophies, Zen and Taoism in particular, have for thousands of years believed in the integration of mind and body, in the reality of "the unmoved movement," of "unity in polarity." These beliefs are grounded in an entire life style. The skepticism of Westerners stems in large part from an analytic rather than an experiential approach to philosophy, science, and experience in general. Westerners are talkers, not doers, and there is strong objection to accepting things that cannot be explained. The experience of satori, or the mystical union of mind and body, sport and player is difficult to communicate and highly suspect as valid. To be "understood," these Zen-like experiences must be experienced in the sense of "letting things happen," giving up the self, and suspending judgments. The process must start and develop within each person. The striving to achieve inner wholeness, inner peace and unity, and inner freedom replace Western goals of superiority, status, fame, material acquisitions, and ambition. However, it is easier and often more acceptable to talk of what we want to become or how great we are than it is to talk of spiritual matters.

> I think it is makyo [mystical union] that are described in the sport, dance, and exercise literature. It is quite possible, however, that these athletes, dancers, and joggers have in fact experienced mystical union in those activities, but in their reluctance to speak of Oneness, a knowing state, compassion—matters so close to one as to want to protect them from skeptical listeners—they confine themselves to speaking to those altered states popularized by the drug culture. (395:105)

Those who achieve flow or mystical union in sport come to know the experience in a unique way, and, from all reports, it is significant and meaningful enough to strive to repeat the experience.

DISCUSSION QUESTIONS

1. Superiority and excellence have been described in the chapter as two different concepts. Is it possible to strive for both at the same time? Explain. What are the "pay-offs" for the participant in each of these achievements? Is one better than the other as an intent and in what ways?
2. Suppose you have a team that has a squad of 20 players. For some, self-testing is important; for others it is superiority, and for the rest excellence is the reward they seek. Is it possible for all these intentions to be compatible in a team setting? Explain.
3. What factors in a person's lifetime may influence change or the kinds of things that are meaningful in the sport experience?
4. Have you ever experienced "flow" or a "peak experience" as it was explained in the chapter? If so, try to describe it.
5. What kinds of chances, or risks, do you like to take in a sport situation? Why?

DIRECTED READING

Alvarez, A.: I like to risk my life. *In* Sport and the Body, edited by E.W. Gerber. Philadelphia, Lea & Febiger, 1972, pp. 203–205.

Ravizza, K.: Potential of the sport experience. *In* Being Human in Sport, edited by D.J. Allen and B.W. Fahey. Philadelphia, Lea & Febiger, 1977, pp. 61–72.

Stone, R.: Of Zen and the experience of moving. Quest, 32(1):96–107, 1981.

Thomas, C.: Personal equations of sport involvement. NAPECW/NCPEAM Joint Conference Proceedings, Orlando, 1977, pp. 262–269.

Weiss, P.: Chapter 1: Concern for excellence and Chapter 3: Challenge of the body. *In* Sport: a Philosophic Inquiry. Carbondale: Southern Illinois University Press, 1969, pp. 3–17, 37–57.

White, D.A.: Great moments in sport: the one and the many. *In* Sport and the Body, 2nd ed., edited by E.W. Gerber and W.J. Morgan. Philadelphia, Lea & Febiger, 1979, pp. 207–213.

Chapter 8

SELF-KNOWLEDGE

Few people nowadays know what man is. Many sense this ignorance and die the more easily because of it. I have been and still am a seeker, but I have ceased to question stars and books; I have begun to listen to the teachings my blood whispers to me. My story is not a pleasant one; it has the taste of nonsense and chaos, of madness and dreams—like the lives of all men who stop deceiving themselves.

Each man's life represents a road toward himself, an attempt at a road, the intimation of a path. No man has ever been completely and entirely himself. Yet each one strives to become that—one in an awkward, the other in a more intelligent way—each as best he can.

We all share the same origin, our mothers; all of us come in at the same door. But each of us—experiments of the depths—strives toward his own destiny. We can understand one another; but each of us is able to interpret himself to himself alone. (167:4)

In Chapter 7, potential sources of meaning such as superiority, excellence, challenge, risk-taking, and a sense of oneness were examined. The realization of personal meanings found in any or all of those experiences often tells us something(s) *about* ourselves, but the acquisition of self-knowledge as a result of sport participation, or anything else we voluntarily commit ourselves to do, is not a guarantee. We must be willing, as the writer Hermann Hesse suggests, to "listen to the teachings my blood whispers to me." We must also be willing to suspend bias and the psychologic defense mechanisms we all use to protect ourselves in order to look and listen openly to what is revealed to us as a result of our sport commitments. The resolution and outcomes of the experience are only part of the story. What we do and who we are in all stages of the sport experience go to make up possible answers to the existential question: Who am I? It is not, however, always an easy or a pleasant task. As Metheny warns:

> . . . A man may learn much about himself—and about all men—on the symbolic field of sport. In those self-revealing moments of commitment to the values of human action he may know himself at his best—but equally he must also know himself at his worst. (274:233)

THE JOHARI WINDOW

It is possible to come to some formulation about who we are from two fundamental perspectives: from our interactions with others and from our experiences. In the social science literature, these perspectives are called the "social self" and the "phenomenal self." Luft's (252) paradigm of the Johari window can provide us with a perspective.

	known to self	unknown to self
known to others	OPEN	BLIND
unknown to others	HIDDEN	UNKNOWN

Johari Window

The four areas shown in the model represent the interactions possible between the individual and others in coming to a knowledge of the self. The "open" dimension represents those aspects of our self that are known to self and others. Others may observe these qualities, or the individual may choose to share feelings, perceptions, and ideas with an outsider to the extent that the "other" can come to know the individual. Tallness, shortness, or shyness would be very obvious and "open" characteristics. The individual comes to "know" these things as a result of others telling him, previous experiences, or social comparison. While the model shows all four segments equal, they are not, for just as the process of personal identity is dynamic, so are the dimensions of the Johari window. The longer and better we are acquainted with a person, the larger the "open" area becomes and the smaller some or all of the other areas may grow.

The "hidden" area represents knowledges we have about ourselves but to which others may not have access. We often hide, for example, our feelings and beliefs of bigotry or chauvinism. Depending on the individual, this hidden dimension may be a small or a large area of the self. Whether we choose to self-disclose is also dependent on the individual, the situation, and the extent we may know and trust the "other" with the information. Such self-disclosure is a selective process and depends on who the "other" is. The hiding of the private self may be grounded in negative feelings about "who I am," i.e., not liking those parts of me; or, it may be that the private knowledge is either too personal or too difficult to communicate in ways that would be accurately understood by the "other." When the knowledge is brought out of the hidden dimension and shared, however, the hidden area grows smaller and the open area grows larger.

The third area of coming to know self resides in the knowledge that others have about us which we may not have ourselves. Luft refers to this as the "blind" area. Others watch us, listen to us, and from an objective and rational standpoint often "put things together" that we may not be able to see or know for ourselves. A simple example may be that we are swinging late with a club or racquet or that some aspect of technique is faulty. Although others may know this, we may not. In this dimension, it is possible for others to serve as a "mirror" for us to see ourselves, and this is a fairly straightforward means of coming to know self and of increasing the open area between self and the selected other. It is also possible that what others know, they may not transmit back to you. Such knowledge of technique or strategy may, in fact, be used against you by an opponent. The use of game films to detect such lapses in our personal knowledge is a common practice. The other possibility is that people come to know an individual in this dimension and may evaluate such knowledge and even unknowingly bias their observation before passing it back to the individual, so that the data come back not as a mirror of what is actual but as a reflection of what we should be or what someone else would like us to be or know about ourselves. The bias may be unintentional, but it is not uncommon. The other option the outsider has, either out of indifference or negative feelings, is to fail to pass the information on to the individual. As we gain knowledge about ourselves from these outside "others," the open area expands. We may also choose to put this "new" knowledge in the hidden category as we confront others, but in either case, the "blind" area diminishes.

The fourth area is the area of the self which is not known either to ourselves or others. This area includes things that we may not have encountered, and hence we have no bias for making judgments or knowing. If someone asks you if you are capable of murder or cannibalism, you most likely would say "no"; yet you do not really know. Like many other less dramatic behaviors, until you experience yourself in certain ways and in certain encounters, you are free to believe what you would *like* to believe about yourself, but you do not really *know* for sure a number of things about yourself. Depending on the individual, the quality, quantity, and variability of one's life experiences and the kinds of "others" with whom one interacts, the "unknown" dimension of the self may be large or small at the time of death.

THE RELATIONSHIP OF THE "OTHER" TO PERSONAL IDENTITY

The public self is available for interaction with the "other." The "other" takes many forms. In our everyday world, significant others such as parents, peers, siblings, teachers, and friends provide considerable feedback about who we are. In addition, the other is more generalized and may take the form of laws, institutions, religion, social roles, or cultural patterns. The sport setting provides parallel significant "others" which include coaches, teammates, opponents, officials, rules, sport roles, team and spectator expectations. Mead, who was a chief proponent of social self theory, believed that the self, or one's identity, evolved as a result of interactions with others and with the more generalized social structure.

> . . . there are two general stages in the development of the self. At the first of these stages, the individual's self is constituted by an organization of the particular attitudes of other individuals toward himself and toward one another in specific social acts in which he participates with them. . . . At the second stage . . . the self is constituted . . . by an organization of the social attitudes of the generalized other or the social group as a whole to which he belongs. These social or group attitudes are brought within the individual's field of direct experience . . . (263:104)

From this context of social interaction as a source of knowledge for the individual, there are a series of impacts on the individual related to the identity he/she eventually assumes. The diagram shows the immediacy of such external impacts:

```
┌─────────────────────────────────┐
│      Cultural Patterns and      │
│           Limitations           │
│  ┌───────────────────────────┐  │
│  │     Laws, Institutions,   │  │
│  │      Role Expectations    │  │
│  │  ┌─────────────────────┐  │  │
│  │  │     Significant      │  │  │
│  │  │       Others         │  │  │
│  │  │  ┌───────────────┐  │  │  │
│  │  │  │       P       │  │  │  │
│  │  │  │       E       │  │  │  │
│  │  │  │       R       │  │  │  │
│  │  │  │       S       │  │  │  │
│  │  │  │       O       │  │  │  │
│  │  │  │       N       │  │  │  │
│  │  │  │               │  │  │  │
│  │  │  └───────────────┘  │  │  │
│  │  └─────────────────────┘  │  │
│  └───────────────────────────┘  │
└─────────────────────────────────┘
```

These kinds of relationships, which have the potential to assist in the formation of personal identity, or a realization of self, represent a value-based source of knowledge in that they tell us who we *should* be. Who we should be may be different from or the same as: (1) who we *are*, (2) who we *want* to be, (3) who we *can* be. When there are no discrepancies, there are no problems, but when there are discrepancies between or among these aspects of our identity, there is often anxiety, uncertainty,

doubt, and despair. Many literary and philosophic themes center around
the dissonance between who one should be and who one actually is. An
example which cuts across many boundaries is the expectation that in this
culture people will be monogamous and heterosexual. To love more than
one person, to have more than one spouse, or to love someone of the
same sex goes against legal, religious, cultural, and social standards. To
have these feelings or to know one fits in an "outlaw" category as a result
of experience is a real possibility. One is expected to be a "good sport,"
to be gracious in defeat. If we are not, we come to know ourselves as
something different from the standard which is set.

In the sport situation, we give and take, act and react. Our actions and
our physical being become public. We are under the influence of the
"look" when the body and its behaviors are the objects of reflection. The
spectator, the opponent, or the coaches may be the interactors and observers, or, upon reflection, the athlete may become audience to his/her
own acts. The knowledge gained through such interactions may be publicly exchanged between self and "other," or it may remain a private
reflection of the athlete despite its objective nature. The audience may
see you during the act and come to "know" something about you. They
may know that you missed an easy shot or that you took a cheap shot at
someone, and they may tell you about it. They know what you did (public
knowledge) but not necessarily why you did it (private knowledge). As
an athlete committed to the sport act, there is not time to think about
who or what you are at the moment. After the fact, however, it is possible
to think about *what* happened (public knowledge) but also, as the participant, to reflect on *why* it happened.

The process of knowing self becomes, at the objective level, an interface
of what and why. The feedback from coaches, teammates, and fans about
what happened often leads to an enlightened evaluation of performance
in terms of technique and even temperament. For example, the admonition to "relax" or forget about it (a mistake) is a reminder that someone
outside yourself knows something about how you feel by observing the
way you are behaving. The after-the-fact reflections of the athlete may
further lead to evaluation of performance but also to an examination and
evaluation of feelings, meanings, and responses to the outcome of the
sport experience that has just transpired. We may know fear in the midst
of roaring whitewater, but we may only come to realize its full meaning
when we sit in the stiller water that comes after the rapids. Similarly,
assessments of a variety of sensations, or the fixing of responsibility in
accepting credit or blame for our actions may be best known in relationship
to ourselves when we become an objective "other."

Kleinman argues:

> . . . a self is a becoming. It is a coming to be. It becomes itself independently,
> yet obligated. An 'other' is a necessary condition for this process to take
> place. . . . A self is actor, yet acted upon, performer and audience. (207:45)

While it is possible to turn inward on our own experiences and be introspective, Kleinman sees the "other" as necessary to the search for self. Knowledge does not occur in a vacuum. It results from experiential encounter with people and things. Whether the "other" tells us things or not is irrelevant. Our own coming to know is contingent on the other being there as a dialectic co-actor.

> Exploration of the nature of the other, which constitutes a necessary and essential part of the dialectic, has been for the most part, avoided or perhaps taken for granted. . . . It is the 'other' which signifies people and things which are essential to the nature of human relationships. I am contending here that it is these human relationships, man's dialectic with people and things, which provide an avenue for man to become a self. . . . an essential ingredient of kinesis [movement toward self] is encounter. (207:46)

To philosophers like Heidegger and Buber human existence is a "being-together-with-others," either in the development of a social interest in the individual or in the development of a dialogue between man and man. Buber, predominantly, insisted on the importance not only of this dialogue but on man's moral need to be accepted by his fellow men and to seek out settings and life projects that would facilitate both dialogue and acceptance.

In sport, the "other" is often the opponent who provides the possibility for dialogue through test and contest. The search for challenge or the achievement of excellence or even the formulation of precontest intent is contingent on either a confrontation or encounter with something or somebody else. The "other" involved may also be teammates of one kind or another with whom cooperation is essential and with whom kinship and bonds of knowing are possible. I cannot play a game of singles tennis without an opponent nor can I play a game of doubles without both a partner and a pair of opponents. From this standpoint alone, the "other" is necessary and important in any quest for self that may be potentially available in sport.

It has been most common to view the opponent as the "enemy," as a barrier to achieving one's intent in sport, but it is the quality of the opponent which has the potential of calling forth the intensity of an involvement, for determining commitment, and for demanding the best in a performer. Ultimately it is the best in us which measures who we are at any given time. The opponent as a rival, as someone to be beaten down, as "bums" who are to be booed during the introductions by the home crowd is a very narrow and inauthentic perspective of what sport is about. What real value is there in any victory when the opponent is unworthy?

Kretchmar (217) and Hyland (177) have written about the possibilities for the opponent to call forth the best as well as the worst in our sport involvements. When viewed as an experiencing of sharing rather than hostility, competition, despite the inevitability of a winner and a loser, can be seen as a source of self-knowledge and meaning. The possibility of the I-Thou exists. Characterized by mutuality, directness, intensity, and dialogue, an I-Thou relationship between player and opponent in sport can be achieved. As Gerber (131:132) summarizes: "The nature of the game, and of sports in general, is that this kind of relationship tends to occur. Thus, through the medium of the game man approaches his fellow players as *Thous*, and finds meaning in his own I."

Bannister speaks to the desire that athletes have to be with others who share the same needs and goals when he says: "There is a desire to find in a sport a companionship with kindred people. Friendships which are formed under the baptism of fire, if I can use that phrase, have a curious permanence." (22:65) Kleinman also points out that the camaraderie achieved by teammates and opponents provides a means of communication and being "in touch" that endures beyond the playing days.

> The bodily person in touch with the other is much more complete and fulfilling. The sensual experiences of having been there in sport also provides a unique way of knowing self and other. It achieves at times a level of communication not easily reached or often found. (207:49)

"Being there," whether it is some championship game, a 10-kilometer race when the temperature is 10 degrees below zero, or the rapids of the Middle Fork of the Salmon River may, as Kleinman suggests "constitute a fundamental change in the mode of being itself." (207:49)

Relative to teamwork, Meier has written about the "kinship of the rope" that binds mountain climbers together as a symbolic bond of trust and common purpose. As much as the rope represents physical safety and protection, Meier regards it as "a desirable and vivid symbol of the common purposes and mutual interdependence of individuals engaged in the enterprise." (267:56) As the basis for lasting bonds of friendship and communication, Sayre points out that:

> The companionship provided by climbing together is almost universally valued by mountaineers. The friendships established are lasting and irreplaceable. . . For the deepest friendships spring from sharing failure as well as success, danger as well as safety. . . Men are made for the close warmth of friendship tested in danger and adversity. It is not impossible without this testing, but it is much more difficult. (366:214)

Meier continues in his suggestion that sport has the potential to be a "loving struggle" and that such a struggle fosters an authentic and unique communication. Such communication and any subsequent understanding achieved as a result of it occurs in an environment of openness and uniqueness. He claims that the interpersonal intimacy available in sport, particularly in something like mountain climbing, leads to authentic exchange among people (267:59–61). Sadler reinforces this position when he says that such an intimate and powerfully intense interpersonal relationship has the "creative power to develop the best in persons and to establish a new personal world where individuality is fulfilled in a complementary union." (358:185)

While such a "complementary union" may be more generally expected and accepted among teammates, competition can, says Hyland, yield friendship among opponents. (177) Similarly, Kretchmar sees opponents as potentially being more than "two persons who create tests for one another." (217:19)

Hyland maintains that two possibilities exist in competition relative to the relationship between two opponents. The first is the most common.

> On the one hand, we have experienced that situation in which our competitive play breaks down into alienation. This can, of course, take on a variety of forms and degrees of intensity. (177:29)

The opponent is viewed with hostility, ranging from irritation to fisticuffs. Competition is viewed in the economic sense of being "better than" and as having its roots in a "winner take all" perspective which seeks to alienate the opponent.

The other possibility is friendship, and competitive sport is seen as a relational rather than monadic event. Even though this aspect of sport is both less obvious and less prevalent, it is a way of being and knowing available to the player. (177:28–30) While these two possibilities exist in many facets of everyday life, "the play situation, by its natural intensity and its sometimes arbitrary delimitation in space, time, and purpose, can make certain themes more visible than in our ongoing everyday lives." (177:29) Like Kleinman, Hyland argues that the "other" is important and the relational I-Thou possibility increases the possibility of achieving a sense of fulfillment and achievement.

> *All* situations in which we strive to overcome experienced incompleteness, whether of sexuality, of political power, of wealth, of creativity, or of wisdom, all are testimony to our erotic nature. . . . we are both relational and monadic . . . We *are* a relation to others—to all other things but especially to other humans—insofar as we see in those others the possibility of fulfillment. (177:33)

The conception of competition that Hyland and Kretchmar have is not without its hope or desire to be victorious. It is, however, what happens on the way to the outcome that has implications for what we come to know about ourselves. Competition as a relational event, as a coming together, would appear to have greater potential for self-understanding than if it is entered into with the intent to alienate or to tear apart. Kretchmar believes it is possible to give oneself to another in going after the same goal even though only one may achieve it. (217:20, 22) Hyland sees "competition as a questioning or striving together . . . grounded in our eros, our sense of incompleteness and striving for fulfillment." (177:35) Friendship and a positive cooperative relationship stem from the demand that each player be the best he can be, that he play hard and play fair.

In other words, you should be as good as you can be and make me be the best I can be to overcome you. "Competition, as a striving or questioning *together* towards excellence, *in so far as it most adequately fulfills its possibilities,* does so as a mode of friendship." (177:36)

The kind of fellowship among opponents who are each dedicated to excellence and/or victory is grounded in trust, cooperation, and honesty. What we are saying is that: I have trained for you, for this event; I will play with you. Trust me to give you the best contest I can. Trust me to be fair. I will expect these things from you.

> In sport the successful coming together of 'will' and 'grace' cannot guarantee victory, excellence, or productivity to anyone. It cannot ever assure that two persons will have a 'good' (closely contested) game. But it does promise human affirmation even though a word may never pass from one athlete to another; skillful gestures serve to communicate one's personal dreams, thoughts, questions, and statements. (217:27)

The "other" may tell us who we should be. Sometimes we use it as a mirror to see ourselves, our strengths and frailties, in objective ways. We are given feedback, some of which is rational and "clean" and some of which is biased about what and who we seem to be with others. The "look" of the I-It relationship is informative, sets expectations and standards that mold who we, at least, think we are. In the "kinship" of teammate or opponent it is possible to achieve an understanding of our humanness and to develop a unique and an enduring communication. We are made available to ourselves for our own self-understanding through our dialogue with the "other" in sport.

THE PHENOMENAL SELF

Seeing ourselves through others as a result of their "look" is the most public and least personal of the modes of self-understanding. Except for the intimacy and intensity with teammates or opponents which may become the for-the-moment I-Thou, the body and its actions are objectified and remain in the analytic second dimension, in the I-It relation. Yet the understandings gained from our interactions with others are a complement to what we may come to know as a result of direct experience. Either the immediate sensual knowledge acquired as we play or the evaluation of behaviors and feelings after the fact, as audience to our own acts, is the more personal and private dimension to self-knowledge. The sport experience, says Metheny, is too immediate and reactive to contemplate as it is occurring and requires later reflection for full understanding.

> In the moment of commitment to the values he attached to his own human actions, no competitor has time to rationalize about his own feelings and his own motivations. In that moment of all-out action he must experience himself as he is, in all the complexity of his own feelings about himself, his gods, and other men who claim the right to share the universe of his existence. (274:233)

The knowledge and meanings derived from this after-the-fact examination of action are contingent on honest introspection and evaluation. One of the recurring themes evident in the writings of Metheny related to meaning and self-knowledge is that you are what you are in sport and there is no place to hide. In the man-made and self-directed circumstance of sport, all attributions of success and failure must be accepted by the player. Since the player comes to the sport experience voluntarily and committed in the sense of being an embodied entity, silence and the hiding of ignorance is impossible inasmuch as the body and its actions speak for all, including the player, to evaluate.

> Stripped of all excuses, he must demonstrate his ability to perform a well-defined task of his own choosing; naked of all pretense, he must demonstrate his own talents for using those talents under circumstances which permit him to function in the wholeness of his being as a fully integrated person.
>
> Within this performance, he cannot delude himself about his own capabilities . . . he may find an image of himself at his best, and equally he may find an image of himself at his worst, but he cannot escape the implications of either image, because it is an image of himself at his utmost.
>
> Neither can be escape his own feelings about that image as it is revealed to him within the performance. (271:65)

The phenomenal self is that identity created from experience and from past and present self-observation and evaluation. Humans are creatures who not only do things but think about what they do premeditatively, prereflectively, or reflectively. In sport, premeditative thought about the upcoming experience is most commonly found in the intent and preparation stages and to a lesser degree in the involvement stage. Prereflective thinking about the experience is the central focus of the commitment stage where the union of the mind and body, player and the act, may preclude analytic and cognitive thought. Reflective thinking occurs most commonly in the resolution stage where an examination of the entire sport experience and our responses and feelings may come under analysis. (See sections on Sources of Knowledge, Chapter 3, and Stages of Participation, Chapter 6, for details on these concepts.) While the "other" cannot be excluded from our experiences, the source of knowledge is the phenomenal or experienced, self. As a result, this knowledge about ourselves may be more private and would, most likely, find itself in the "hidden" dimension of the Johari window until such time as self-disclosure to others brought it into the open.

There is no guarantee of self-understanding as a result of the sport experience, or any experience. For most people, personal identification comes not as a sudden revelation, an effortless gift, nor as a gradual natural growth. Rather, if it occurs at all, it is likely to come as an achievement, sometimes a slow, laborious, painful emergence accompanied by doubt, fear, confusion, and anxiety.

> Who am I, really? is a project guided by uncertainty, ambiguity, and mystery. The man who seeks an answer is condemned to struggle, sentenced to tentativeness. And yet the search goes on. Men want to know. (147:126)

The necessity to retreat within ourselves, to introspect, to "listen to the whisperings my blood teaches me" is not welcomed by all people. It is often viewed as self-indulgent to turn our focus inward, to examine ourselves, for the personal feelings and internalizations stemming from such introspections are often difficult to communicate or people fear they will appear romantic or out-of-control of their lives. Critics of the poet Rod McKuen cite his writings as "mushy rantings." However, for many people his sentiments come close to home in their truth and applicability. The view that personal truths may be "too soft" or may somehow make us vulnerable in a competitive world often stifles introspection. Instead people stay active, seek thrills, and chemically alter their minds so they don't have to think about themselves, about wars or rumors of wars, about the economy or the mortgage, about the alienation or boredom that is part of the urban technology in which they live. While the "who I should be" is a product of the social self, who I am and who I can be is a product of the phenomenal self. Knowing that part of the self requires reflection, authentic evaluation, or, at minimum, self-awareness.

T.S. Eliot described the writing of a poem as "a raid on the inarticulate" that was attempted within "the general mess of the imprecision of feeling undisciplined squares of emotion." The attempt to turn inward to understand self may be a similar experience. Further attempts to verbalize any feelings may also be problematic in that few of the feelings and knowledges can be commonly shared. But in at least general terms, some areas of potential knowledge can be identified. However, before it is possible for an experience in sport to yield meaning and/or self-understanding either prereflectively or reflectively, a number of prerequisite conditions must exist.

In the first place, the participant must truly "enter into the experience" and achieve the commitment stage. This is, however, not always an easy task to accomplish. Meier points out that in a society committed to work and productivity, there is a tendency to try and measure sport in these same terms.

> Man is what he does; his identity is his productivity. Thus, personal satisfaction, value and meaning are direct products of man's labor. (264:26)

Since one of the characteristics of sport is its nonutilitarian nature, many attempts are made to make sport accountable in terms other than personal satisfaction which is qualitative in nature.

> . . . an obsession with objectivity and productivity in physical efforts and activities renunciates the lived body; represses muscular sensuousness for expressive rather than instrumental ends; focuses exclusively on quantifiable matters to the exclusion of qualitative questions on bodily freedom, sensual

gratification, and sexual expressiveness; desensitizes movement as a distinctive source of creative impulses and aesthetic experience; and finally, alienates the individual from his body. (264:29)

Similarly, Fetters argues that it is difficult for the player to enter into the experience and to be what she calls "self-creative." "Implicit in the process of self-creation is a sensitive awareness and responsiveness to one's experience, a curiosity and spontaneity in one's approach to the world." (100:37) It is this awareness, curiosity, and spontaneity that makes it possible for the participant to become more aware of the qualitative, aethestic, sensuous, and meaningful dimensions of the sport experience.

To participate in one's own self-creation requires that one be "in touch" with those delicate qualitative modes of human experience, the depths of personal feeling, imagination, and meaning. (100:37)

Fetters goes on to cite a number of cultural factors that intrude on our ability to focus on the qualitative aspects of sport. She identifies a number of "myths" which must be overcome to permit prereflective awareness to be heightened and for reflective analysis to include qualitative considerations. First, there is the myth of objective measurement previously described by Meier. The second myth, the myth of abstraction and generalization, stems from the myth of objective measurement. It assumes that "*all* knowledge and *all* experience are subject to verbal explication. . . . He learns to abstract each personal experience, to generalize it to the point of losing its personal uniqueness . . . to fit into a neat category with a label. . . ." (100:38)

The myth of separateness is much like Hyland's concept of alienation. Where superiority is the focus of the experience, Fetters maintains that meaningful relationships will be difficult if not impossible to achieve in that sport setting. "When the athlete views himself as competing *against* rather than *with* the opponent [he creates] an antagonistic world of reciprocal hostility rather than a shared world of mutual affirmation." (100:41) Entering *into* a complete and mutual sport experience is denied by such beliefs in separateness and superiority as the main objective. Stemming from this is the fourth myth that Fetters identifies as the myth of power and control over others. Spurred by the need to win, the "inherent drive to question, to wonder" is usurped by the emphasis on power and control to achieve victory. "When success means winning, the coach cannot afford to relinquish control; he cannot allow the game to be *played* by the players; he cannot permit them the spontaneity and freedom to make their own decisions." (100:41–42) Creativity and introspection cannot flourish when freedom and choice are removed. Self-evaluation is minimized when external evaluation replaces it.

The "inner game" concepts have been enlightening despite their varying degrees of philosophic and psychologic applicability. From the standpoint of the inner game advocacy to suspend judgment during and after the experience, a "let it happen" and "trust your body" attitude lends itself to qualitative understandings of the experience. Fetters and Kleinman have advocated that to be "in touch" with our "self" we need to be in touch with our bodies. We must allow the body to be our access to the world, allow it to experience fully without chastising it or controlling it or overanalyzing it. The body as subject, as a union of mind and body, and as a union of play and the player would seem to be another essential prerequisite for prereflective and introspective self-realizations. The body as a being-for-itself rather than an object in being-for-others "reflects and expresses our attitude regarding the whole world. In and through our bodies we ultimately witness that which we are and that which we want to be in our most profound verity." (361:162)

Despite the advocacy for entering into the experience with "others," it is also necessary to experience sport alone in the sense of minimizing outside interference with choices and consequences. In surfing, says Slusher, "if a man makes an error, he is 'wiped out'. But it is his error. It is this experience that counts. Tradition and history can do little to assist him. He must determine his own destiny. He is solely responsible." (383:33) Away from the everyday hassles and interruptions of others, it is possible to be alone in sport despite any simultaneously on-going I-Thou relationship. Harper says that when we are actively involved in sport, the choice is to play or not to play and if the choice is to play then we are alone in the sense that personal success and failure depend solely on the individual. (147:126)

> Whether he is hurling a javelin, soaring off a ski jump, performing a double back flip off a diving board, or screaming towards earth in a free fall sky dive, man is alone. He is beyond the world of public determinations; of self-deceptions and of everydayness. And in the solitary state of oneness, man can meet himself. (147:127)

Being alone can provide the individual with information knowable only to himself. "It is I alone who feels the bat as I alone can sense it. It is I alone who 'knows'." (379:59)

In speaking of the body as a source of knowing Van Kaam notes:

> My hands reveal to me a basketball as spherical, solid and leathery; my throwing hands unveil to me its bouncing quality; my pressing hands reveal its elasticity. Bodily behavior as gesture, movement, and language *is* my being-in-the-world, my immediate presence to people and things. Bodily behavior is not a symbolication nor meditization of myself or my desires; it is I, it is my desire, it is the loving me. (431:229)

With regard to such subjective aloneness in sport, Metheny says "that each man's connotations are his own and he is is not obliged to find each other's meaning in any [sport] form." (271:69) Aloneness in a solo effort or in the company of others is a necessary but not sufficient condition of self-realization. Too frequently in sport we are not left alone in sufficient enough ways to achieve a union with sport, to experience our bodily expressions with awareness or to reflect on our choices, actions, and the consequences.

PREREFLECTIVE KNOWING

> . . . my body is already a meaning-giving existence, even if I am not yet conscious of this meaning-giving activity. My body invests my world with meaning even before I think about this meaning. . . . my body makes the world and the other available to me. . . . (431:229)

The experience of the body as self provides a source of information that occurs even before one has the opportunity to reflect on what has happened. When you bounce a basketball, it is possible to "know" roundness, elasticity, angle of rebound, hardness or softness just by doing the bouncing. The body is aware before cognitive processes even begin to analyze what is going on in the experience. Sport, like many other experiences, provides the opportunity for direct movement experiences and for a number of encounters, or self-relationships to exist. "The self-relationships are assumed to be the relationship to the mover's body as an object in a physicochemical universe, the relationship to the other persons in a defined social structure, and the relationship to personal uniqueness." (110:55) The first of these two relationships has been treated previously in this chapter. Gerber maintains that "sport experiences can elicit an intense awareness of one's body" (134:187) and one's self. Fraleigh (110:53) also argues that "man becomes available to himself for his own self-understanding" as a result of his movement, or sport, experience.

If we turn our attention to the examination of the personal uniqueness that it is possible to come to know as a result of moving in a sport situation, there are an infinite number of possibilities. For as we have previously noted, each person comes to sport with a different history of experiences, different intents and motivations, and varying degrees of commitment. As a result the kinds, degree, and quality of self-understanding are highly individualistic. Perhaps the easiest aspect of self-understanding to examine is that of physical prowess, or the sensations we are made aware of first on a prereflective level and later on a reflective and/or evaluative level. Metheny projects *possibilities* that suggest an individual's initial involvement, but as she finally comments, "Who can account for the likes and dislikes of human beings?" (274:235)

> Perhaps a contestant may find a particular sport particularly meaningful because it does formulate a conception of a man who performs certain kinds of work . . . . because it formulates the patterns of his own personality structure . . . . because his physical being is so admirably designed for the performance of that action . . . . Perhaps he chooses to ski because he likes the feeling of the cold air as it stings his face, or because he likes the whiteness of the snow and the blueness of the sky. Perhaps he chooses to swim because he likes the sensation of being supported by the water. (274:235)

The physicalness of football, the communion with nature in hiking, the "skinny-dipping" sensation of skydiving, the open air and green grass of the golf course—any of these factors can be motives to participate but also become physical sensations that the player becomes aware of as a source of knowing self and the physical world. You can watch a thousand golfers and a thousand swings, but when you hold the club in your hand and swing, you are a uniqueness among commonality. This is *my* shot. You ski down a mountain that thousands have skied before you. Yet you come to know speed, balance, grace, and timing as unique aspects of who you are or what you are. Meaning of the self-knowledge variety is an individual "coming to an awareness of his own identity as an individual and as a member of humanity who is, simultaneously similar and different from other beings." (117:108)

> The experience of the body as self is crucial to the individual's self-identi-fication. It relates to the experience of self as a strong, skilled [or weak, unskilled] person who is [or is not] able to accomplish certain physical tasks with a high degree of excellence. To to able to feel good about one's physical performance is to be able to feel good about oneself—and the converse is also true. (134:186)

Before anyone tells you or before you think about it, you as your body experience yourself as a moving being and all the physical components which comprise movement. There is no way you can know what static balance is or whether you are capable of static balance unless you experience a situation that demands it. Your body tells you what it is to achieve it or not achieve it. It is not an experience requiring reflection or evaluation as it occurs as part of the on-going experience.

Fraleigh, in his classic paper, "The Moving I" (117), examined six possibilities of what he called "meanings of the self-knowledge variety." These meanings included freedom, necessity, violence, tenderness, competition, and cooperation as they were potentially found in the direct sport experience.

Necessity

The self as "necessitated" is experienced (1) as the body becomes subject to physical laws and gravity, (2) when the body is experienced as deficient or not skilled/trained adequately enough to meet the demands of the situation, (117:109) and (3) when there is a restriction on actions which are permitted in a particular sport activity. (117:130) Fraleigh argues that the condition of necessity "tells me" that there is a sameness among humans and that despite our greatest wishes, we are not unconditionally free. Many of my movements, like those of all humans, are determined or limited by such physical forces as gravity. Despite the Jonathan Livingston Seagull admonition to "break the chains of your mind and you break the chains of your body," we share an identity with all humans of not being able to go beyond certain physical principles. (117:130)

Motor inability, whether from lack of training or preparation, necessarily limits the potential of the performer. This is necessity as a "personal condition." For some this is a relative necessity, and one can be "freer" through more practice or skill development. For others, it is a more deterministic limitation as the necessary skills for performance are not available to the performer. (117:132) An individual, for example, may not be free to win a marathon. You may be free to participate in a marathon, but despite all the training and desire in the world, physically you just do not have what it takes to win it. Knowing either that you were not ready or that you did not have the necessary skills to achieve your intentions in sport is a possible revelation of self which comes as a result of participation.

The third of the necessities in sport are those "restrictions on choice of movements performed." While I am free to enter into the game of volleyball, I then must accept the rules, techniques, and restrictions that are part of that game. (117:111) I may not, for example, walk off the court during play and get a drink of water, kick the ball, or punch an opposing player in the mouth. We learn that we must act in necessary and specified ways in order for the game to go on. More broadly we identify with it being necessary that some things and much of who I am may have to be the way they are in order to get along in the world and to have any freedom at all.

Freedom

> My personal human identity is at least partially a product of my will to free myself. . . . And it is in entering such a world [sport] that man may know himself symbolically as a powerful agent in being since, in that world, he literally uses externally controlling necessities. . . . to serve his own purposes. (117:114)

Both in contrast to and as a complement to necessity having meaning for our personal identity, "the lived body experience of the self as free is also a very basic source of human identity meanings." (117:113) Slusher was one of the first sport philosophers to consider the concept of freedom is sport. In *Man, Sport,* and *Existence,* he attempts to demonstrate that freedom and sport are inseparable. Slusher contends that "freedom is a pivotal force by which man can comprehend the perspective of sport" and as such demands that the participant choose, act, and take responsibility for his own involvement in the sport experience. (379:186) Additionally, Slusher believes that an awareness of freedom is essential to sport and that this awareness is the foundation for authenticity and self-realization within the sport environment. He says:

Deny freedom and sport is denied any meaningful place in the realm of existence. . . . As the sport event unfolds, each situation presents itself with a number of potential choices. . . . Choice is a function of awareness . . . . the performer develops through it and, in the process, sport develops because of it. (379:188–189)

It is important to note that while Slusher maintains that freedom is an integral aspect of sport involvement, the awareness of freedom is not guaranteed.

Sport generally does not free man by itself. Rather, man is *left alone*. The guidelines are present, the rules are established, but he is there in the vacuum of his existence to inquire and discover his own truth. (379:182)

Within the sport experience man is faced with numerous opportunities for choice; for example, to enter or not to enter the sport situation, to cut right rather than to cut left, or to play for a tie rather than for a win.

Where necessity shows us there is a sameness among humans, freedom allows us to experience self as unique. "Basic to the element of freedom in sport is the fact that sport . . . is freely chosen and freely engaged in." (67:69) While it is necessary for the player to adapt to the necessities of the game in order to play, there remains the freedom to be creative and spontaneous within the context of the rules. Freedom in movement activities demonstrates that there is a uniqueness among us. (117:114) If every person who played halfback had the blocking that O.J. Simpson had, there would still be only one Simpson. There was only one with the unique freedom to "pick the hole" the way he could, and yet any football player is free to make choices once the ball is handed off. While the rules exist and the play may be designed, the player remains free to express movement options. The choices and the consequences become a source of personal identification.

Fraleigh also points out that the player is free to realize personal intentions. (117:135) If it is possible for me to win a marathon by training hard enough and by being coached well enough, then I am free to train and be ready. I am also free not to train and to impose a state of necessity (limited development of ability) on myself.

The person who is free to realize personal intentions understands his identity as a being partly dependent upon his own personal will as manifest in effort. The person who is free to create new personal intentions understands his identity as a being who transcends himself and other humans by his personal will in conjunction with his personal creative levels and new strategies. (117:137)

Becoming a self, establishing a sense of personal identity is a process or movement from knowing what is possible to what is actually part of who we are. Such a transition, says Kleinman, takes place in a state of freedom.

Nowhere is freedom more clearly manifested than in sport. 'You call the signals. You lay the strategy. You make the improvisations and adjustments.'

The description clearly captures the freedom inherent in self becoming a self. (204:152)

Violence and Aggression

In discussing violence in sport, the "collision" sports of ice hockey and football immediately come to mind. Generally, violence is viewed as a negative means (since it usually involves fighting, brutality, or cheap shots) to achieve the highly desired end of winning. Within this context, violence has its roots in ethical behavior which will be examined in Chapter 10. Although the term "violence" with its premeditated intent to hurt someone else usually takes on negative connotations in sport, acts of aggression are commonly accepted as part of the game. Boxing is an extreme example of a sport where aggression, violence, and brutality are accepted by the participants and many of the fans as an integral part of the game. Many people refuse to watch boxing and, in terms of the number of participants it draws, it is not considered a popular sport.

Although pop singer Olivia Newton-John's 1981–82 hit song "Let's Get Physical" was not sport-related, it does reflect an attitude among today's youths who are seeking many varieties of physical encounter and want to let their "bodies talk." The expression of physicalness in the form of aggression or violence or physical contact in sport is only one outlet for such expressions, which came out into the open and were accepted during the self-introspecting 1970s. Many sports, which by definition and by rules are noncontact sports, do allow for contact and for acts of aggression and violence. Basketball is, in fact, a contact sport in which the rules allow for "incidental" contact, but the fans, officials, and players can extend the interpretation of incidental contact to mean "let's get physical." Games like football, lacrosse, hockey, and wrestling are generally acknowledged as contact sports where physicalness is a predominant part of the game. Sports like volleyball, racquetball, tennis, or badminton are generally thought of as noncontact sports. Fraleigh points out, however, that even these sports allow for violent actions. (117:117–118)

Many people choose to play certain sports and either choose or end up playing certain positions because they like the contact; they like to "hit" and be hit. The value of sport in this regard is that for these individuals, the violence is controlled. In ice hockey, checking hard is an important defensive tactic. A "good" check is one that is hard and puts the opponent into the boards and out of the play; yet there is a limit to what the player can do with this physical aggression. The rules are designed to stop the violence short of allowing players to be injured. The permissible violence does not include tripping, slashing with the stick, hitting someone over the head with the stick, or punching the opponent in the face. Up to that point and within the rules physicalness in the form of aggression and violence and just plain body contact is an acceptable expression of who I am and what I am capable of being. Expressing violence allows me to realize first of all that I am capable of violent acts. Secondly, it gives an indication of whether I am willing to control my violence and stay within the rules. Out of anger, fear, or the desire to win it is possible that what I might like to do to someone, i.e., hurt them, and what I end up doing to them are either the same or different. In either case, both private feelings and public behavior are sources of self-understanding.

In noncontact sports, Fraleigh gives examples of violent acts which occur in technique or through use of implements. "Executing the smash in badminton or tennis and the spike in volleyball are good examples of this." (117:117) He goes on to say that "for the person executing such violent action the experience is one of intense concentration of one's being to the extent that the self becomes a unity of violent intention and violent action." (117:117) In power volleyball, there has been an increase in the specialization of positions. Players are now known for their defensive skills, their ability to serve, as setters, as "hitters." Substitution and court positioning are often based on these player specializations. While there may be some differences in physical technique between a setter and a "hitter" or spiker, some of these differences may come down to the ability to see oneself as "violent." Most men players really like to hit but far fewer women players hit well or want to. A woman collegiate player once remarked, "I love to hit, to pound that thing so nobody can touch it, watch it hit the floor or the other side and bounce a mile high. Sometimes I'd really like to just stuff it down somebody's throat. I get the urge but I don't do it. I hate setting. Too mushy. But I love a good set so I can put it away." Perhaps part of this behavior is not authentic. If she would like to hit someone with the ball but does not, there are any number of factors which modify intent, but knowing you would like to "stuff it" is also knowing that you could if the circumstances were different.

Our reactions to the violence we direct at others or to violence which is directed at us can be potentially self-revealing. Do I enjoy it? Can I handle it? Am I afraid that I will be hurt or that I will hurt someone else? Do I temper my violence toward less skilled players or toward members of the opposite sex? It is possible to know ourselves as violent in ways we enjoy and dislike, in ways we accept, rationalize, or reject, but when the sport situation demands acts of aggression or violence, either we are capable or not capable of being violent. Our actual involvement provides an inescapable answer. ". . . Positive self-identity meaning of being a powerful agent achieved through the experience of violence is mixed with negative self-identity meaning of being fearful of the responsibility for the exercise of such power." (117:121)

Tenderness and Compassion

In contrast to physicalness expressed as violence or physical contact is physicalness expressed in a "softer" way. The usual associations made about moments of tenderness or compassion in sport frequently relate to injury, to consoling teammates during a loss, or to sharing moments of good feelings. Those expressions of touching and caring seldom capture the attention of the fan, as they are often private or not part of the immediate action of the game, or they are considered "sissy stuff" that gets in the way of beating the other team. Toughness and tenderness are usually viewed as antithetical possibilities.

The expression of tenderness is seldom discussed or even recognized among players; yet touching is a very real dimension of the support system in sport. While the meanings of the touch may vary among athletes and be highly situational, the fanny-patting, "high five," and arms around shoulders all reflect a "we're in this together" or "I care" or "It's great" or "I'm sorry." Watch a field goal kicker who has missed an easy field goal. As he walks back to the sideline, many will avert their gaze or walk away, but every once in a while, someone will touch him in much the same way as an injured player is touched, as if to say, "It's OK."

> Beyond informing me of my capacity for tenderness, executing or receiving tender actions allows me to reflect on my own reaction. . . . If I enjoy the tenderness, then I know something of my identity as a being who is fulfilled in this way. If I am threatened . . . then I know something of my identity as a being who is fearful. . . . (117:121)

Some people do not like to be touched, though they may or may not touch others. Other people are what we call "touchers." Of all the senses, touch is the most primordial and direct. It allows more "feedback" and provides more information and, as a result, transmits more information. Touch is also honest communication. The touch is either one of tenderness and compassion or it is not. Either individuals are capable at a given time of demonstrating tenderness or they are not. Many athletes turn their backs on an injured player, thinking "I'm glad it wasn't me," while others reach out in some way to say "I'm sorry it was you." Why don't we like to be touched? Why is it so easy or so hard to reach out in joy, sadness, or injury to show our compassion? The sport experience provides the opportunity to demonstrate whatever compassion exists in us. Regardless of whether it is a fulfilling or threatening possibility, it is, nonetheless, a self-revealing one.

As with the violent possibilities of technique, Fraleigh also examined the potentiality for tenderness in our expressions of technique. He used the examples of the hairpin shot in badminton, the set in volleyball, and the short putt in golf as expressions of tenderness. (117:119) These, among many others, are skills where finesse and "caress" rather than power are the primary demands. "Beyond informing me of my capacity for tenderness, executing or receiving tender actions allows me to reflect on my own reaction to such experience. The bodily experience of tenderness [and tender expression] may be reacted to as most enjoyable or fulfilling in that the person may relish the feeling of soft, non-threatening sensitivity." (117:121) Power and powerful performance have been integral aspects of men's sports perhaps for as long as they have been played. Women have been generally seen as using skill, finesse, and good mechanics to accomplish what men have been able to do with sheer power. Golf, tennis, and bowling may be good examples of the sex differences in style and approach to achieve the same ends in the same game. While the tenderness-violence dichotomy can break down along sexist lines, a new androgyny in sport may soon find increasing numbers of men who find tenderness a viable and fulfilling physical expression and women who enjoy powerful and violent physical expressions. Since behavior is, essentially, bisexual and all people are capable of all behavior, sport may provide the outlet to experience self in an androgynous, human way free of the strong socialization and "shoulds" which exist in the everyday world.

Competition/Cooperation

Competition in its various forms as it is related to a potentially meaningful and self-realizing sport experience was discussed in Chapter 5. In addition to the possibilities that were already examined, other forms of competition and their meaning potentials are discussed by Fraleigh. The experience of competing alone, with one other person, or as a member of a team may yield different perceptions and understandings. Whether the opponent is equal to our ability, far superior to it, or far below it may make a difference in our attitude, performance, and what we come to see in ourselves. Where a superior opponent may cause feelings of inadequacy, an equal may create a sense of challenge, and an inferior one may generate feelings of indifference or dominance. (117:122) In any case, an honest introspection will reveal these attitudes and approaches to the player. The nature of the competition—family picnic softball game or varsity game—may determine intensity and establish a differential intent. Then again it may not. The "jock" with the "must win" attitude has spoiled many informal games, and the player without the "kill" instinct has failed to win the "big ones" because he wasn't "hungry" enough.

Sport requires a minimum of cooperation in the sense that all players involved must agree to certain things before the game can even start. For example, when and where will the contest take place, will there be officials or not, are there ground rules or "house rules" or "winter rules" in effect? We also agree to play a specific game and to follow the rules of that particular game. Beyond those initial points of cooperation, Fraleigh suggests that a more fundamental and humanistic possibility for cooperation exists within the competitive experience:

> This experience occurs when participants approach a sports contest with the predominant attitude that they wish to be there primarily for the joy of the game itself rather than the result of the game expressed in winning or losing. In such events, the self is experienced as a cooperative agent in a mutual

endeavor. . . . Even though single points may be heartily contested, the competition itself serves to enhance the mutual and cooperative joy, mirth, and diversion function of the sport for all participants. (117:124)

Does the player in the competitive or the cooperative setting come to view the self as adequate or inadequate and how does he/she feel about these knowledges? How do we view a superior opponent—as lucky, as better, as skilled? How do we treat those who lost to us? How do we view poorly skilled opponents—as lesser skilled, as motor morons (M and M's) or as a joke? Any of our thoughts, feelings, or reflections about ourselves and others in the competitive situation have the potential to direct us toward a more personal understanding of ourselves, our motivations, and our behavior. While it is not always possible to put these knowledges in a rational, orderly model that is transmitted to others in words, we still "know" from our experience in sport a little more about the hidden and blind parts of the self.

DISCUSSION QUESTIONS

1. How do the meanings found in sport differ in the spectator and the participant? What factors in the sport experience may account for these differences?
2. Excellence is often seen as an external objective standard against which a performance may be measured. It is also seen as a "personal best" which may be inferior when compared to an objective standard. What factors might dictate the standard of excellence that is applied in a particular situation? Is the spectator more likely to apply one form of excellence as a criterion more consistently than another? Is there a justification for doing this?
3. From your experiences as a player, in what ways has an "other" been instrumental in allowing you to come to know yourself in the sport context? In what ways does the opponent as either a barrier or a "friend" aid in your self-understanding through the medium of sport participation?
4. What do you think is possible for an observer to come to know about you as a player or a person that you may not already know?
5. In what ways is it possible to argue that what we learn about ourselves or our human capabilities may or not have transfer value to dimensions of life outside the sport situation?
6. It has been stated that sport is amoral in the sense that it does not make someone something he/she is not in the first place. In what ways is it possible to argue that we make sport in our own image and that our playing may reveal much of who we are as persons?

DIRECTED READING

Fraleigh, W.P.: The moving I. *In* The Philosophy of Sport, edited by R.G. Osterhoudt. Springfield, IL, Charles C Thomas, 1973, pp. 108–129.

Gerber, E.G.: My body, my self. *In* Sport and the Body, 2nd ed., edited by E.W. Gerber and W.J. Morgan. Philadelphia, Lea & Febiger, 1979, pp. 181–197.

Hyland, D.A.: Competition and friendship. J. Philos. Sport, 5:27–37, 1978.

Metheny, E.: Symbolic power of sport. *In* Sport and the Body, 2nd ed.,edited by E.W. Gerber and W.J. Morgan. Philadelphia, Lea & Febiger, 1979, pp. 231–236.

Metheny, E.: Movement and Meaning. New York, McGraw-Hill, 1968, pp. 57–82.

Chapter 9
AESTHETIC DIMENSIONS

Art is a very cherished part of almost every known culture. Man seeks beauty and the aesthetic experience, as spectator and as performer, in the simplicity of nature and in the complexity of structural forms. He has created forms to communicate symbolically, to express his feelings and the feelings of a society around him. He has created forms which meet his needs. I think it is possible now to view sport as a meaningful form in which man seeks and has sought that which is beautiful about himself and his existence. (406:79–80)

Art historians place the origin of aesthetic and art theories as far back as the sixth century B.C. Plato referred to them as "the long standing argument between poetry and philosophy." It was not until the eighteenth century when philosopher Alexander Baumgarten applied the new name "aesthetics" to the old argument. Richter (340:14–21) points out that aesthetics, which originated as the science of beauty, has branched into many diverse approaches to the study of art and the aesthetic experience. These varying perspectives lie in the fact that theoreticians disagree as to what aesthetics is, or should be, and have often interjected moral or metaphysical dogma. A secondary factor in the diversity of theories has been the varying degrees of competency among aesthetic theoreticians in dealing with various art forms. A similar problem exists among philosophers and sport philosophers who try to examine the aesthetic possibilities of sport. Some may understand aesthetic theory and some art forms but do not understand all art forms. Still others do not have a sound cognitive and/or experiential understanding of what sport is. Relative to sport, two basic questions arise which are complementary but not synonymous: Is sport an art form? and Is sport an aesthetic experience?

Traditional aesthetic theories and philosophies of art have been concerned with the art object and usually with the beauty of the object via some mode of sense perception. The artist has been considered only in relationship to his having produced the object. Some dancers, for example, suggest that dance as an art experience is essentially a creative process. However, often this definition and aesthetic which examines, or is based upon, the process still concerns itself with the object—color, space, shape, flow, time and continuity—rather than with the dancer's experience of dancing. In short, the aesthetic experience and its examination have almost always presupposed an object. Although the sport aesthetic necessarily presupposes an object—the body and its movement—it seems necessary to examine the potential of sport as an art form separately from the potential of sport as an aesthetic experience.

To follow traditional aesthetic theories in the development of a sport aesthetic, we would focus on the beauty of the human body in motion and would consider the grace, efficiency, and effortlessness of movement achieved in skilled performance. Some sport movements that have dance overtones, such as those in gymnastics, figure skating, synchronized swimming, and diving, have often been termed beautiful and artistic. However, in other sports this expertise and "beauty" conjures a utilitarian, structured, and mechanistic process rather than the expressive reactions that have served as criteria for aesthetic theories. Since it is theoretically apparent that this objectification of the body and its movements can be considered artistic, the necessity arises to look toward the art object as well as toward the experience and the nature of the aesthetic experience in the examination of a sport aesthetic.

The aesthetic experience has been defined broadly as a feeling attributed to an experience in which the sensuous, qualitative aspects are encountered apart from all mediation by ideas and independently of any determination as to whether or not anything else exists. Use of this definition from the experiential perspective points the way toward a possibility of an aesthetic experience in sport. Although any single definition of art is necessarily limiting and inflexible, the following operational definition is the synoptic result of definitions offered by many aesthetic theoreticians. Art is the object of the aesthetic experience, i.e., from the audience perspective, it is the object which is the cause of the aesthetic experience or from the artist's perspective it is the object which results from, or symbolizes, the aesthetic experience. This resultant object can be defined further as a concrete representation via some medium. (434:3–5)

Aesthetics, in general, is concerned with the nature and significance of art. Study within this area is broad and touches on a number of topics and issues, some of which have social, political, economic, moral, or metaphysical implications. Osterhoudt delineates these issues in an exhaustive yet succinct manner:

> Most important among the major issues in aesthetics are: the metaphysical status of the arts; the form, content, and subject matter of the arts; the criteria of aesthetic judgment (criticism); the relation of the arts to natural phenomena; the role of intellectuality and emotionality in the arts; the nature of the aesthetic experience and pleasure; the relation of the art product to the process by which it is created; the role of technique and expression in the arts; the role of the artist, performer, and audience in the arts. . . . (309:303)

There are two dimensions to be considered in sport, art, or the aesthetic experience. One perspective is that of the audience and the other is that of the performer. As discussed earlier (Chapter 6: The Nature of Experience), the audience view (the Apollonian) has the capability of being removed from the actual "lived experience." This detachment leads to objectivity, the possibility of the establishment of performance standards, and criticism. It is an "outside in" view of sport and art that allows judgments based on criteria established to evaluate that which is observable in a performance. From this standpoint it is possible to look at experience, at a performance, and make judgments or comparisons in an unbiased way. The difficulty the audience has is in determining motivation, intent, or in assessing the qualitative aspects of performance that may be important parts of the experience and which, if known, would influence judgments and comparisons of performance. The second perspective, which is the performer's orientation (the Dionysian), really has two possibilities. On the one hand it is an "inside" view which is a result of the on-going "lived experience" and is feeling-based and nonanalytical. Attention may be directed to the sensuous and qualitative aspects of the experience. Then, upon reflection, performers can become audience to their own acts. While they do not have the unbiased overview of the spectators, performers do have the benefit of "having been there" directly and can integrate many of the unobservable parts of the performance with many, but not all, of the observable parts available to them upon reflection.

SIMILARITIES BETWEEN SPORT AND ART

> In the action and rhythm which testify to mastery of space and time, sport becomes akin to the arts. . . . No athlete can accomplish a genuine feat without such perfect control, in time and space, that his movements and the rhythm of their timing are not to be differentiated from the finest ballet, the most splendid passages of prose or verse, the most glorious lives in architecture or the loveliest harmonies of light and color. Lastly, in art as in sport, we find in the protagonist the same inimitable assertion of personality we call style. (259:14)

At the outset it should be understood that whatever purposes the existence of art and sport are considered to have, the fact remains that art is done by artists and viewed by audiences for different reasons than sport is done by athletes and viewed by audiences. What Huizinga defines in the following passage is the nature of play, but the definition, as Hein (160) points out, could just as well be of the aesthetic experience.

> . . . a voluntary activity or occupation executed within certain fixed limits of time and place, according to rules freely accepted but absolutely binding, having its aim in itself and accompanied by a feeling of tension, joy, and consciousness that it is different from "ordinary" life. (174:28)

Huizinga has cited a number of features common to both play and aesthetic experiences: spatial-temporal characteristics, arbitrary rules, nonutilitarian qualities, affectivity, and the fact that it is marked off, as Dewey has noted, from everyday and ordinary experiences.

Competition, whether direct or indirect, against self, others, or some arbitrary standard, is a dominant characteristic of sport. There is present an intent and desire to win if winning is the nature of the specific activity, achieve what has not been achieved, or attain some standard of excellence whether this standard is internally or externally imposed. "It is a relative matter, the victory being over self and previous performance or over fellow competitors of comparable standard rather than against an arbitrary standard or a record." (21:77) Similarly, the artist has an intent and desire to reach goals of achievement and excellence. Despite the absence of score, there is an internal competitiveness to do well or to express what was intended. Within this context of self-imposed competition, little distinction can be made between the artist and the athlete. The product of these efforts, be it a score or an art object, is similarly "measured" and evaluated, albeit with different tools and scales, by outside observers and critics. Those who suggest sport is not an art form or an aesthetic experience argue that the competitive element in sport negates its aesthetic possibilities. This will be discussed later in the chapter.

Huizinga and Hein both note the voluntary nature of play (sport) and the aesthetic experience. Although there are philosophic and definitional distinctions between sport and play as outlined in Chapters 4 and 5, both share the common element of voluntary participation by the performer. Voluntary involvement means freedom from external force and a choice by the performer to participate. However, it may be feasible that the performer will participate due to an internal compulsion, or drive, which may, in that sense, render participation an involuntary function. The "scratch," the "bench," and the "understudy" are integral parts of the sport world and the art world, since choosing *not* to participate is an option for the performer.

Both the aesthetic and the sport experience are characterized by the structures of time and place. Where sport has its courts, fields, and stadia, art has its stages, canvases, and concert halls. Although it may be argued that the proscenium arch is being eliminated in the staging of the dramatic production, a stage of some sort is a boundary for the production. It may be similarly noted that in such activities as skiing, frisbee, and a variety of outdoor pursuits formal boundaries give way simply to a place where the event is staged. Most sports are marked off in periods, quarters, or halves or, at least, in the case of mountain climbing and skydiving, by a definite beginning and ending. Most art media in which the aesthetic experience occurs are also characterized by temporal separation into acts, measures, beats, or in the cases of painting and sculpture, by a beginning and ending. Kuntz argues that this time and space are not only functional but symbolic. "It is useful to consider sport and theatre in the same category. . . . It is because both employ props that help create symbolic reality. It is otherwise silly to contend, in sport, for a ball or defend territory or to pretend that a costume makes a king." (226:307) He says the same is true of time when actual time is secondary to what time may mean in measuring performance. Weiss states in his *Nine Basic Arts* that space takes on a meaning in both sport and art beyond being just a specified place to carry out the activity. The performances of sport and art are:

> "the space of action, of events . . . the space of values, educational space . . . a space of positive and negative affiliations, of oppositions and frustrations, adoptions and rejections, of subjugations and enrichments. (434:16)

Relative to time, Weiss claims that it is a matter of how interested one is in the performance whether or not time has any significance. For some who are uninterested the time seems long; for others intimately involved in the performance, time seems short. "Eventful time is distinct from both perceptual and scientific time. It embraces a set of unit occurrences, turbulent on-goings in the extended present." (434:20) The symbolic importance of the "two minute warning" in sport or the dramatic "pause" in theatrical performances makes time in sport and art different from the time of our daily lives.

Sport and aesthetic experiences share the commonality of being "outside" daily experiences. In comparing artist and athlete, Weiss sums up what has been stated about the aesthetic experience and what many have said about the sport experience:

> The athlete's world is set over against the everyday world. Economic demands and the satisfaction of appetites are for the moment put aside. . . . Artists and historians similary bracket off their distinctive, dynamic spatio-temporal worlds. What he (artist or athlete) is and what he does is for the moment thereby severed from the rest of the world. (437:243, 245)

Hein's (160:70) main thesis in her comparison of play and the aesthetic was not only that the two are nonutilitarian and autotelic in nature but that they both have the quality of being detached from reality, i.e., artificial restrictions are imposed upon real situations by social convention or by the arbitrariness of a group or an individual. These restrictions can take the form of previously mentioned spatial and temporal dimensions or of rules which are specific to the movement or art form and understood by the performer prior to the performance. Rejection of these rules or failure to comply fully can result in a variety of individual penalties, expulsion, inhibition of others' performance, or ineffective execution of a work. Even jazz improvisation requires that everyone play in the same key.

Maheu (259) saw sport as a cultural expression spawned from leisure in much the same way that the arts fulfill leisure pursuits. Philosopher

Thomas Munro considers sport as a "field which borders on the arts." As a performance he noted sport as being similar to the arts as a spectacle for spectators and as an entertainment in our culture. (293:148–149) Both the game and the work of art are as Weiss says "outside the web of conventional needs." (438:6) However, they both provide an expression of what our culture is about while attracting participants and spectators seeking the opportunity for expression in their leisure time.

The artificiality of the sport and aesthetic experience has also been noted as providing grounds for self-realization and as a special way of knowing self and the object. With regard to the artist, Lipman reiterates a viewpoint that Metheny and Slusher held for the athlete:

> The art form (media) represents a searching, a casting about for oneself, and when, out of this, an organized poem or painting emerges, the sense of personal achievement permeates the entire situation as the immediate qualitative experience of self. Creation implies self-creation. . . . (241:46)

This way of knowing is seen to be based on the experiential *process* rather than the result or *product* of the experience. It is a process which is immediate and present rather than past or future, concrete and affective as opposed to abstract and cognitive, lived rather than reflected.

Weiss (435:605) insists that the process of the performing arts and the activity of the artist/athlete in this process be a central focus. Performance is concerned with "the creative expression of the texture and meaning of a genuine process of becoming. . . ." (436:75) Sport and art are "infected by human interests and values" and from a metaphysical standpoint they reflect human actualities and human potentialities. Weiss (438:8–10) notes that it is possible to learn what existence is from sport or art because, essentially, they are both concerned with the creation of a space, a time, and a way of becoming.

A last commonality between sport and art is the use of symbols. Although through different media and in different ways, the expression of an idea, an intent, a feeling, a motive, or an ambition is common to sport and art. The study of symbols in art by Langer (232), Goodman (139) and in sport by Metheny (269) and Roberts (344) reveals complex attempts to understand language, feelings, forms, and movements which mean something to the performer and which are efforts to convey something to an audience. There are various positions and interpretations relative to what these symbols may or may not mean. The role of the audience in interpreting the symbols or if, in fact, an audience is even necessary in symbolic expression is also not clear. However, it is generally accepted that symbols of expression exist in sport and art. The elements of performance may include: color, shape, flow, movement, use of an implement, gesture, symmetry. Tranquility may be expressed by use of blue or pastels in painting; in the soft, light, indirect gestures of the theatre or dance; or in the curves and continuity of a sculpture. Use of these symbols may be intended or unintended, picked up by an audience, or they may exist only as part of the artist's feeling at the time of creation. For the athlete, sport movements may not represent feelings and ideas in the same way that symbols of color, line, and gesture serve to represent the artist's theme; yet feelings are expressed in nonverbal gestures and movements of the body. An astute and interested observer comes to read such body language and subsequently to "know" to some degree what an athlete is feeling or intending. Intensity, joy, anger, and frustration can be read with the same degree of accuracy one interprets the intent or feeling of the dancer or painter. The athlete may not intend such a symbolic representation for an audience, but as a symbolic expression of human intent and idea it does, nonetheless, exist in sport as well as in art.

These commonalities do not suffice to make sport acceptable as an art, and it may or may not be necessary that sport in its various forms and with its multitude of intents be considered a full-fledged art form. It may, however, regardless of its status as an art, have many aesthetic qualities. A sunset on the ocean that produces a lavender and orange afterglow is an aesthetic experience for most people, yet by critical artistic standards, this "natural beauty" does not really qualify as an art form. Gerber sums up a central problem in dealing with art and aesthetics:

> Much of aesthetic inquiry centers around the appreciation and evaluation of artificial art—that is, objects deliberately created to be beautiful, to catalyze an aesthetic experience. Nevertheless, most people have had the pleasure of experiencing beauty in a natural setting, with no artist intervening. . . . Somewhere between the natural and the created art object is the structure created for utilitarian purposes, such as a building, which happens to be beautiful and evokes an aesthetic experience.
>
> Sport may be an example of the latter category, or it may be considered a phenomenon of natural beauty. (136:315)

DIFFERENCES BETWEEN SPORT AND ART: CRITICISM

What is aesthetic quality? What is an aesthetic experience; is it the same as an art form? Does sport because of its commonalities with art qualify as either an art form or an aesthetic experience? A classic view of aesthetics is that there are certain standards and principles against which a work of art is measured to determine its artistic or aesthetic value or potential. Such standards are based on the values of a society or may be cross-cultural standards that are more classic. A photograph or painting of a Campbell's soup can may or may not have aesthetic qualities by North American standards but almost certainly would not by Nigerian standards. On the other hand, a photograph or painting of a nude woman may have greater possibilities as an artistic endeavor regardless of where, geographically or culturally, it is judged. If sport can meet standards which are based on normative principles of excellence and taste, then it may be considered "art."

While sport and sportsmen have long been the subject of artists through painting, sculpture, photography, and prose, sport itself has not often been considered art. In some sports which use the body as the instrument of expression—diving, gymnastics, figure skating, and synchronized swimming—artistic possibilities have been more strongly espoused. Some of this has to do with body as medium but also the use of criteria or standards of scoring which objectively measure excellence have a bearing on the belief in a potential artistry. Style and grace in addition to technical performance are primary in these sports and are usually seen as unimportant in other sports. Fetters (102:32) suggests that the *way* in which either the performer or the audience views the body makes it potentially aesthetic. As an object doing things, the potential is limited, but as a subject expressing itself, the aesthetic potential is enhanced.

> The capacity to view one's body and the body of the other as a source of "identity and dignity" and as an expression of the richness and fullness of humanity, what Keen calls that "common grace," takes one beyond the world of objects. This sense of the body both as an expression of uniqueness and of human mutuality engenders the respect and reverence necessary to aesthetic appreciation. (102:32)

In contrast to objective criteria for art and its inherent criticalness is the belief that art and the aesthetic experience rest on the ability of the work of art to evoke an emotional reaction in the audience and to serve as a form of communication between artist and audience. From this perspective, something "ugly" could be considered aesthetic in its ability to evoke response or communicate. If sport evokes a response or communicates, perhaps it is an aesthetic experience. Viewpoints among aestheticians differ regarding whether the "message" must be intended or unintended.

Three major factors are consistently cited in the philosophy of sport literature related to the differences between sport and art which preclude sport from being considered as either an art form or an aesthetic experience. These include the agonistic nature of sport; the lack of concern for style, grace, and form in deference to technical efficiency; and the motivation of the athlete to seek only an end product without concern for or attention to the process or the environment.

Competition as it is evidenced in the desire for victory is perhaps the strongest objection to viewing sport as an art form and divesting it of aesthetic qualities. While Best (35) and Ziff (454) concede that some sports such as diving, gymnastics, and figure skating may have some ancillary aesthetic qualities, most sport has none. Best makes the distinction by posing a question to a player:

> Which would you prefer, to score three goals in a clumsy manner, or to miss them all with graceful movements? There is little doubt what the answer would be, at least in most cases. In sports such as these the aesthetic aspect is subordinate to the main purpose.

On the other hand, there is a category of which the aim cannot be specified in isolation from the aesthetic, for example trampolining, gymnastics, figure skating, and diving. (35:348)

Elliott claims that every athletic act is primarly for the sake of victory. If there is any beauty at all, it is more like the beauty of nature. In art, he claims, beauty is the primary goal, but in sport it is an incidental occurrence. (85) Best would agree that the lack of beauty as a central aim makes even technically excellent sport impossible as an art form, but aesthetic possibilities exist from the spectators' standpoint when excellence in technique is achieved.

> However successful a sportman may be in achieving the principal aim of his particular activity, our *aesthetic* acclaim is reserved for him who achieves it with maximum economy and efficiency of effort. (35:349)

Reid (338) and Ziff have a more restrictive conception of art which does not lend itself to considering sport as art nor as an aesthetic experience from the spectators' standpoint. Reid sees the motive of art as producing an object for aesthetic contemplation and the motive of sport as the seeking of victory. As these two motives are incongruous to Reid he cannot consider sport as art. Although some secondary aesthetic qualities such as style might be part of sport, Reid sees these aspects as very superficial. Ziff sees sport as grounded in the reality of winning, oblivious to the environment in which it is conducted, often violent, and obsessed to the point that style, grace, and even technique are lost as aesthetic aspects. Only in sports where form is graded is it possible for an aesthetic dimension to emerge. "But even though gymnastics has an aesthetic aspect, aesthetic factors have at best an inconsequential ancillary role to play in sport." (454:101) In comparing ballet to gymnastics he suggests that "brute strength is an aspect of gymnastics but not of ballet," (454:101) and such strength is directed not toward any artistic end but toward scoring to win.

In answer to the critics who argue that competition kills art, Kupfer suggests that competition is not divisive but provides an opportunity for man to achieve wholeness:

> Aesthetic values also emerge from human interaction. The activity which constitutes competitive sport involves tension between opponents and coordination with a team. A 'good' game includes both team cohesiveness and balance between the teams. . . . In the context of the opposition necessary for engaging in such sports, individuals come together to form a whole. As in art proper, the antagonism between part and whole is overcome. (227:358)

The agon produces the potential for drama which will be examined at length later in the chapter. Weiss (434:194) says that both a game (agonistic) and a stage play create tension which is eventually resolved but that conflict, rage, skill, and power in either setting have artistic potential.

> The resolution of contest in victory and defeat is the way in which competitive sporting episodes are completed-in-themselves. When aesthetically rich, the

game builds to consummation. . . . In this way, competitive sports exhibit . . . oppositions, pivotal situations, inclusive rhythms, denouements, and consummations that are real. . . . The wholeness and finality possible in competitive sporting events, paradigmatic in the artistic, answer the human desire for completeness and unity, if only in symbol. (227:359)

Todd argues that with the desire to win as the chief motive some aesthetic aspects may be lost but that others may be achieved. More from the standpoint of the performer, he states that the intensity of competition provides a focus for action that is a prerequisite for excellence. Such intensity is not unlike that of painters, musicians, or dancers who narrow their focus, perfect their technique in search of the ultimate performance, in search of perfection. What may be lost is some of the sensuous pleasure available in the joy of motion, since attention to these aesthetic qualities distracts. However, under the intense conditions of competition, "the actors [players] by concentrating entirely on those motions, have been able to culminate and encapsulate years of training in a single moment." (420:18) What the viewer may see and what the athlete may experience is perfection or excellence in performance, a coming together of intent and achievement that has strong aesthetic possibilities.

In testing himself or seeking the prize of victory, Weiss says that athletes are urged to become mean, aggressive, and warlike. (437:32–33) Art, on the other hand, does not divide its participants into agonistic camps. Keenan summarizes the case against the agon:

Unfortunately, at least from an aesthetic appreciation excellence in athletics has been equated with quantitative measures. . . . The fetish for the scoreboard does not accurately define the conditions of the contest, or man as athlete engaged in the athletic phenomena. (196:310)

Kuntz argues back that the dramatic potential of man's struggle with inequity and paradox can be as much attended to as the score, nor is the striving for excellence restricted to the dimensions of *citius, altius, fortius.* (222:24–25) If "beauty is in the eye of the beholder" then either as performer or spectator it is possible to attend only to the quantitative striving for victory, to look at and for the qualitative aspects of the performance, to see the agon as a framework which serves to produce rather than reduce aesthetic possibilities.

The second objection to sport as art stems from its lack of style, grace, and form. Technical efficiency is seen as the optimal and desired outcome, and such efficiency while achieving excellence of one kind cannot be considered artistic or aesthetic. Weiss has maintained that in the agonistic event, skill and accuracy are the most important features. If style and grace are also possible, then the athlete has achieved a degree of excellence. "A man can be accurate without having either skill or grace . . . be skillful without accuracy and grace . . . be graceful without being skilled or accurate. . . ." (437:127–128) Of the three, grace is the least important in the athletic performance; yet from an aesthetic standpoint, grace and style are significant features. They are the deliberate aims of many artists. In her early paper "Athletics in the Studio," Metheny (269) contrasts the dancer and the athlete. The athlete is concerned with movement in its functional and utilitarian sense, "getting the job done," regardless of how it looks. The dancer, i.e., artist, on the other hand, is not at all concerned with outcome but with "how it looks." (269) "How it looks" is a stylistic concern that is secondary to the athlete as long as the goal is accomplished. Ziff maintains that mechanical efficiency may or may not be aesthetic but such efficiency is not intended by the athlete to be beautiful. A lack of intention to be beautiful thereby disqualifies sport as potentially aesthetic. (454:45)

Kuntz answers this charge with the argument that "the mechanistic approach stresses quantity at the expense of quality" (223:25) and that many sports are taught with attention to stylistic concerns. The two—style and efficiency—may, in fact, be interlocking concepts.

> Perhaps mechanical efficiency is the by-product of the grace required of the awkward novice in his canoe. It looks better to kneel than to sit and also happens to lower the center of gravity. It feels neater to feather the paddle on the forward return and happens to spend [less] energy propelling the craft. (223:25)

Those who argue against sport as an aesthetic experience based on style and grace see sport performance as awkward and inelegant attempts aimed at accuracy and efficiency. To this charge, Maheu answers:

> In the action and rhythm which testify to mastery of space and time, sport becomes akin to the arts. . . . No athlete can accomplish a genuine feat without such perfect physical control, in time and space, that his movements and the rhythm of their timing are not to be differentiated from the finest ballet, the most splendid passages from prose or verse, the most glorious lines in architecture or sculpture or the loveliest harmonies of light and colour. (259:14)

Accuracy and efficiency are fundamental to all technique in sport and in art. Once the basics are mastered, artist or athlete can concentrate on stylistic concerns. It is possible for critics to criticize such famous artists as pianist Van Cliburn or opera star Luciano Pavarotti as giving a performance which is technically sound but stylistically lacking. The same criticism can be leveled at any artist or athlete. A dunk-shot by Julius Irving or the skyhook of Kareem Abdul-Jabbar combines efficiency, accuracy, style, and grace. Others "get the job done" but lack the style and grace of the "masters." From an audience perspective, it is altogether possible to see an athletic performance aimed at winning which also features style and grace. The athlete who has command of his skills *likes* to "look good" and strives to do so in combination with scoring. Style and efficiency in athletic endeavors are not necessarily either/or situations. The advent of instant replay and slow motion cinematography has perhaps done a great deal in demonstrating the grace, fluidity, and style that are often overlooked in the "heat of battle." A more complete treatment of technique as aesthetic will be undertaken later in the chapter.

The third major problem with sport as an art form is that critics sense the agonistic outcome and that dedication to it destroys process considerations. Sport is essentially a technique or discipline, specifically a craft in which the objective is winning a contest that has no way of revealing the meaning of a world beyond. Critics would argue that rules, the necessity for utilitarian and efficient skills, and training negate problem-solving and concerns for process. Comments by Ziff are representative of the additional belief that not only is the process of little concern but so is the environment:

> Doesn't fishing have an aesthetic aspect? Think of casting in a trout stream, crystal water, aromatic pines, surrounding mountains and so forth. All very nice, all irrelevant. . . . and one could also fish . . . surrounded by garbage smelling smog. Something is not an aspect of an activity unless it serves to individuate that activity. . . . standing in a stream of crystal water in a piney forest is not an aspect of fishing or even of trout fishing for one could be fishing or trout fishing even if one were not there but surrounded by garbage and knee deep in sludge. (454:100)

What is fishing? What is basketball? Certainly these things are defined by rules and evaluated by quantifiable means. Would a person go fishing in a sewer treatment plant even if fish could live there? The recent literature describing sport experiences would suggest that people run, ski, golf, fish, or play football as much for *where* they are doing the activity as for *what* they are doing. Scuba diving in the Bahamas would have more aesthetic appeal than scuba diving in Lake Erie. The context of the sport experience is significant in contributing to one's pleasure and fulfillment. From a spectator standpoint fishing may be fishing whether it is in Idaho's Clearwater River or the Boise Sewage Treatment Plant. From a participant standpoint, where it happens may, indeed, make a difference about whether or not it does happen in the first place. As Kuntz notes: "Ziff has given us far less than a *complete* angler." (223:24)

With regard to the lack of problem-solving or creative process opportunities, Gaskin and Masterson respond:

> In our view Reid's argument is not only too 'object-oriented', but it also hinges on aesthetic contemplation [by the audience] of the art work/object as the primary reason for its existence. . . . For we believe that it is through the resolution of problems posed by a chosen medium that the artist strives for excellence in a search for self-fulfillment. (127:42)

They cite many examples from art history related to the complexity and persistence involved in "getting it right"—pigments for making colors, composing problems, poetry writings, rehearsals for plays. Wulk suggests that the complex, confusing, and ever-changing nature of the sport experience requires constant reaction and innovation: "Invention, improvisation, and experimentation by the participants are necessary for adaptation in the ever-changing vista of a sport situation." (444:342) Gaskin and Masterson suggest that the nature of art is problem-solving in combination with mastery of technique rather than the production of objects for contemplation. This view suggests that the artistry and the aesthetic experience may be *best* known though not exclusively known by the artist/actor/performer. In describing the performance of a musician Keller relates it to sport:

> The performer's own experience in surmounting the technical difficulties, his own satisfaction, is palpably an aesthetic one which is closely related to the satisfaction that the skier experiences when for example he surmounts the difficulties of a very steep downhill run or slope. (cited in 127:54)

There is a further argument that sport has its technical and strategic problems requiring the same problem-solving and process skills demonstrated by the artist. Even for the spectator, the contest provides an aesthetic quality in seeing the ability to "cope with the novel immediately and skillfully." (188:312) While the artist and athlete may be headed toward different ends, excellence is a concern, and the process of "getting there" is not very different. Every art has its own language, its own idiom, but parallels between arts can be seen. (127:59) To evaluate painting on the same basis as theater is an error, for both the language and the criteria are different. Yet they are both art forms. Similarly to "attempt to identify art in sport by applying the language of another art form would be a mistake." (127:59) Todd provides an analogy of photography which historically was a functional "taking of pictures" to aid memory. It has, however, become recognized as an art form in and of itself. "Somewhere in the process it was realized that there was room for much the same sort of imagination and creativity that was present in the established art forms . . . [and that] some pictures were more aesthetically pleasing than others." (420:20) Sport has the same potential if the concepts of feeling, imagination, intensity, technique, and the creative fervor find an expanded and specific vocabulary to describe the unique qualities of sport.

Criticism of sport as an art or as an aesthetic experience has left the door open to view sport in *some* ways as aesthetic but not necessarily in the *same* ways as other art forms. Within what are considered the traditional art forms, however, there is wide variability of expression, technique, creativity, and purpose. Each is judged by standards applicable to that art with a language that describes that form. Sport may have potential as an art form and as an aesthetic experience if it can be considered in terms of the elements it possesses rather than in a strict and formal comparison with other arts which are not, in the first place, necessarily compared among themselves. Gaskin and Masterson sum up:

> So it is then that the superlative action of individuals or of groups of players, resolving the problems imposed by sport within the rules and ethics of the event and stimulated by the drama, tension, uncertainty, and mood of the occasion can give rise to displays of human skill coupled with courage, power,

strength, and effort which manifest beauty and the sublime, thereby creating Art in sport. (127:60)

In light of the similarities and differences which have been identified in sport and art, three performance-based possibilities appear to be prominent possibilities in considering sport as an aesthetic experience. Two of these, drama and excellence in technique, have potential appeal as an aesthetic experience for both the performer and the audience, although from a different cognitive and feeling perspective. The third possibility, the sensuousness of the sport experience, is more restricted to a performer aesthetic.

TECHNICAL EXCELLENCE AS AESTHETIC

The most arresting feature of sport *is* the grace of the human form. Economy and efficiency of effort are accomplished in movement which is continuous and fluid: sport provides us with balletic values. . . . (227:358)

Concern for form and the body-as-object are primary in considering physical prowess as an aesthetic dimension. It is the physical prowess aspect of form that has drawn the attention of aesthetic theorists. However, the form and technical excellence of sports which use the body as the primary medium of expression and which have a scoring system for such physical excellence have drawn the greatest attention. The "perfect pass" in soccer, basketball, or football has rated little attention for its potential as an aesthetic experience or as an aesthetic move. All art forms require some kind of technique in order to express an idea, a feeling, or a simple space-time relationship. It has already been noted that skill, style, and grace are independent possibilities, but all are essential when we consider "good form" or excellence in technique. While one player may "look different" from another, it is possible for both players to achieve a standard of excellence, not only in being successful but also in terms of the perfection of their technique. It is also necessary to point out that a "good" pitcher, for example, will not always be in good form. Fernando Valenzuela, 1981 Cy Young winner, was considered an excellent pitcher, yet he was not technically excellent during every start. For some, his "form" was not beautiful, but his mastery of technique and his control were examples of excellence. Kuntz suggests that "all of us could *share vicariously in excellence* and were lifted to heights comparable to those of great dance, music, and theatre." (226:308)

There is a tendency in the spectator to be more aware of poor technique, as it usually results in a misplay or in an awkward movement. In football, the snap of the ball from the center to the quarterback is usually executed with flawless precision, but such precision is obvious only when technique fails because there is usually a fumble or a "broken play." A spectacular play may be a one-time example of technical excellence but lacks the consistency for mastery and aesthetic potential. The athlete must have sufficient enough mastery to be able to focus away from technique and begin to make innovative space-time decisions, to be creative within the context of the rules and the strategy, and to develop a style. A broad working knowledge of the norm is essential before the player can control deviations, changes in defenses or offenses. The process which produces innovation and excellence is based on wide and deep experiences and knowledge. From an audience standpoint, Kaelin argues that "like the virtuosity of a musical performance . . . sport technique is best when it is noticed the least." (188:28)

Weiss has viewed one of the major similarities between sport and the arts as that of performance excellence. While not guided by an idea or a need to communicate, excellence in sport means much the same as it does in the arts. Both reveal what can be done. (435:3) The skills of the athlete are primarily those involved in mastery of the body and of the implements needed for the performance of the specific sport skills. The kind of physical coordination and mastery, as well as the kinds of implements, may differ in sport and art, but nonetheless, such physical mastery is essential to excellence. The process of achieving an intended and desired end has the potential for excellence, and it is this process which, Weiss says, holds the qualitative possibilities for performance excellence.

> Excellence excites and awes. It pleases and it challenges. We are often delighted by splendid specimens whether they be flowers, beasts, or men. A superb performance interests us even more because it reveals to us the magnitude of what then can be done. Illustrating perfection, it gives us a measure for whatever else we do. (437:3)

The body-as-object when viewed for its technical excellence or for its achievement of fitness and beauty in a physical entity is often a source of aesthetic pleasure for those who watch the sport.

Excellence in technique is not the strict domain of the professional player. There are runners whose training and technical mastery allow them *optimal* performances for their age and body type. There are weekend golfers who can putt as well as many pro players. There are high school and collegiate volleyball players who can consistently "set" the ball with accuracy, style, and grace. There are teenage swimmers like Tracy Caulkins whose performance in the turns is beautiful and technically close to perfect. Yet the audience for these participants is not a concern or the technique is not visible. Who sees Caulkins turn unless there is an underwater camera? Who goes out to see the weekend golfer except the other people in the foursome? It is in these circumstances as well as in the more visible displays of technical excellence that the athlete experiences the aesthetic feeling of having achieved excellence. It may be in only one play of the game that excellence is experienced, but at the moment of its occurrence, there is a beauty that results from the perfection of motion and the coming together of action and intent.

> However successful a sportsman may be in achieving the principal aim of his particular activity, our *aesthetic* acclaim is reserved for him who achieves it with maximum economy and efficiency of effort. . . . the highest aesthetic satisfaction is experienced and given by the sportsman who not only performs with graceful economy but who also *achieves* his purpose. (35:349)

Such moments may be infrequent for any player, but they remain the objective of training and practice: to do something right, to do it perfectly, to have the skill. To have the skill to play the game and meet its end objective is a primary and quantitative aim in sport, but to have enough skill to be able to "play" creatively, deceptively, efficiently, and as close to perfection as possible is the aim of any artist and the possibility for many athletes.

> The concept of personal style of moving also adds drama and complexity to sport performances. Functional perfection, the mastery of bodily movements, allows the performer to move smoothly and fluidly with appropriate rhythms of tension and relaxation. Once this is achieved, then the performer can give the movement expressive form. . . . (444:342)

The film *Ski the Outer Limits* visually describes the poetry of motion that is possible in a skilled performance. At one point the narrative in describing skiing in powder suggests that "it is not often given to man to create poetry let alone recognize the act at the time of its creation." Athletes engage in sport for different reasons than artists engage in art, but it is apparent that the athlete has, at times, recognized the aesthetic aspects, for as Arnold Palmer comments:

> What other people may find in poetry or art museums I find in the flight of a good drive—the white ball sailing . . . into that blue sky . . . suddenly reaching its apex, curving, falling, finally dropping to the turn to roll some more just the way I planned it. (311:29)

While these aesthetic moments may or may not mean something to the athlete or to the audience, they do bear a significance in that sensuous or qualitative feelings are generated. In many instances they are what draws the player back to the sport. A sailor may race a boat for many reasons, but a warm day, a steady wind, and a perfect tack may make it more memorable. "Flying a hull is the closest thing to orgasm there is. No artist could paint a better picture or write a lovelier song. The beauty of it all makes you ache and feel alive," says a Hobie aficionado. The athlete may experience technical excellence as part of the "lived experience," the immediacy may be prereflectively recorded, and attention is directed back to the action. Often sport is too reactive to stop to think about things even if the feelings were "great." After the fact the aesthetic experience that occurred may change with reflection, but even in reflection the image of perfection, mastery, and achievement provides an aesthetic dimension to the sport experience. "Having an aesthetic experience is not dependent on having the time during the event to contemplate it." (35:351)

There is no time whilst the operation is going on to dwell upon aesthetic qualities. . . . Afterwards the participant may look back upon his experience contemplatively with perhaps some aesthetic satisfaction. . . . But to produce strokes for contemplation is not part of his dominating motive as he is actually engaged in the game. . . . (338:252, 254)

Where Reid has argued that contemplation of an art object is essential for an aesthetic experience, Best suggests that contemplation either during the act (by the audience) or after the act (by the performer) may be a necessary but not a sufficient condition for the aesthetic experience. (35:351) He points out as have others that technical excellence is aesthetic when it is in keeping with the objective of the game. "We say that a stroke felt 'beautiful,' and it was so to the extent that it was efficiently executed in relation to the specific purpose of the action in the sport concerned." (35:351) The coming together of technique and purpose serves to provide an aesthetic potential. Skilled performance without intent or desire has limited aesthetic appeal. It remains a form of exercise.

. . . although the winning or losing of the game is aesthetically irrelevant, the *desire* to win is never aesthetically irrelevant. (188:328)

Winning without technical excellence is not aesthetic, for it ignores the process. There is a difference between the drawings produced by a third grade class and the drawings of the masters; between the White Plains Little League and the New York Yankees. In either case there is an end product, a drawing or a winning game. There is not, however, the technical excellence that implies mastery, consistency, and potential perfection among third graders or Little Leaguers.

. . . the game is made an aesthetic event by the opposition of strength in the wills to win. But desire itself is not sufficient. . . . In any game defined by the opposition of power, skill, and determination in its players, the power and skill cannot be lacking. (188:328)

POTENTIALS FOR DRAMA

To be an aesthetic event . . . the athletic contests must within the limits of the rules set down for the game become a unique contest of tensional wholes. This it does by building up tension, sustaining and complicating it, and ultimately releasing [it] into a state of peace. Well-played, i.e., successfully played, games and they alone succeed in this aesthetic ideal. (188:330)

Metheny has pointed out that man is drawn or driven to sport by his own psychologic need to test the limits of human ability. (271:74) The inherent nature of sport is its competitiveness. There is a conscious intent on the part of the individual to pursue personal excellence and to measure the "self" against goals set by the player and represented by an "other." These goals or intents may stem from the concrete motivation to demonstrate superiority or from the more tacit need to identify personal uniqueness. In either case, a struggle and a "contesting" is an inevitable feature of sport.

In many respects the dramatic possibility and the tragic potential of sport follow the pattern of Greek and Elizabethan tragedy. Conceptually and functionally Aristotle viewed tragedy as the poetry of universals: struggle, effort, confrontations of good and evil, success and failure. The plot is ordered action with powerful elements of emotional interest, and the characterizations are intended to show the moral purpose of the hero. There is structure, order, and direction. And, says Aristotle in his classical work, *Poetics*, "Tragedy is an imitation of action which is serious, complete in itself, and of a certain magnitude which creates a purging of emotions." The player defines the contest through his/her own acts and must then accept the consequences of those acts as the drama is resolved. The dramatic resolution may be manifest in either fulfilled or unfulfilled intent, and the consequences may be success or failure. Intent, preparation, and commitment are the prerequisites for sport to have dramatic potentialities. In some respects it is this need to "give all and see what you get back" which separates the trite and mundane drama of many athletic contests from those which are highly dramatic and reveal to us the true nature of people in general and the quality of the human spirit which has traditionally been played out on stages and pages instead of on playing fields.

From a spectator's standpoint, Keenan examined Aristotle's six formal elements of tragedy as they related to sport. These included plot, character, thought, diction, music, and spectacle. (196) From least important to most important, Keenan compares the spectacle of sport with the spectacle of the theater. Although the music of the pregame, halftime and postgame is not essential, it does provide entertainment, color, and pageantry to the event. The Rose Bowl parade and the Orange Bowl halftime have nothing to do with the actual athletic contest but have become an integral part of the "game." "The integrity of the contest as a tragedy remains intact without music or spectacle." (196:325) Relative to thought and diction, the language of the athlete is bodily movements, says Keenan, and "execution is the diction of the athlete's language." (196:324) Skilled performance enhances the articulation of the language and diction and is an important aspect in both how the character (the athlete) is capable of acting and how the plot, or struggle, is carried out.

> The 'character' of the tragic contest is conveyed through the plot, through adversaries vying with a necessity which decrees that one side shall win and one lose. When the players are excellent performers, as actors are excellent performers, they bring greatness to their roles. Good athletes give us good action in the plot. They characterize well the purposiveness and the seriousness of the plot. (196:323)

The athlete also characterizes a full range of emotional responses to the ongoing plot. The audience can readily see the anger, disgust, frustration, and joy during the dramatic sport event.

The plot of the tragedy in both sport and theater is most important. The ending is uncertain for the audience but consists of actions and events which either intentionally or unintentionally demonstrate the "frailty of human existence." Weiss points out that both a game and a stage play create tension where conflict ranges and struggles are waged within a connected scheme. This tension eventually finds some resolution. (434:197) Kaelin suggests that it is possible for some but not necessarily all contests to be aesthetic in the dramatic sense if it is apparent to the audience that there is a dramatic unity and continuity between preparation and climax. In addition, a skilled and well-played game which is closely contested adds to the sense of drama for the spectator. (188:326–328)

> The game itself considered as an aesthetic object is perceived as a tense experience in which pressure is built up from moment to moment, sustained through continuous opposition, until the climax of victory or defeat. The closer this climax occurs to the end of the game, the stronger is our feeling of its qualitative uniqueness. Sudden death play-offs—and perhaps extra-inning games—are as close as a sport may come to achieving this aesthetic ideal. (188:329)

Sport as a form of dramatic tragedy does not imply only sad endings or morbidity about defeat. Tragedy reveals the fighting spirit, and such positive and inspirational qualities as courage, will, and gallantry. (196:323) "The tragedy symbolizes man's struggle with the inequalities and paradoxes of life." (196:323) Some, but not every, sport contests may demonstrate these tragic qualities in a way that is visible to a spectator. When it is seen, then like any good theater or piece of literature, the spectator is privileged to witness the full range of human feelings, strengths, weaknesses, meanings, and possibilities. Some of this dramatic potential, however, is not visible to the spectator but remains among the contestants. "Through conflicts, collisions of interest, climaxes and Dionysian rituals, sport reveals itself as an extremely intense experience for both the performer and spectator. Aesthetic values related to the intensity of the experience arise from these human interactions." (444:343)

While a superbly skilled performance, tension, and conflict resolution are accepted and easily perceived aspects of the drama, there is more to the tragic dimension of sport. The intensity of interaction may be known only by the participant, since it stems from desire, will, and commitment and a variety of internal drives and feelings. Where Sophocles viewed drama as the "instrument for achieving sublime knowledge," contemporary playwright Arthur Miller sees drama as the stage for the "common man" to seek to achieve some measure of status, or nobility. Miller asserts that the potential for tragic consequences resides in many "life projects," of which sport can be one, as a result of a person's commitment to them and the need to evaluate the outcome of his efforts. In his "Tragedy and the Common Man," Miller states that "tragedy is the consequence of man's total compulsion to evaluate himself justly. The commonest of men take on tragic stature to the extent of their willingness to throw all they have into the contest." (280:1) The "need to know" coupled with a desire to be superior and the possibility of a skilled struggle makes commitment to the contest an act of focused intensity.

The stage is set in sport for the "common man" to act and the "tragic feeling" to occur. "The tragic feeling is evoked when we are in the presence of a character who is ready to lay down his life, if need be, to achieve one thing—his sense of personal dignity." (280:3) Viewing or participating in sport generates a broad range of feelings and a strong identification of the fan with the player, of player with player. In examining literature and the theater which are two art forms with greatest dramatic possibility, Miller writes that if tragedy is to have meaning for people in general, most of whom are ordinary, then it must deal with thoughts and feelings that have some universal base of understanding. (279) In sport, the stage is set for the "common man" to act. There is intent, a willingness to do whatever is necessary, and a total reliance on self. The rules are there. The plot and the strategy have been outlined, and the elements of excitement and spectacle surround the event. The questions become: How will the characters perform? How will the plot turn out? What will be the tragic flaw, and downfall, of the players? Tactical errors, skill deficiency, failure to stay "cool under fire" or simply not being good enough become the evident shortfalls.

Not all sport is intense enough to become drama. Some remains mundane in much the same way that daily struggles are—perhaps significant but not dramatically revealing. When there is a passionate intensity to want something "out of" sport whether it is excellence, superiority, status, or some sort of satisfaction or distinction, then sport, from an aesthetic standpoint, has the potential to be elevated above the mundane. There is a risk in a committed sport endeavor. It may not necessarily be a physical risk, but a risk in failing to achieve one's goals or desire, the risk of seeing oneself as less than we strive to be. These are significant risks in any society that rewards and applauds success. To want something from sport badly enough to risk obvious failure is to achieve tragic status in the most classic sense.

When the athlete has truly given all because he wanted to and because it was important and necessary to do it, he has put himself on the line. When he cannot retreat anywhere to hide his ignorance or incompetence in a "world" uncomplicated by the outside world, perhaps we have a true test and one of the cleanest confrontations of man, will, and fate—perhaps truer than the representational forms of theater and literature. The moments and necessity of choice in the contest are not unlike those in life except that they are more direct, immediate, reactive, and clear. One might wonder if it is not this reactive aspect that is perhaps most self-revealing. No time to be phoney. No time to think and cover up. Perhaps it is on this kind of "stage" that the "common man" can come to realize that it is not the fates, the consequences of his choices, or his failure but his *reaction* to these things and his ability to deal with them that make the real difference in how he assesses his own authenticity.

While success or fulfillment of intent has its potential in revealing man's capabilities, often it does not have the impact that failure has in self-realization. Failure is more difficult to come to grips with, more easily rationalized. Again, it is not man's confrontation with the fates but his reaction to them that demonstrates the authenticity of his being, the trueness of his identity. To know one's self is, for Sophocles and for Greek tragedy in general, to know that one is powerless and that one is destined to error, failure, and misery despite one's wisdom. Yet it is out of this suffering that the mirror is held most clearly and man can potentially see himself with a clear eye. The winner is tragic if he/she comes to believe that his/her total identity and/or self-esteem depends on physical prowess or that the world "owes" him/her something because of it. Athletes who live in the past and cannot get on with the "real" business of living productive lives after their athletic careers are over are also classic tragic figures. Winners or losers who cannot separate the outcome of a contest from the personal feelings of self-worth live out a tragic drama long after the game is over and the fans have left the stadium. The response to winning and losing is as much a part of the drama as how you play the game or whether it is won or lost. From an aesthetic standpoint, these responses to dramatic resolution characterize both the beautiful and the ugly.

THE SENSUOUS AS AESTHETIC

> The performer's body demonstrates at once one's objective and subjective orders of being. It is, in a sense, a 'thing among things,' quantitative and visible but it is also a subject who sees and feels and is sensitive to the world. . . . Performer's experiences of their bodies can be said to be experiences of beauty incarnated as they delight in an integral unity of a multitude of sensuous qualities: the firm and muscular with the gentle and sweet; the light and free with the strong and bound; the sustained with the quick; the direct with the indirect. (99:8, 9)

Skilled performance, drama, action, form, a symbolization of feelings and meanings are all aesthetic possibilities for both the performer and the audience in sport. Qualities like perfection and style become available to the athlete upon reflection. There is, however, one aesthetic dimension of sport that will not stand for reflection by either athlete or audience. It is that aspect that is feeling-based and sensuous. While it is true that the aesthetic experience may not be considered wholly sensuous, it does have a sensuous dimension. In these instances, the body is no longer the object of observation. The body as subject becomes the source for the aesthetic experience, and it is an aspect of sport reserved for the performer and not accessible to the spectator. A sensuous experience in sport is not guaranteed, and it may be an infrequent occurrence unless the individual has met the necessary prerequisites. Fetters points out that this sensuous possibility stems from the fact that "experience is a function of the whole body acting as a synergetic unity." (99:9) She goes on to identify body sensuality as being based in the performer's visual, tactile, and kinaesthetic perceptions as they occur *within* the experience. (99:9)

Literature on aesthetics has been primarily concerned with the audience and with their perceptions of some art object. The *expression* of feeling has been viewed as possible and appropriate as long as the audience sees the feeling as the artist has intended it. The awakening of the sensuous in the audience by the performer or art object is also seen within the boundaries of the aesthetic, but the *experiencing* of the feeling, or sensuality, by the performer has not been a serious consideration in aesthetic theory. This thinking has followed the nineteenth century philosophies of Veron and Tolstoy.

> . . . art is the manifestation of emotion, obtaining external interpretation, now by expressive arrangements of line, form or colour, now by a series of gestures, sounds, or words governed by particular rhythmic cadence. The measure of a work of art can be finally measured by the power with which it manifests or interprets the emotion that was the determining cause. (432:88–89)

While it was agreed by such philosophers that art addressed all feelings, its main function was to embody the emotions the artist experienced and communicate them to the audience. The emotions, feelings, or sensuality of the artist in the process of such transmission were of little or no concern except as they manifested themselves in an art form.

> To evoke in oneself a feeling one has experienced and having evoked it in oneself, then, by means of movements, lines, colours, or forms expressed in words, so to transmit that feeling that others may experience the same feeling—this is the activity of art. (421:43)

There has been consistently a confusion over the nature of feelings and emotional discharge. Expressions of anger, for example, may have sensuous overtones and be potentially aesthetic if they *symbolize* a fundamental humanness. On the other hand, kicking the family dog because one is angry about one's job is not existential symbolism. It is an act of psychologic displacement that is an emotional catharsis with no sensuality or symbolism intended or inherent in the act. "Feeling . . . is an act, in which there is a referent . . . to an object that is intentionally present." (50:156–157) The nature of the sensuality and feeling in sport stems from the direct and complete involvement of the body in the experience, as well as from the structured and nonutilitarian nature of sport. The sensuous in sport requires a full commitment to engage, to interact with the sport world. The feelings generated are results of that interaction and that commitment. Fetters describes the sense of "oneness" necessary for sensual feelings to occur in sport as an absence of opposition and an achievement of harmony.

> The sensuous experience of one's athletic energy as dynamic form has often been characterized as this experience of intimate relation between body and the world. Totally immersed in the sensuous feeling qualities of his medium the athlete has described his experience as a 'oneness' of body in the world. The skier becomes part of the mountain as he glides effortlessly through the soft, cool powder; the surfer feels one with his wave as he rides it gently.
>
> Sport offers numerous opportunities for this experience of oneness as a sensual dialog with the world and with others. . . . a oneness with one's medium, a oneness with the earth, a oneness with environmental elements, and a oneness with others, such as teammates and opponents. (101:257)

These reactions are individual feelings that are often spontaneous, private, and difficult to communicate. The sensuality of the sport experience is not sufficient to make it an art form, but perhaps it falls within the same qualitative, sensuous, and aesthetic experience that occurs while making love or watching a sunset. It is not enough to justify the existence of sport on any basis other than such sensuality as the basis for pleasure and an awareness of the self as human and not merely as an object among objects in the world. As Meier elaborates:

> . . . the texture of the being of the participant arises, by means of the body's power of expression. The player, through exuberant, delightful, joyous and spontaneous movement, gestures, and actions, confronts the world in a fresh manner, engages in dialog with it, and explores it and himself in a manner pregnant with individual significance. (264:32)

Skill and training play an important role in the experiential aesthetic. "No longer struggling to be there at the right time the performer delights in dynamic rhythmic form." (99:10) The commentary from *Ski the Outer Limits* that "powder is the ultimate in sensuous experience," T-shirts that advise you to "Get High on Rock," and descriptions of running "highs" in such periodicals as *Runners World* suggest that if you are ready, the pleasure is possible. "To experience this organic flow of movement during a flawless performance is, indeed, to experience beauty incarnated." (99:10)

Todd suggests that "one of the most basic pleasures associated with sport can be called 'joy of movement'." (420:9) Often obscured in the performer's perception by the agonistic aspects of the struggle, both the environment and contest can be ignored in enjoying the movement. (420:9–11)

> Such pleasures may also be associated with, and be simultaneous with, other pleasures such as the enjoyment of a summer day and the feel of grass on the bare feet. Still, the joy of movement derives almost entirely from tactual and somatic sensations, and very little from other kinds of sensations. (420:10)

While nature may be a welcome addition to the sensual aesthetic of moving, it is the *physical* joy of movement which is sensual. Even the "squalor of the gymnasium of a typical inner city YMCA" (420:10) cannot squelch the sensuality of moving, playing, contesting. Awareness of the joy of movements is not a highlight of outcome-oriented coaches who believe such "mush" detracts from the main purposes of sport. Many people exercise, play, and contest because they feel a physical need to move, because they like "how it feels." For some, the goals of the activity are secondary to the movements that are required. A swimming coach reports that: ". . . . in swimming, there is an additional beauty, the marvelous physical sensation of being in the water, of feeling power turn into speed as one pulls through the water." (373:18)

> Participation in any sport has the potential for being an intensely beautiful and very satisfying experience. In dedicating their performances to the gods, the Greeks may have been giving religious expression to an aesthetic truth. The beauty is of several kinds.
>
> There is a beautiful feeling in meeting a challenge, in pushing one's limitations outward, in going faster or harder, or longer than one had ever done before.
>
> There is beauty in feeling one's mind and body working together at full capacity in complete harmony.
>
> When one realizes those different kinds of beauty all at once, it is absolutely wonderful, an aesthetic experience of the highest order, a celebration of life. (373:18)

DISCUSSION QUESTIONS

1. Much of what is considered "aesthetic" is affective or "feeling based." As a means of expression or as a sensuous experience, in what ways is it possible to consider sport as an aesthetic experience?
2. Technical excellence is often described as "beautiful." What factors are usually considered in calling a technically excellent performance beautiful? Does "beautiful" in this context mean the same to the spectator as it does to the performer? What differences might exist?
3. There is some argument about whether sport is an art form in the same sense that the performing arts of music or drama are considered artistic. In what ways can sport be seen as artistic as an independent kind of performance or when compared to music, dance, and drama? In what ways does it fail in achieving status as an art form?

DIRECTED READING

Best, D.: The aesthetic in sport. *In* Sport and the Body, 2nd ed., edited by E.W. Gerber and W.J. Morgan. Philadelphia, Lea & Febiger, 1979, pp. 345–354.

Kaelin, E.: The well-played game: notes toward an aesthetics of sport. *In* Sport and the Body, 2nd ed., edited by E.W. Gerber and W.J. Morgan. Philadelphia, Lea & Febiger, 1979, pp. 324–331.

Keenan, F.: The athletic contest as a tragic form of art. *In* The Philosophy of Sport, edited by R.G. Osterhoudt. Springfield, IL, Charles C Thomas, 1973, pp. 309–325.

Kupfer, J.: Purpose and beauty in sport. *In* Sport and the Body, 2nd ed., edited by E.W. Gerber and W.J. Morgan. Philadelphia, Lea & Febiger, 1979, pp. 355–360.

Thomas, C.: Sports as drama. J. Phys. Educ. Rec. Dance, 53:39–40, 1982.

Thomas, C.: Toward an experiential sport aesthetic. J. Philos. Sport, 1:67–91, 1974.

Chapter 10

ETHICAL CONSIDERATIONS

The realm of ethics, then, is *right action*. The central concept of this domain is *obligation* and what *ought to be done*. The "ought" here is not individual but a universal principle of right.

Moral action presupposes *freedom*. Ethical meaning does not attach to coerced, purely habitual or mechanical, accidental, unconscious, or compulsive action. It is conduct that is deliberately executed as an expression of what one is committed to personally. Such action is self-determined rather than determined by outside factors. In this respect, personal knowledge (of the self) is essential to ethical meanings since personal maturity is the ground of freedom. Being a free person is prerequisite to moral action but not all free action is moral. (321:220–221)

Axiology has three interests: beauty, morality, and the common good. Aesthetics, the study of the nature and value of beauty is treated in Chapter 9. Moral philosophy, or ethics, focuses on the concern for determining what is right and wrong, good or bad, virtuous or evil. Ethics is prescriptive in the sense that it establishes what should be (potentiality) rather than what is actually occurring (actuality). In this regard ethics serves as guidelines for action and establishes obligations involved in and criteria for moral conduct. Against such guidelines of good and bad it is possible to examine behavior and intentional actions to determine their rightness and wrongness, appropriateness or inappropriateness. To some extent, theory and practice are related, since our theories about right and wrong aid in evaluating our practices. On the other hand, our value theories are grounded in practice. In that values reflect the practice of society, they are specific to a given society and have social roots. If this were not the case, value theory would be a matter of superstition or mere personal preference. This basis in reality is a key point because it holds that ethical standards are not generated in a vacuum but that ethics is a practical matter. Ethics is a discipline built on a reasoned conception of reality and based on logic and fact. We arrive at a perspective of what is, and we infer from that what ought to be and then judge our behavior accordingly. Axiology, in general, deals with social well-being and questions of freedom. What is good for this society? What is good for the individual? But there always exists the antithesis between the need to conform and the need to be free and an individual. Many moral decisions stem from these two positions: How can I be a good person in a society and meet the demands of that society and still be free to do and be what I want?

Three major categories exist for guiding ethical behavior. The first applicable standard is legal which is, in theory, stringent and strictly applied in all situations to all people. The law and the written rules are explicit in what actions are allowed and what actions are not only bad or inappropriate but illegal. The legal orientation usually carries with it specific penalties or consequences for actions which go against the rules. There is little room for a "judgment call." Murder is murder; tripping is tripping. Legal standards are usually clearly defined and applied across the board. The severity of the penalty imposed may be open to judgment when, for example, a choice may be made between life imprisonment or the death penalty or between a 5- or 15-yard penalty. Although a jury or a referee may be lenient, the rules are clear about what is acceptable and not acceptable behavior.

The second set of standards is moral and has more to do with social acceptability. Although these standards are not as tight or as stringent as legal standards, they do provide society with a relatively firm set of rules for right and wrong behavior. Moral standards are not as clearly defined as legal standards and are often open to more interpretation. They also tend to be situation-specific. Since these standards are looser, what may pass as acceptable in Los Angeles may be viewed as inappropriate in Des Moines. The struggle to define "obscenity" in the United States is an example of the inability of the courts to establish a legal standard and to rely instead on the moral sensitivity of a community in setting standards of right and wrong. Similarly, the kind and amount of contact permitted in a street game of basketball may be unacceptable in a fraternity intramural game. Morally acceptable standards vary among subcultures but within the situation stand as guidelines for right and wrong behavior.

The third set of standards is professional. Most professional associations—lawyers, doctors, teachers, coaches—have some set of standards and guidelines for the conduct of people who engage in that profession. These standards may be legalistic and strictly imposed or enforced or they may be loosely defined and based more on a moral conscience. Nevertheless, professional standards represent values and beliefs that a particular group has about the way the group should behave in the best interests of the people whom the profession serves as well as the society in general.

Many legal standards stem from the values and beliefs of a society and serve to impose those values in a strict and specific manner. For example, equal rights and equal opportunity are values of a democratic society and exist as part of the moral standard of such a society; yet without the legal standard that carries the strength of punishment with it, the moral standard historically had failed to provide equal opportunity and equal rights. The most prominent legislation in the United States of the last two decades has sought to guarantee equality by law in cases where the moral and professional standards had failed. In some ways the legal standard reflects social preference, but it also changes social attitudes. At one time women did not vote in the United States, but today it is *assumed* that everyone has the right to vote. To deny voting privileges to any person would be viewed as wrong, but it was not always viewed as wrong. Democracy did not change; the law did and over time, so did attitudes.

Sport has all three standards operating simultaneously. In its organized form, rules abound and legal standards and sanctions are plentiful. The "unwritten rules" that are the moral conscience of sport reflect a given situation as well as the attitudes and beliefs of the participants in that situation. The "courtesies" of many games may be ignored, but the sportsmanship of any player who ignores the courtesies and unwritten rules is highly questionable. Tennis players Ille Nastase and John McEnroe may be winners of tennis games but they are considered "losers" by many people who see tennis as more than the final score. The professional aspects as they relate to the relationship between coach and player, player and player, management and player all have ethical dimensions that are guided by legal, moral, or professional standards. Recruitment violations, deception, the administering of drugs, and playing injured players are examples of decisions based on ethical beliefs.

DEFINITIONS

moral—relating to the principles of right and wrong behavior; conforming to a standard of right, or good, behavior.

immoral—positive and active opposition to what is moral.

amoral—neutral; outside the sphere where moral judgments apply.

ethics—system of morals and values dealing with right and wrong, duty, and obligations.

values—abstract ideals not tied to any specific situation but representing beliefs about ideal modes of conduct and goals.

attitudes—an organization of beliefs focused on a specific object or subject predisposing one to respond in some preferential manner.

belief—a conviction of the truth of reality of some object or situation or event often based on experience, authority, or evidence.

KINDS OF BELIEFS

Beliefs about what is right and wrong not only form the value structure which guides individual ethical behavior and decision-making but serves as the foundation of culture and civilization. Phenix delineates five main areas where beliefs and moral obligations are primary concerns. These include: human rights which are intended to secure the freedom, integrity, and dignity of the person; sex and family relations; social relationships that may occur within class, ethnic, racial, religious, and vocational groups; economic life which has to do with property rights and the equitable distribution of goods and services; and political life where the just deployment of power requires moral action. (321:222–223) While sport is not directly reflected in this list, sport cuts across many lines in the need of its participants to establish various human rights, social and power relationships which are moral and appropriate for the particular sport setting.

Figure 10–1 provides a perspective for looking at the relationships that exist among values, beliefs, attitudes, and action.

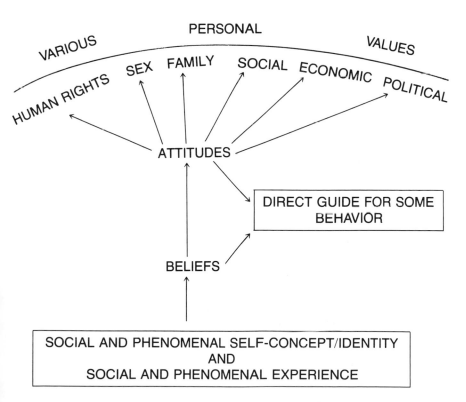

CONSISTENT ACTION AND BEHAVIOR
IS BASED ON THE
ETHICAL SYSTEM OF THE INDIVIDUAL
WHICH IS COMPRISED OF

PERSONAL

VARIOUS   VALUES

HUMAN RIGHTS   SEX   FAMILY   SOCIAL   ECONOMIC   POLITICAL

ATTITUDES

DIRECT GUIDE FOR SOME
BEHAVIOR

BELIEFS

SOCIAL AND PHENOMENAL SELF-CONCEPT/IDENTITY
AND
SOCIAL AND PHENOMENAL EXPERIENCE

Fig. 10–1. Diagram of relationships among values, beliefs, attitudes, and action.

Later in the chapter, the sources of beliefs, attitudes and values will be examined. In general, beliefs are situation-specific and vary on a continuum of being very central and unchanging to being peripheral and subject to constant change. Rokeach (347:6–10) has studied this range in the belief system and identified five kinds of beliefs:

1. Primitive, 100% consensus beliefs are most central in the belief system and are usually the most important, the most stable, and the most difficult to change. They are developed by direct encounter with others and as a result of experience. These kinds of beliefs represent the individual's "basic truths" about physical reality, social reality, and the nature of self. They are grounded in social consensus. "I believe this is my mother," and all data from a consensus of sources leads the person to believe this is true. Then, depending on other beliefs and attitudes about how one would relate to one's mother, various values are formed. Since this belief is central in the belief system, moral decisions based on values and attitudes will be fairly consistent, stable, and difficult to change. For example, if I value respect toward my parents and I believe this is my mother, then, in all probability, my mother will be treated with respect in a consistent manner. If, however, as I mature and the family is replaced with other values, some of the feelings about how I should relate to the family may change, but the belief that this particular woman is my mother will not change. The more central the belief, the more resistant it is to change. And, the more central the belief that *is* changed, the more widespread the repercussions in the rest of the belief system. If one believes for 15 years that "this is my mother" and is then introduced to the "fact" that she is not, the psychologic and philosophic questioning of all beliefs as a consequence of being "lied to" about a central belief is a fairly common reaction.

2. Primitive, zero consensus beliefs also rely on direct encounters with others and on experience, but maintenance of these beliefs does not depend on their being shared with others. Beliefs based on faith such as a belief in God or beliefs related to personal identity, e.g., I am intelligent or I am affectionate, are central beliefs. They are fairly stable once established and difficult to change. While they are not as central as beliefs based on social consensus, the fact that there is little reference outside personal experience tends to give these beliefs an emotional base. The emotional centrality serves to guide moral behavior from an egocentric base. The validity of the beliefs which have such a self-centered basis become an important factor in whether the values and behavior which result are appropriate, authentic, or justifiable. For example, a person who believes he/she is highly intelligent and has leadership qualities (for whatever reason) may then opt to "take charge", "give orders", or "make decisions." In social relationships such persons may view themselves as superior and decide that it is their duty and obligation to tell other people what to do and how to do it. They value themselves as leaders and the

others as followers. Now, if they are, *in fact*, what they think they are, it may be "right" or appropriate for them to behave as leaders. On the other hand, if they are not leaders and/or are not very intelligent except in their own eyes, then it may be an inappropriate social relationship and a wrong ethical choice to take over.

3. Beliefs based on authority also have their source in direct encounter with others. In experiencing the positive and negative authority of significant others, reference persons, and reference groups, beliefs are developed. These beliefs are on the midpoint of the central-peripheral continuum in that while the authority is viable, the belief is central but as the significant others lose their significance or potency and others replace them, then the beliefs also become subject to change. In this context, a belief may be central at a given time but peripheral in another situation with another authority figure. If a player's junior high school coach tells the player that intentionally fouling to get another player out of the game is essential to being a "good" player and is part of the game, the player will likely believe this because the coach is the authority. If the coach is also respected by the player, then the coach's status as a significant authority centralizes the belief and at that time such a belief would be difficult to change. During the period of this coach's influence, the player's ethical decisions would be guided by this, among other, beliefs. However, changing coaches or reference groups (teams) who hold different views on fouling will influence the centrality of that belief. If the new coach or the new group take on greater significance and replace the authority status of the former coach, new beliefs are likely to be formed.

4. Derived beliefs are formed through secondhand identification with authority rather than through direct encounter or actual experience. For example, *Runners World* or the *New York Times* said so. These beliefs are highly subject to change, since the authority source is not significant in the way a personal encounter with an "other" may be and it does not have the emotional base that faith and ego have. Many ideologic beliefs are developed by reading a book, and it is easy to identify with the author's position, especially if the tenets of the position match up with some of our already established values; but then if we read another book, with opposite ideals, it is just as easy to change our minds and believe in something else. The variability of facts serves as the basis for the peripheral nature of derived beliefs. However, in the absence of facts or another position, it is possible for a publication such as *Runners World* to be a bible upon which a belief is based and upon which subsequent moral choices are made.

5. Inconsequential beliefs have few or no connections with other beliefs. These are the most peripheral and are subject to change. In general they are considered arbitrary matters of taste and seldom develop into attitudes and values that impact on moral decision making. For example, to believe chocolate chip cookies are the best kind of cookie or that autumn

is the nicest season of the year are really matters of preference and are inconsequential as beliefs that have moral impact.

ATTITUDES

While it is possible that a single belief in isolation may lead a person to act in certain ways or to make a moral choice, usually several beliefs about a particular situation come together to form an attitude about the situation. This attitude then guides our behavior toward a specific situation within the context of a value system. For example, we may believe that the government is a waste, or a rip-off, or corrupt. This belief, however, when taken in isolation seldom leads to specific action. We may also believe that the income tax structure is unjust. Taken alone as a belief, this probably would not lead to action. Taken together, and perhaps combined with other related beliefs about government and taxation, the beliefs help to form an attitude. The attitude is situation-specific, and the ethical decision that may have to be made relative to the beliefs and the attitude is: Should I cheat on my income tax return? This situational decision is then considered within the context of my overall value system. The value system represents the ideal. How should one behave? What are the ideal modes of conduct? What ought to be done?

In the case of the income tax decision, honesty is the value in question. I may value honesty in all situations and believe that it is important to be honest and truthful. My moral choices become to remain true to my value system and override my negative attitudes toward the income tax or, on the other hand, to view the income tax as a situation that justifies my cheating. If I believe the income tax and the government are just, no moral problem would exist. While the overall abstract ideal of honesty exists, cheating at golf, cheating in one's marriage, and cheating on the income tax represent situations where honesty "should" exist but where honesty may be attitudinally based on beliefs that are situationally different. Valuing honesty as a moral ideal does not preclude situational application: I will cheat at golf and on my income tax but not in my marriage. The rightness or wrongness of these decisions will be examined later in the section on ethical theory. The fact remains that behavior is based on the *interaction* of the attitudes (series of beliefs) that we have toward an object or person *and* the attitudes that we have toward the situation in which that object or person is present. Both the person or object and the context have impact on the decision.

SOURCES AND DEVELOPMENT OF VALUES

The values an individual acquires have the same two bases that the self-concept, or personal identity has—a social base and an experience base. (See Chapter 8 for a full treatment of the social and phenomenal self). Because of the influence of social and experiential factors, values (the abstract ideal of what *ought* to be) have both a static and a dynamic quality. Inasmuch as they have both an enduring quality and are subject to change, personal value systems represent complex expressions of thoughts, feelings, and behaviors which reflect social influences, maturity, age, and health. What is of value to a college student may change over time or cease to be of importance as one grows older or changes reference groups. Other core values such as a respect for human life may endure over a lifetime once they are established. The value system also represents a hierarchical organization with some values being more important than others.

Rokeach (348) divides values into two categories which are related yet separate. Instrumental values reflect "means" or modes of conduct. These include such values as altruism, ambition, competence, courage, honesty, independence, love, responsibility, and fairness. Terminal values refer to end states of existence that the individual views as important. These include health, equality, an exciting life, true friendship, a sense of accomplishment, inner harmony, and a meaningful life. Terminal values generate other values. For example, if health is a strongly held terminal value, then it is possible that the person will also value exercise. In this respect, exercise is valued in an instrumental fashion as a means to an end and not as an end in and of itself. The examination of play in Chapter 4 highlights this difference. It is possible to view play as serving another end—releasing surplus energy, developing skills or fitness—or it is possible to view play in its existential fashion as an end state, valuable in and of itself.

The relationship between terminal values and instrumental values may be seen in the use of instrumental means to achieve an end state. For example, if a terminal value is true friendship, it may be possible to see the instrumental values of love, altruism, honesty, and fairness as values directed at meeting the desired end state. Sport has often been seen as a secondary instrumental value in achieving health, a sense of accomplishment, a meaningful life, an ambition, competence, or an exciting life. It is seldom seen as a terminal value, an end state toward which people strive. Aspiring professional athletes may be the exception, but it is more probable they are seeking something sport can make possible (thereby using sport as instrumentally valuable) rather than seeking out the sport as an end in itself. Sport becomes a valuable *means* in many situations for people to achieve or demonstrate either instrumental or terminal values.

Based on the belief that the values of a society need to be transmitted to all members of that society, it has been common practice for those in authority positions to pass on the values of the institution. Values are assimilated by the individual by virtue of family membership; the institutionalization of the individual in schools, churches, social groups, sport groups; and by the learned familiarity with the legal constraints of a given society. The inculcation of values has been traditionally viewed as a one-way street where the parent, teacher, or some expert or significant other "tells" the neophyte what is important. In this respect, right and wrong, instrumental and terminal values have been taught in much the same way as mathematics and history. The church, the school, and sport as an institution have felt a particular need and responsbility to teach values. Simon (377) and Raths (332) identified moralizing, modeling, and laissez faire as the three classic approaches to the teaching or transmission of values.

1. Moralizing is the direct, sometime subtle inculcation of adult societal values upon the young. It is a telling of what "should be," what is right and wrong, appropriate and inappropriate. It is also an effort to establish for the individual what is important in life, what goals are significant and what terminal values are important. Moralizing does not have a universal character in that it reflects the values of a given subculture, the family, a particular neighborhood or socio-economic class. The problem with this approach to values transmission is that there are often many moralizers with different and discrepant messages for the individual. Such discrepancies often lead to confusion, inconsistency and superficial compliance. Moralizing does, however, remain a strong social influence in the development or refinement of an individual's value system.

2. Modeling is an attempt to show rather than to tell the individual what is important. The significant other becomes the example of appropriate behavior, and values are inferred from this behavior. The individual is again faced with many models whom he/she may emulate for a variety of reasons. The potential for the creation of basic value conflicts among models is highly probable and creates contradictory, inconsistent, and superficial value-related behavior. While modeling is often an intentional means of value transmission, many values are transmitted unintentionally as a result of the imitation of role models, particularly by children and young adults. Many of the values associated with competitive behavior are instrumental. The Little Leaguer sees big league manager Billy Martin throw dirt at an umpire and sees Martin able to intimidate to get his way. The association is made and the belief is formed that it is necessary and rewarding to use intimidation to get your way in a competitive setting. The value is formed unintentionally. The "model" is unknowingly effective. Using that data and adding his/her own experience, the player then forms an attitude about competition and what is a valuable end state. Winning becomes a terminal value for any number of reasons, but intimidation becomes an instrumental value because it works, it is rewarded, and it aids in achieving the terminal value of winning.

3. A laissez faire approach grew out of the belief that each person has to develop his/her own values and that the moralizing and modeling approaches are producing inconsistent personal value systems. The ad-

vocacy was to leave people alone to experience the world and put together their own set of values and priorities. As a popular approach in the 1960s it failed in its assumption about the maturity of young people to understand values and conflicts without some guidance. Confusion resulted and highly egocentric values evolved.

In response to the failure of these approaches in the development of values, humanistic philosophers and educators of the early 1970s advocated the process of values classification as a practical approach to the teaching of values. Realizing that the development of a system of values was a personal and unique process for each person, the concept focused on individual clarification. It was an attempt to teach the person what was important without necessarily laying out a set of established societal or universal values. The role of the significant other became the identification of the moral problem, helping the individual realize there is a problem or a conflict of values and identifying what values are at stake.

For the purposes of values clarification, the valuing process is defined in an operational fashion, in terms of how it works. The valuing process includes seven elements clustered in the three action processes of *choosing, prizing,* and *acting.* These seven elements can be used as a set of criteria to hold up against a choice or a decision a person makes to determine the nature or depth of value commitment.

CHOOSING: 1. Choosing from alternatives
2. Choosing after considering the consequences
3. Choosing freely
PRIZING: 4. Considering what one prizes and cherishes
5. Affirming one's choice publicly to others
ACTING: 6. Doing something, acting in terms of one's choice
7. Doing so repeatedly as a pattern of one's life

As a clarification process, the approach is intended to help sort out existing values and to refine means-ends possibilities. Existing values develop and take shape but are not transmitted.

A more controversial approach to the teaching of moral thinking is that of Lawrence Kohlberg, (211) who has been reviewed by Muson (295) and Kurtines and Grief. (228) Following the thinking of Piaget, Kohlberg identified six stages of moral reasoning that were contingent on both the motivation and the maturity of the individual and moved from dependence on and dictation from others to autonomous decision making and from a strict concern about self to concern for more universal values. While the stages are not necessarily sequential or separate, they do provide a model for looking at ways people operationalize value systems.

Kohlberg's stages reflect his belief in a hierarchy of stages which depends on an increasing capacity to think with sophistication and to empathize with others as a result of social interactions.

Stage 1: Punishment and Obedience Orientation. In this most primitive and egocentric orientation, the individual defers to the superior position and power of the other. This deference is most common in the parent-child relationship where the child does what he/she is "supposed" to do out of fear of punishment or rejection. This stage is a strong socializing agent and remains as a basic response in many situations throughout life. Even in situations where sophisticated thinking may tell us to value or do something else, we may behave "appropriately" and give up freedom or integrity out of a fear of punishment or social rejection.

Stage 2: Instrumental-Relativist Orientation. The individual in this stage agrees to obey a rule or behave in certain ways because he/she anticipates that there will be some benefits in return. It is a reward orientation. The moral reasoning at this stage is still very self-centered and unsophisticated. Little attention is paid to what is being valued or why but only that in Stage 1 I won't be punished and in Stage 2 I will get something of value in return. In these two stages, we may be doing the "right" things, or at least what someone else thinks is right, but we are not doing it because we value the behavior as either a means or an end. We do "good" because it either reduces pain or increases pleasure that is related to something else. We *use* moral behavior to get or to avoid something else, but we do not value the behavior in and of itself.

Stage 3: Good Girl/Nice Boy Orientation. In this stage the approval of others becomes important. We do what others want us to do or what they think is right so that they will think well of us. We seek to be a good person. In a religious context, the "good person" concept carries with it the approval or the wrath of God and combines Stages 1, 2, and 3. All three stages are grounded not only in Piagetan developmental theory but based also on operant learning principles of reward-punishment-approval.

Stage 4: Law and Order Orientation. This is the first stage where the individual goes outside his own personal gratification to be concerned about the "good" of society. It is a stage where maintaining the system by the fair and equal application of rules and the punishing of transgressions for the good of the social order is seen as important. Moral decisions are based on legalistic principles and conformity to existing standards. This stage reflects a concern for the wider community but retains punishment as the motivation for ethical decision making.

Stage 5: Social-Contract/Legalistic Orientation. Moving beyond the straightforward law and order stage is a concern for justice. As a social orientation that reflects sophistication beyond the reward-punishment mentality, this stage has as its primary focus civil rights, human rights, and equal rights. The moral principles that guide law in its constitutional form are seen as basic concerns of the Stage 5 moral reasoning.

Stage 6: Universal Ethical Principle Orientation. This most abstract of the stages deals with universal laws and principled behavior regardless of ideology. These beliefs about right and wrong are reflected in such documents as the United States Proclamation on Human Rights or the Geneva Convention. This stage represents the ultimate in social conscience, as it often has little to do with personal values in daily life but reflects a set of beliefs and attitudes about what is appropriate behavior for all humans.

ETHICAL THEORY

As a perspective it may generally be said that there are two basic approaches to ethical decision making, emotive and cognitive. On the emotive level, most arguments are based on interest, on changing the values and beliefs of one party to match the interests of another party. The side that a person takes is based on feeling and not on data. What is "good" or "right" is not a clearly defined fact because it is believed that the undefinable (good) cannot be defined. Often there is an emotive and connotative use of language to create bad feeling against one thing or person to sway feelings toward another thing or person. For example, to call persons jocks, dykes, or niggers is to also call them deviant or inferior and to attempt to create bad feelings about their life styles or ethnicity. Inasmuch as interest serves as the basis for what is good, there is a tendency to define good in terms of what gives one pleasure. Ayer (17) holds that ethical statements are neither true nor false but merely expressions of personal preferences. In a similar argument Stevenson (391:21) says that ". . . you might regard 'this is good' as meaning 'I approve of this; do so too'—for in saying that something is good one means, partly, that one approves of it and, partly, that one wants one's hearers to approve of it as well." An example of this is to say physical fitness is good because it facilitates longer life. One would have to universally agree that a "longer life" is good for this statement to be valid. Or to say that a good game is a victorious game. One would need to stipulate the characteristics of victory to determine whether it matched up with what is meant as good. Is winning while playing poorly still considered a good game? Is winning by cheating still a good game? Use of these emotive kinds of value arguments often decreases understanding of situations by the absence of fact. Emotionally grounded interest arguments may also lead to a standoff in the resolution of issues. However, to the extent that experience is frequently illogical and irrational and many beliefs and values stem from experience, the emotive approach may be justified to some extent.

Zeigler (447:15) points out that in the emotive approach ethics are normative and cannot be scientifically factual, since "good" appears to be indefinable. However, he argues that an ethical dispute or decision must be elevated above interest, feeling, and emotion by distinguishing factual statements from value statements and attempting to resolve the issue on a factual level. The separation of fact from value, meaning from substance, and denotation from connotation is a cognitive approach to ethical decision

Table 10—1.   Major Philosophic Approaches to Ethical Decisions

Ethical Approach	Underlying Presupposition	Criterion for Evaluation	Method for Determination of Ethical Decision	Probable Result
I. Authoritarianism (or legalism)	Absolute good and rightness are either present in the world or have been determined by custom, law, or code	Conformity to rules, laws, moral codes, established systems and customs	Application of normative standard (or law) to resolve the ethical dilemma or issue	The solution to any ethical dilemma can be readily determined and then implemented (acted upon)
II. Relativism (or antinomianism)	Good and bad, and rightness, and wrongness are relative and vary according to the situation or culture involved	Needs of situation there and then in culture or society concerned	Guidance in the making of an ethical decision may come either from "outside," intuition, one's own conscience, empirical investigation, reason, etc.	Each ethical decision is highly individual, since every situation has its particularity; there are no absolutely valid principles or universal laws
III. Situationism (with certain similarity to I above)	God's love (or some other summum bonum) is an absolute norm; reason, revelation, and precedent have no objective normative status	"What is fitting" in the situation is based on application of agapeic love; subordinate moral principles serve to illuminate the situation	Resolution of ethical dilemma results from use of calculating method plus contextual appropriateness; act from loving concern; what is benevolent is right	The best solution, everything considered, will result when the principle of God's love is applied situationally

From Zeigler, E.F.: Application of a scientific ethics approach to sport decisions. Quest, 32(1):14, 1980.

making. Zeigler (447:14) has termed this approach "scientific ethics." Strong efforts are made to identify the facts in the situation and tentative hypotheses are developed relative to what is good or right. Empirical verification and testing of the hypotheses bring truth to the validity of the value statement. Analysis, logic, and the seeking of substance are the primary methods. An effort is made to know what a thing or a statement *is* and not what it *means*. Meaning changes but reality does not. For example, if we examine use of the word "jock," the definition or substance of that word is "athlete," but in using the word "jock" instead of "athlete," a meaning or evaluation is attached and what is being said is something about being inferior. Cognitive approaches to ethics make an attempt to break down the situation or thing under consideration to get at substance and fact. The problem with this approach, as some philosophers have noted, is that fact and moral obligation are of essentially different logical orders. It would be argued that one can never correctly make an inference from what *is* to what *ought* to be, nor vice versa. Similarly, G.E. Moore argued that all attempts to reduce values to facts result in a "naturalistic fallacy."

> This fallacy is committed whenever one *defines* value concepts in factual terms, as for example, when the statement 'This is good' is said to *mean* 'This gives me pleasure.' The first statement asserts that something is valuable, or praiseworthy, or desirable, all of which meanings are logically different in kind from the factual impact of the second statement. The statement of value is logically independent of and incommensurable with (though not necessarily inconsistent with) the statement of fact. (283:216–217)

In addition to the basic cognitive and emotive approaches, Zeigler (447), and Fraleigh (112) have outlined three additional theoretical approaches to ethical decision making. These include: authoritarianism or legalism, relativism or antinominianism, and situationism. In a recent paper (447), Zeigler has outlined these three theories as shown in Table 10–1, "Major Philosophic Approaches to Ethical Decisions."

Authoritarianism or Legalism

"The *legalistic* approach is perhaps the cleaner and easier in its approach to decision-making . . . that the application of the appropriate rules provides a rather clear, direct answer." (112:6–7) The agent of decision in the legalistic approach is the law or, in the sport setting, the rules of the game. Good and right are decided by one's behavior as it is consistent with the rules, for it is assumed that the laws and rules were made with the "good" of everyone in mind. It is not necessary to have a great deal of knowledge, insight, or feeling about a situation, since the rules are clear about what decision *should* be made. Freedom and choice are minimized in the sense that the individual is subject to the norms of the group. Individualism is secondary to the utilitarian principles of "the greatest good for the greatest number." From an existential perspective choice is available, but one also chooses to accept the consequences for going against the rules.

Despite the explicitness of the rules in the legalistic approach, interpretation still remains a possibility. Consideration of the difference between the letter of the law and the spirit of the law often causes difficulty. Fraleigh identifies other difficulties:

> . . . This ease and clarity of decision is not, however, without difficulty. First, abstract rules seldom fit each case perfectly since cases are composed of differing set of variables. Second, cases occur for which there are no directly applicable rules. And most important, third, rules sometimes become idolized even when intentional violation may be the most humane action in a particular case. Although rules are not intended to be broken there appear to be cases when rule breaking is both intelligent and humane. (112:7)

In his paper, "Why the Good Foul is Not Good," Fraleigh (120:41) delineates the three ways in which rules function in a contest: (1) they tell the participants what they must do and what they are allowed to do; (2) they identify the within-the-contest goals toward which performance is aimed; and (3) they define illegal actions. Violation of the first two functions may inhibit playing the game in the first place. Violation of the third function may get in the way of achieving the end result of an ethical or "good" win, since such violations may require penalty.

Cheating, taking unfair advantage, or manipulation of the rules as in intentional fouling, fighting, deception, or the use of drugs to enhance performance are all behaviors that are legislated against in sport. Yet while the standards of what is appropriate are very clear and definitive in a legalistic approach, the decision-making process is not always as easy as simply following the written rules. (See Table 10–1 for criterion, method, and probable results in the legalistic approach.)

Relativism

Fletcher (105:22–23) describes relativism or antinomianism (against law) as the approach to ethics in which the individual is the sole agent of decision. There are no principles or rules to guide the decision-making process. It is believed that every situation is unique and requires the decision maker to rely on the conditions of the situation in a "here and now" time frame to arrive at an ethical decision. The emphasis is on individual decisions and the elimination of law, codes, or moral principles to guide decisions. This approach is based on the assumption that there is no absolute or universal good and, as a result, no real coherence in moral decision-making processes. Since one cannot view the greatest good for the greatest number as a viable moral principle, reliance on self and the conditions of the situation are paramount. Freedom and choice are unconstrained possibilities. Within the sport setting, all ground rules and game rules would need to be delineated each time the game is played and would be subject to change as the game went on. Anything not specifically covered would be subject to interpretation by each player. In some respects, this approach governs "sandlot" or "pick-up" games and many of the "New Games," although the "Play Hard, Play Fair, Nobody Hurt" maxim of "New Games" would have to be accepted at the outset. Table 10–1 plots out the basic elements of the position.

Situationism

Situationism, first advocated by Fletcher in his *Situation Ethics*, is relatively recent in the development of ethical theories. The agent of decision is the individual rather than an external formalistic standard or legal code of behavior. Yet the decision-making process has a guiding principle beyond the conditions of each situation. That condition is love and the situation ethic is based on the assumption that love is necessary to improve the human condition and that if love is the criterion of good, then the right decision will be made regardless of the variability of the situation. The situation ethic responds to the uniqueness of the situation and allows for individual freedom and choice by placing the responsibility for the ethical decision on the person rather than having it imposed by a set of legalistic standards. Love as the guiding principle does not imply romantic love, sexual love, or even the necessity of liking the "other." It is a feeling of reciprocity, of mutuality, of concern, and caring for one's fellow human. In some respects, the characteristics of Buber's I-Thou enter in when the decision is made. Situationism is analytic and practical seeking to examine means, ends, motives, and consequences within the context of the situation with decisions being based on what is "fitting" and loving at a particular time and in a particular situation. Table 10-1 traces the criterion, method, and results.

TERMINAL AND INSTRUMENTAL VALUES IN SPORT

Terminal values, as was previously explained, represent desired end states toward which a person is willing to direct time, energy, and resources. Sport participation may be valued instrumentally in achieving these end states. In Chapters 6, 7, and 8 some reasons for participation in sport were explored. In some respects, any or all of these reasons (meanings) may have do do with what are terminal values or desired ends in a person's life. Some of the terminal values that might be achieved by using the sport medium are: a sense of purpose, an exciting life, status, a sense of competence, a sense of achievement, a sense of superiority. In deciding about ethical behavior in sport, it is first necessary for individuals or groups to decide what ends sport is serving. For example, sport would be approached differently or different *means* would be used if I am trying to achieve a terminal value of feeling superior as opposed to achieving an exciting life. On the one hand, winning games may be very important, and on the other the "thrill of the chase" may be my dominant concern.

If winning is my terminal value, then there are many instrumental values which would come into play such as discipline, hard work, skill-development, persistence. Negatively expressed, deception and cheating may be valued over honesty and fairness. A value conflict may occur if I value superiority as a terminal value and fairness as an instrumental value if the situation arises where one or the other value may not be achieved or has to be sacrificed. A terminal value of "an exciting life" may be met in sport, but the approach and the means may be altogether different than in the case of valuing superiority.

Loy et al. (250:89–90) studied attitudes toward agonetic activities and identified a number of values that people would consider either terminal or instrumental in their lives. Sport was viewed as instrumentally valuable primarily in achieving a desired terminal value (end state of existence) such as being healthful or in meeting other instrumental values such as sociability. Their list is as follows:

1. Sport as an aesthetic experience. Participating in sports which provide for the expression of ideas and feelings through graceful and artistic human movement.
2. Sport as an ascetic experience. Participating in sports which require prolonged, painful, and strenuous training and call for stamina and endurance.
3. Sport as a cathartic experience. Participation in sports for personal relaxation and release of pent-up emotions.
4. Sport as a combative experience. Participating in sports which require the use of a weapon against an opponent, target, or quarry.
5. Sport as an environment experience. Participation in sports which test the individual against the elements such as mountains, water, ice, and snow.
6. Sport as a fortuitous experience. Participating in sports which involve a great deal of chance or luck.
7. Sport as a healthful experience. Participating in sports to improve one's health or level of physical fitness.
8. Sport as an experience of physical contact. Participating in sports which involve direct body contact with one's opponents.
9. Sport as the experience of skilled performance. Participating in sports in order to perfect physical skills.
10. Sport as a social experience. Participating in sports for the purpose of meeting people and having a good time with friends.
11. Sport as a strategic experience. Participating in sports for the purpose of developing and demonstrating tactics and strategy.
12. Sport as a vertiginous experience. Participating in sports characterized by high speeds, constant change of motion, danger, and thrills.

These kinds of values have been typically used by physical educators to justify sport, dance, exercise, and play in school settings. However, it is important to remember that sport is being *used* to meet life values that the individual holds and is not necessarily seen as important in and of itself. It should also be noted that sport and other physical activities are but *one* medium available to meet terminal and instrumental value needs. The fact that people find ways other than sport to achieve a sense of purpose in their lives or a sense of superiority is not a denigration of sport; it merely reflects a preference for activities which are more valued.

ENDS VERSUS MEANS

Do the ends justify the means? This has been a long-standing debate in both sport and nonsport settings. Winning may be the amoral object of the game, but should we go about it the same way in PeeWee swimming as we do in professional athletics? A consideration of what is important as an outcome other than winning (if anything) may give direction to means and methods. Keating, in his look at the concept of sportsmanship has been instructive in his advocacy that while there is an element of sportsmanship present in both sport and athletics, the same code is inappropriate or not applicable for both. (191:266–268) The outcome and the means by which the sportsman and the athlete differentially prepare require different standards of evaluation relative to sportsmanlike behavior. Even if one does not accept Keating's sharp dichotomy between sport and athletics, his point about differential evaluation seems valid.

> Since the sportsman's primary objective is the joy of the moment, it is obvious from that very fact that he places no great emphasis on the importance of winning. It is easy for him to be modest in victory and gracious in defeat and to play fair at all times. . . . The strange paradox of sportsmanship as applied to athletics is that it asks the athlete, locked in a deadly serious and emotionally charged situation, to act outwardly as if he were engaged in some pleasant diversion. After an athlete has trained and sacrificed for weeks . . . dreamed of victory . . . literally exhausted himself physically and emotionally in its pursuit . . . to ask him to act with fairness in a contest, with modesty in victory, and an admirable composure in defeat is to demand a great deal. (191:269)

Jack Scott (372) identified three ethical positions which were distinguished by their focus on the primacy of ends or means. In his concept of the Lombardian ethic, winning is the most important outcome and the end result justifies the means of achieving that end. In this ethical view, the opponent is viewed as an enemy, and concepts like fair play are secondary to overcoming the obstacle of the opponent. Scott admits that such a system has demanded and received the sacrifices and hard work of many athletes and has produced an excellent product. (372:73) Developed at the expense of a player's freedom and individuality, self-expression, and spontaneity, decisions are based on authoritarian and legalistic approaches. (372:73). Kew (201:106) observes that in the Lombardian ethic, dominated by the work ethic and the emphasis on winning, ". . . all movements within a game must be directed toward the attempt to win and that any movement not so motivated is inappropriate and counter-productive."

As winning becomes the dominant theme, it overrides the moral ram-ifications of behavior that might occur within the game. Right and wrong have a tendency to become blurred, and the inappropriateness of behavior is lost in the heat of the battle. "Did I do something wrong?"

> As the emphasis on winning increases, so the value of the actual playing of the game decreases. The means being to justify the end result. . . . basic moral tenets which, by common consent, govern all human action, cease to apply within the realm of the game. (201:107)

The Lombardian ethic is an example of the instrumental use of sport to achieve values outside the activity—a terminal value of compe-tence/superiority. The cost of achieving this value is at the expense of others. The potential for dehumanization comes with the focus on winning as the exclusive outcome. With varying degrees of intensity players be-come "meat on the hoof" subject to use and manipulation, sales, and trade by coaches, owners, and athletic directors. The recruitment of out-standing players to a campus fills stadiums, wins games, gives a school "visibility," and prompts alumni support. Kew reminds us that in its extreme application winning blinds us to what happens to us as a person.

> . . . individual players are valued only insofar as they contribute to a suc-cessful outcome. The individual is valued purely instrumentally and his effectiveness and worth are synonymous with his single-minded dedication and contribution to winning. His own motives for playing the game, the meaning of the game for him, his personal and private experiences, and feelings, aesthetic satisfaction, and so on are of no consequence if they neither contribute to, nor detract form the main aim of winning. (201:107)

The antithesis of the Lombardian ethic is what Scott calls the "coun-terculture ethic." This view holds that winning is an extrinsic reward and that the value of sport rests in the process of the activity itself rather than in its outcome.

> . . . the counterculture ethic takes every value of the Lombardian ethic and puts forth the exact opposite value as its position. Cooperation replaces competition, an emphasis on process replaces an emphasis on product, sport as a coeducational activity replaces a concern for excellence, and an oppor-tunity for spontaneity and self-expression replaces authoritarianism. (372:74)

Scott points out, however, that while this counterculture perspective of sport as pure play has served to highlight many of the abuses of com-petitive sport, it does not accurately reflect the values and attitudes of the society in which sport is conducted. (372:74) It is, however, appro-priate to use the counterculture ethic to highlight values that the com-petitive setting may potentially facilitate when winning is viewed simply as the outcome of the game rather than as its central preoccupation. As a means of consciousness raising, as an experience of freedom, and as a source of meaning the process of sport has potential value to many who play. With regard to the potential for freedom in play Sartre (365:85) remarks:

> The act is not its own goal for itself; neither does its explicit end [winning] represent its goal and its profound meaning; but the function of the act is to make manifest and to present to itself the absolute freedom which is the very being of the person.

The sport act itself is the important focus for the achievement of values other than winning. The focus on process to increase body awareness is very much in keeping with counterculture (Con III) beliefs in self-understanding and self-actualization which replace values related to dominance and superiority. Kew summarizes the contribution of process to achieving counterculture values.

> Sport, in general, is freely chosen and freely engaged in; the rules are freely accepted, one is free from the everyday world and, most important, one is free to be oneself—to actualize one's potential. The performer may gain many complex conceptions of himself and many sources of meaning. (201:108)

Between the exclusive attention to either product or process is what Scott has labeled the "radical ethic." In attempting to keep sport in its perspective as a reflection of broader social values which include success and competition as important elements while heeding Morford's (288) admonition that "we have made of sport a place where I will prove myself rather than know myself," Scott has sought the best of both worlds. The radical ethic holds that there is nothing fundamentally wrong with the essence of competitive sport. It sees sport as neither an extreme of competitiveness or cooperation, product or process. "The radical ethic recognizes the excellence of outcome as important but holds equally important the way the excellence is achieved." (372:75) The means are as important as the outcome and winning is hollow if the means used to achieve it lack integrity. "The radical athlete has an intense desire to achieve excellence and victory, but he just as intensely wants to seek and experience the agonistic struggle." (372:76) The radical ethic represents a balance in values which are sought as they relate to means and ends. It also represents a striving toward the "good" game where playing well within the context of the rules, viewing the opponent as worthy, the struggle as valuable, and striving to win all go to make up the "ideal" of sport. Kew summarizes the position by saying:

> To have a good game and to play well is the foremost aim. . . . In order to have a good game all players must have a respect for the rules; they must cooperate effectively with others. . . . The desire to win is an essential prerequisite. The radical ethic thus recognizes that playing well and winning are complementary and mutually conditioning aims. (201:104)

Gallwey (124) suggests that in true competition, no person is ever really defeated. Rather we overcome the obstacles that the other person presents to us. The opponent is a friend who does his/her best to make things difficult for you and requires of you your best possible effort. From this standpoint the process of overcoming the obstacles is of value, and taking advantage of a friend who is attempting to elevate you to your greatest potential is inappropriate in the competitive setting. (124:153) Although each player attempts to defeat the other, "winning is overcoming obstacles to reach a goal, but the value in winning is only as great as the value of the goal reached." (124:153)

Often the decision between seeking excellence or seeking superiority makes the difference in approach, means, attitudes, and ethical decisions. From a legalistic standpoint, each player enters into a "contract" for a contest and thereby freely and voluntarily accepts the rules and conditions under which the contest will be played. Violation of the contract produces some direct and indirect consequences and penalties. Some penalties are "bad" because a player gets caught and disadvantages the team by being penalized. Some penalties or fouls are viewed as being "good" because the penalty benefits the offending team rather than the offended team. From a legalistic perspective, the rules are being broken, manipulated, or bent, and they are being used in ways in which they were not intended to be used. Pearson argues that the purpose of the game is to determine who is more skillful and any act which deliberately interferes with that purpose can be considered unethical.

> If the purpose of the contest is to determine who is more skillful in that game we can say that a player has entered into a contract with his opponent for the mutual purpose of making that determination. . . . a particular game is defined by its rules. . . . a player who deliberately breaks the rules is no longer playing that game. . . . These kinds of acts are designed to interfere with the purpose of the game in which they occur. (318:273)

A "friendly" round of golf may give the player "understood" or explicit permission to improve the lie of the ball without it being considered cheating. A tournament round of golf is not perceived in the same way. The spirit of the rules in any consideration of "fair play"* creates a complexity in any consideration of what is right and wrong in sport-related behavior. The rules attempt to establish fairness and equality in the structure of the game, although Brown (44) points out that there will always be an inequality in the participants who play the game—equal opportunity but not equal ability. The contest is intended to test ability and to determine who is superior. The rules are intended to provide the same opportunity to all players. A test of ability rather than a test of using the rules may have been intended, but "strategy" has come to include reducing the effect of the rules in maintaining equality of opportunity and creating advantages by *using* the rules.

---

*See Peter McIntosh: *Fair Play: Ethics in Sport and Education*. London, Heinemann, 1979, for a full treatment of complexities of ethical behavior in sport.

When the "spirit" of the rules is considered or when unwritten codes of conduct which revolve around sportsmanship or "courtesies" of the game are considered, moral decisions increase in their difficulty and complexity. How one views the opponent and what a player values in the game itself become the background against which decisions are made. In addition, the situation and the rewards are confounding variables. If an individual is operating in Kohlberg's (211) first three stages where egocentricity is the primary motivation, consideration for the "other" and for the integrity of the game may be secondary to "what's in it for me" by way of a payoff or achieving personal terminal values. The advocacy of the situation ethic to make decisions based on what is the "loving" or most concerned thing to do often fails to be a valid criterion when all consideration is given to the "I" and little is given to the "we" or the "Thou." Through a rather complex socialization and experiential process, we are taught what is important to achieve and what are appropriate means of going about achieving these things. Freedom has always implied responsibility, but the boundaries of and criteria for such responsibility remain without universal definition and acceptance. This is not to imply that such boundaries and criteria are without merit, but the way in which each individual conducts his/her sport life and life in general remains an individual matter governed by personal values, interests, attitudes, and beliefs.

CONCERNS UNIQUE TO SPORT

Sportsmanship

Slusher points out the reality of the intent of athletics when he says that:

> Our expressed purpose in sport is clear. It is not comradeship, self-discovery or aesthetics. I don't care what the level of participation is—be it six-year olds or sixty-year olds—man plays to succeed. And success is measured by pushing the other guy down, just a little, so that you, as you harness the forces of nature, climb a little higher. (379:167)

Most discussions of sportsmanship result in a dilemma which involves defining sportsmanship and then applying its codes of ideal behavior in sport to the actual reality of the sport situation. Sportsmanship has been viewed not so much as a set of rules but as a code of living. (57:260) Despite the different goals in sport and athletics and inability to apply the *same* code of sportsmanship to both situations, Keating sees fairness as the possible common base of sportsmanship in both sport and athletics. (191:269) Traditionally, physical educators, coaches, players, and fans have all identified a number of desirable behaviors in sport that have come under the classification of sportsmanship. Representing attitudes rather than rules, Keating delineates these qualities while at the same time indicating that identifying so many qualities has stripped sportsmanship of any real meaning and specificity of application.

> . . . Yet the moral qualities believed to comprise the code have almost monopolized consideration and have proliferated to the point of depriving sportsmanship of any distinctiveness. Truthfulness, courage, spartan endurance, self-control, self-respect, scorn of luxury, consideration one for another's opinions and rights, courtesy, fairness, magnanimity, a high sense of honor, cooperation, generosity. The list seems interminable. While the conduct and attitude which are properly designated as sportsmanlike may reflect many of the above-mentioned qualities, they are not all equally basic or fundamental. (191:267)

Slusher's vision of motive in sport reflects the Lombardian ethic to the extent that achieving superiority makes any means used to get there justifiable. There has been a propagandized belief in physical education for over fifty years related to the role of sportsmanship. It has been believed that in some cases sportsmanship is taught, thereby justifying social claims for engaging in sport and physical education. In other cases, it has been said that sportsmanship is part of the game and that merely by playing one learns to be humble in victory and gracious in defeat. Such concomitant values have been a justification for the existence of sport because it was further claimed that the "lessons" learned in sport transferred to everyday life and made us better and more moral people for having played. The character-building aspect of sport has been challenged recently by social scientists who argue that sport may build character but that such character may have both positive and negative components. In short, while it may facilitate the learning of a trait like generosity, the sport experience may also facilitate the expression and learning of such negative traits as dishonesty. Calisch (57) further notes the specificity of values to sport and cannot support their transfer to daily living.

Specificity in the definition and application of sportsmanship has been difficult in that its characteristics and application in age group competition may be totally different from what it is in professional athletics; yet in each setting there does exist a distinction between what is fair and unfair, what is a "cheap shot" and what is being aggressive within the "spirit" of the rules. A code of fairness in any setting may be specific to that setting and grounded in the common values and intents of the participation in that particular level of play. Royce identifies criteria for fair play which may be applicable to all levels of sport. He calls it a loyalty to loyalty and uses the "love and concern" of situationism as a guide to ethical behavior.

> . . . fair play does not merely mean conformity to a set of rules. . . . Fair play depends upon essentially respecting one's opponent just because of his loyalty to his own side. It means a tendency to enjoy, to admire, to applaud, to love, to further that loyalty of his at the very moment when I keenly want and clearly intend to thwart his individual deeds and to win this game, if I can. (351:256)

Inasmuch as ethical concepts of right and wrong and appropriate and inappropriate behaviors are based on ideals of what *should* be, the writings of philosophers and educators about the complementary interaction of sport and ethics may be understandable. Kennedy summarizes the beliefs of writers over many decades who thought that sport (athletics) had the potential to teach values and sportsmansip that would have applicability outside the sport situation:

> When you pass out from the playing fields to the tasks of life, you will have the same responsibility resting upon you, in greater degree, of fighting in the same spirit for the cause you represent. You will meet bitter and sometimes unfair opposition . . . you will meet defeat [but] you must not forget that the great victory of which you can never be robbed will be the ability to say, when the race is over and the struggle ended, that the flag you fought under was the shining flag of sportsmanship, in victory or defeat, you never lost that contempt for a breach of sportsmanship which will prevent your stooping to anywhere, anyhow, anytime. (199:58 50)

The enduring belief that it is not that you won or lost but how you played the game stands in stark contrast to the reality of playing to win, "getting the job done" and "every man for himself." Recognizing reality, Turbeville notes that while "the object of the game may be to win, [it is] not to exterminate." (422:258)

One of the more recent efforts to establish what is "fair" or moral or sportsmanlike is to take an established ethical system which has been applied to nonsport decision-making processes and extract a system against which to evaluate behavior in sport. Morgan (284) has used Sartre's ethic of ambiguity, Osterhoudt (304) used Kant's categorical imperative and Zeigler (451) has used Dewey's pragmatic approach. Each of these kinds of "implications" approaches seeks to establish principles of moral conduct that will guide sport behaviors.

Morgan's analysis of the Sartrean ethic as a moral guide for sport starts with an examination of the basic tenets of Sartre's ethical position.

> . . . man is that which he discloses himself to be through his actions, that which he wills himself to be, that which he chooses himself to be. . . . man is aware of the free ground of his acts and the moral responsibility that directly flows from this freedom. . . . freedom actually entails responsibility for one's actions. As a result, Sartre's moral theory begins not as most moral theories do with the formulation of specific "ought" judgments, but rather with the exhortation that one accept and live up to the freedom and correlative responsibility of one's acts. (284:84)

There is also belief that human existence has no predetermined meaning and that not only do I have freedom but others have freedom as well. (284:89) In sport there is the freedom to choose to engage or not to engage in sport. Rules which are freely accepted then require a responsibility to abide by what was accepted. To act badly in those things we have freely chosen to accept as binding is to act in what Sartre calls "bad faith." The egotism of "bad faith" turns into a negative rather than positive expression of humanness. In this egotistical sense, sport is made or played in the image of those who play. The sport endeavor itself and one's relations with fellow players become inauthentic and unworthy.

> In this way [bad faith] the pact of freedom that unites the individual athlete with his fellow athletic colleagues, a pact established and overtly attested to by their collective consent to freely abide by the rules, is abrogated thereby encouraging a treatment of one's athletic compatriots not as persons (free beings) who through their mutual contesting efforts make possible the expression of one's being *qua* athlete, but as obstacles (mere objects) to one's freedom who are to be considered only insofar as they can be manipulated to further one's own egotistic impulses. (284:91)

Freedom and a responsibility for that freedom once it is accepted, is the primary moral choice. Respect and responsibility for the freedom of others as a moral guide has the potential to serve as the basis for the "literal survival of sport as a noble human enterprise." (284:93)

Arguing from the Kantian imperative, Osterhoudt sees the fundamental principle for moral behavior as resting, in some ways on the "do unto others as you would have them do unto you" maxim. Osterhoudt's variation suggests that we extend to others what we, as free, self-determining, rational beings, would have extended to ourselves. (304:67) "Respect for each person as a moral agent" implies that the other person is not to be treated as an object or a means to serve our own personal egotistical needs. (304:67) The source of moral decision making is the individual rather than external agencies. Osterhoudt identifies Kant's beliefs that man is rational and free and applies these principles to sport behavior, particularly "sportsmanlike" behavior relative to the rules and the opponent as follows:

> The use of the imperative in sport secures an internal relationship with the laws (rules and regulations) which define and govern it, and with those other persons who also freely participate in it. A regard for these laws as self-legislated, and an intrinsic respect for those others is nonetheless presupposed by a free entry into sporting activity. . . . [It means] the taking on of the laws of sport as one's own, and the cultivation of a divining sympathy for all others who have also made such a choice. The categorical imperative commands that we abide by these laws for their own sake. . . . and that we consequently treat others with a regard that we ourselves would prefer. . . . (304:68)

The athlete *chooses* freely to enter sport and to meet the opponent. The freedom to choose then obligates the athlete to uphold the accepted rules and to treat the opponent in the same way that the athlete would treat himself. Osterhoudt criticizes Keating's belief that competition is ends-oriented in the economic sense and is governed by the Lombardian ethic. "Keating's conception of competition does not, and ought not cmmit us inexorably to the notion that it is excelling or vanquishing of others which is of primary significance in the process." (306:193) Rejecting the self-destructive view Keating holds about athletics in its goal-directedness,

Osterhoudt argues that the common good, generosity, and magnanimity which Keating attributes to sport (and play) but not to a sportsmanship code in athletics is, in fact, a code suited not only to sport and athletics but to life in general. The cooperative attributes that Keating attributes to sport and play reflect a more positive and humanistic view of man than does his athletic conception of man. Osterhoudt sees one code of sportsmanship being applicable.

> Sportsmanship, when regarded as the moral category appropriate to playful behavior, and the whole of life, becomes the all-embracing principle. . . . It becomes one with the sentiments of generosity and magnanimity proper to all forms of human activity. The moral qualities absolutely essential to the sportsman are resultantly those absolutely essential to all humanity. The application of sportsmanship to athletics is, then, not so much an attempt to soften the force of the competitive struggle as it is an attempt to reorder and reform it. (306:197)

A third "implications" approach has been Zeigler's application of pragmatic thought to ethical behavior in sport and physical education. Zeigler (451) sees ethical judgment as the application of reason to the results of scientific investigation. The individual and the context of the experience serve as the basis for the decision, but such individual freedom to set standards and to act is tempered by responsibility and the democratic ideal that there must be respect for the freedom of others.

> Dewey's cognitive theory of value is one in which value judgments are determined experimentally in light of experience. When an ethical problem, or moral dilemma, arises it is always within a social context. (451:257)

Past experience and the present situation and experience aid in the identification and resolution of moral "dilemmas." Zeigler points out that this view sees man as a social being living as a free person in democratic relationships with others. Values have a useful aspect in that they have applicablity to specific situations. They also reflect a social or collective "good." Other people or opponents are not used to meet personal ends, nor are the rules of a particular situation broken once they are accepted as applicable to that situation.

Bending the Rules and/or Cheating

One of the major concerns in a code of sportsmanship or fair play has to do with abiding by the rules. Breaking the written rules extracts a specific penalty, but beyond the legalistic standards of black and white lies the gray area of using the rules and bending or manipulating the rules to put the opponent at a disadvantage or to put ourselves at an advantage. The other gray area which falls within the "spirit" of the rules is getting away with illegal tactics by deceiving or going undetected by the game officials. The common attitude of "play to the whistle" suggests that it is the officials' responsibility to legislate written and unwritten rules and what they don't call is to our advantage. The presence or use of officials in some ways allows the player to abdicate responsibility for upholding the rules, since the officials then become the overseers of moral integrity. This attitude, like the rules themselves, is reflective of a legalistic approach to ethical behavior. Pearson distinguishes between accidental and deliberate breaking of the rules. In the case of an accidental foul or breaking of the rules, premeditation and intentionality are missing. From that standpoint, the "foul" has no ethical significance. (318:272) "We would ordinarily expect a person to accept the penalty for that foul, but we would not place moral blame on him." (318:272) It is not uncommon, however, to see ill-tempered responses by players and coaches to the calling of "accidental fouls" and to complain about the assessment of the prescribed penalty. Such behavior has overtones of "poor sportsmanship" in the sense that the player and the coach fail to accept the consequences or responsibility for their own violation of freely accepted rules and to abdicate the responsibility of calling such violations to an impartial third party (the referee).

Deliberately breaking the rules by direct violation or by using them as a means of strategy against the opponent or in ways not intended by the letter or spirit of the rules interferes with the contracted purpose of the game. According to Pearson:

> A variety of elegant arguments can be produced to indict the deliberate foul. It violates the ludic spirit, it treats the process of playing as mere instrument in the pursuit of the win, and it reflects a view of one's competitor as both enemy and object rather than colleague in noble contest. . . . deliberate betrayal of the rules destroys the vital framework of agreement which makes sport possible. (318:273)

In addition to breaking the contract which was freely accepted by participants, Delattre sees the worthiness of the opponent as one of the criteria for success in sport. Among other things, "opponents, to be worthy, must utterly respect the game." (72:276) He argues that a person may either cheat or compete at a game but to do both is logically impossible. "To cheat is to cease to compete" (72:276), since competition makes sense only within the framework of the rules that define the game and the goal. More importantly, the opponent is demeaned by cheating. Delattre claims that cheating is treating the opponent in bad faith and making ourselves unworthy as an opponent.

> When a person violates the rules which govern competition, he treats his opponents as means merely to his end of victory. The symbols of victory have status or meaningfulness only because they stand for triumph in competition; without the opposition, they are worthless. Attainment of these symbols by cheating is therefore the exploitation of those who competed in good faith. (72:276)

Cheating, whether it is by deliberately breaking or bending the rules, taking advantage of strategy and technique because it "won't be caught" by the officials, violating recruiting policies, or playing ineligible players, demonstrates a lack of respect for the game as it is defined and for the opponent as a person. Leonard has pointed out that winning by cheating is a "hollow victory," since the player has gone outside the rules to win. Take the example of a golf game: One player hits the ball into the woods and has an impossible lie. The moral thing to do is to lift the ball and take the penalty. But no one is looking. The other option is to move the ball and hit it out into an advantageous place on the fairway. Let us say the player chooses the second option. At the end of the round, the player cards an 85 for the round. Irrespective of whether this was the best score among the foursome, this score is basically a lie. The other players do not know it is a lie, but the player knows. What really is reflected in this score? An honest representation of ability? An honorable victory if it was the low score? Success? Triumph? Mastery? No, what the score reflects is one form of cheating—nobody was looking, or everyone does it, or there is no rule against doing it. Many people who habitually cheat under the guise of these defense mechanisms come to believe that what they are doing is not really wrong. The "good" foul becomes a matter of strategy rather than a violation of the rules. Holding or cheap shots or moving the ball to gain an advantage often is seen as OK because no one is looking or the "ref" should catch those things. If nobody knows or nobody sees it, it remains a deliberate deception and violates the "spirit" of the contract. Games require rules to define means and ends. A contest requires an opponent who agrees to play the *same* game. Choosing not to play the *same* game by cheating subtly or overtly is to ignore or demean the contract and the opponent.

Drugs in Sport

The use of drugs and ergogenic aids to enhance the performance and gain an advantage over opponents has been a highly controversial ethical issue for the past two decades. The problem has three major sources of controversy. The first relates to whether there is any physiologic damage done to the athlete, either knowingly or unknowingly, by those who administer the drugs or otherwise alter the physical make-up of the athlete. The second issue has to do with the fairness of permitting athletes who use drugs to compete against those who do not or choose not to alter their physical abilities by use of drugs. The third objection to use of drugs has to do with determining what the essential purpose of athletic contests is: the measurement of the best human potential or the measurement of the best use of chemistry under the stress of human competition.

With regard to the first argument about potential physical damage, two separate problems exist. Athletes may not know there will be damage and may take the word of the physician, trainers, or coaches assuming they would not hurt them. The other problem is that the athlete knows what damage will be done but chooses to take the drugs anyway. According to the American College of Sports Medicine Position Statement in 1977 (9) no conclusive scientific evidence exists related to the effects of the use of steroids on the athlete or on the athletic performance. The athlete's choice to take or not to take painkillers, steroids, or any other chemicals designed to develop, maintain, or "cure" the body in its pursuit of athletic superiority or excellence remains a moral question. Regardless of the question of legality, choice is a central issue.

The concept of "informed consent" has been developed in medicine to provide patients with the opportunity to make choices about their welfare. What is informed consent? One definition of informed consent is fairly broad in its intent. Informed consent is defined as "the knowing consent of an individual or his legally authorized representative, so situated as to be able to exercise free power of choice without undue inducement or any element of force, fraud, deceit, duress or any other form of constraint or coercion." (251:7) Three aspects are included in informed consent: (1) the person consenting must be competent to consent; (2) adequate information must be presented; and (3) consent must be voluntary.

For the most part, a coach, a trainer, a physician, and management in general do take a great deal of liberty with an athlete's body. They ask the athlete to change his/her diet. They ask the athlete to change patterns of weight gain or loss. They ask the athlete to run anaerobic training patterns. They ask the athlete to play while injured. They ask the athlete to think certain kinds of things and to behave in certain kinds of ways. Essentially, management as experimenter imposes change and makes decisions *for* the athlete without the consent of the athlete. The trust of a young player in the judgment of those who run programs is often warranted, but sometimes it is not. Players are vulnerable, and even if they know the "facts" about what is being asked of them, consent is often not as voluntary as it should be. One factor entering in is vulnerability or coercion, which makes it difficult for informed consent to be practiced legitimately. The athlete is in a precarious position in making a free-will consent, because if he does not play he is likely to be benched, traded, or put in less than a positive light by peers, coach, and fans. Thus, the onus is on the athlete to continue playing and to consent to things that he or she would not otherwise consent to, one of which is the administration of drugs for the purpose of killing pain. Coercion, however subtle, makes the athlete vulnerable. It also takes away the athlete's ability to act and choose freely with regard to informed consent. Mandell, the former team psychiatrist of the San Diego Chargers, describes coercion and some of the factors which force players to look for relief and to develop what he called "chemical courage." Mandell says that:

> Even as high school freshmen, athletes are preoccupied with physical activity and tire from workouts so they develop their own society, free from non-jocks who stereotype them as dummies whether that stereotyping is out of

envy or competitiveness, but athletes in their world are also deified, given special favors and then criticized, threatened and made fearful of losing their standing and prerequisites. The alumni and the fans control athletes much as heroin dealers control junkies. From a very early period in their careers, athletes learn that they must perform and please others or they have no place and no worth. Anger and paranoia thrive under such conditions. All the warmth in the world, the athlete learns, cannot substitute for victory. (260:40)

The players therefore learn to play while hurt and request to play while injured because they learn that by not playing they are of no value and that much of their self-concept and many of their feelings of self-worth and self-esteem are based on the fact that they are playing. Coercion becomes subtle, but primary, in the athlete's motivational scheme and the athlete become vulnerable, a victim of management and a victim of the "dealers." The vulnerability and coercion aspects affect not only the "playing hurt" part of the athlete's training but the whole "Yes sir, anything you say" attitude which prevails from junior high to the professionals. Informed consent, legally and professionally, means that the athlete should be told what he is taking and what it means and will mean to be taking drugs of one kind of another. What is the risk? What are the alternatives?

Some drug use has high risk potential for creating physical damage short term or long term. Some training procedures appear to be less risky. The use of vitamins and altered kinds of diet for athletes is certainly, to most people, an innocuous practice; yet in general, vitamin supplements are indicated only for the treatment of a deficiency condition, which many athletes certainly would not have. It is possible that more dangers exist in taking excessive amounts of fat-soluble vitamins such as A and D than in going without them. Is the athlete told what the effects of the vitamins are? Is he told that he should discontinue heavy use after his playing days are over? What are the effects of long-term, high protein diets? What are the effects of carbohydrate loading? Is the athlete told how to return to a normal diet pattern when his career is finished and he resumes normal daily activity in a nontraining state? Often these things are not considered when we tell the athlete to inject chemicals and to eat certain types of food during training and playing sessions. Yet, it seems that a responsibility exists to tell the athlete what the long-term effects of nutritional patterns are when he returns to the nontrained state. Physicians, who are usually paid by management, may help propagate the myth that pills increase performance by the way they freely prescribe some medications. Even if the taking of vitamins is harmless, the prevailing misconception that they improve performance is perpetuated by their continued misuse.

Blood doping became an issue in the 1976 Olympics, and since that time, a variety of investigations have been directed at the effects of such a technique. We can generally conclude that much of the effect of this transfusion is largely psychologic, yet it is dangerous because the athlete runs the risk of serum hepatitis, mismatched transfusion, and infection.

Costs must be weighed before choices and informed consent become viable alternatives. Even in something as common as the use of anaerobic exercise training, it has been noted that short-term anaerobic exercise causes marked changes in plasma hormone concentrations and, even though individual differences are found to be great and the reaction of fit and unfit people to both aerobic and anaerobic exercise quite different, it is difficult to know the possible beneficial or harmful effects of these pronounced alterations in hormone metabolism in individuals who train regularly. At this point in research, longitudinal studies are certainly needed. Yet, we continue to train many individuals in anaerobic patterns without knowing what all the effects are on body function.

Much of the legislation created by the various governing bodies of amateur and professional sport related to drugs has been grounded in a principle of fairness. The physical concerns focus on *abuse* and potential damage to the body. Fairness is concerned with *use* as it gives one opponent who uses drugs a potential advantage over another who chooses not to use drug additives for either personal or legal reasons. Brown examines the concept of fairness in the use of drugs in sport. He argues that there is a built-in unfairness in sport despite the rules. The participants are at the outset inequitable in terms of ability, preparation, and desire. (44:17) One of the problems with considering whether the use of drugs is fair or not comes in deciding what constitutes a "drug" and whether only chemical alterations should be considered. Drugs (chemical additives) can range from foods to vitamins to hormones to fluoride toothpaste to antibiotics. Drawing the line about what is permissible and not permissible is a difficult decision. A second problem is how much of any substance can be permitted without excluding innocuous additives. Is it fair or unfair to bar a competitor who has taken a hayfever medication? It enhances performance in the sense that it restores the performer to a "normal" performance level.

If all performers have the choice to take drugs or chemical additives, is there a question of fairness? Choosing not to take an additive may be considered similar to choosing one training system over another. If we assume that none of the drugs or chemical additives is injurious to one's health, this may be a legitimate position. However, what if it is legally acceptable that person A has access to and resources for acquiring such chemical aids but person B does not? Is this unfair or is it just another built-in inequity like skill or training? A similar case can be made for physical alterations.

There is also the issue of whether this class of substances needs to be restricted to those ingested rather than externally applied. Must they affect metabolic or biosynthetic processes or structural configurations of the body? And if structure and function of the body can be altered chemically, they may be altered physically as well. We might then question acupuncture, ultrasound, and surgery (not to mention whirlpools, taping, and steel braces). . . . (44:18)

Brown argues that regardless of the drug or chemical additive or the physical alteration, the criterion for fairness rests in legality. If one athlete uses drugs and such use is against the rules while the other competitor obeys the rules, cheating occurs and the use of drugs is unfair. Other than for *health reasons*, "the solution to the fairness problem seems to be to provide universal access, not universal prohibition." (44:18–19)

Perhaps the use of drugs is unfair if some athletes do not have access to them? Perhaps. But, then, is it unfair to be born of healthy parents, of a mother who did not smoke or ingest other substances dangerous to the fetus, to be raised in pollution-free environs, to be well-fed, to be encouraged to grow strong and swift, to be free to train at high altitudes, in a dry, safe gym with coaches and equipment. (44:18)

The issue of pitting a "pure human" against another "pure human" as free of chemical and physical alteration as possible remains an issue independent of health, legal, and fairness issues while being at the same time, very much intertwined in the moral decision making about those issues. Again, a consideration of what is terminally valued in the sport experience—ends or means—is central to what one believes is the "essence" of the contest. Taken at one extreme no athlete should train beyond that which is necessary to avoid injury. At the other extreme all athletes should train optimally and alter the body to every extent possible (within health parameters) to extend their performance capabilities.*

Ideally, all participants in any sport should be better off for having played. They should know that what they did in that sport was authentic behavior. They should be able to return to the real world with an authentic self-realization of what they were capable of doing in a sport and what the parameters of their ability and their success were. No doubts should arise in athletes' minds about whether they could have done it without drugs, without pain killers, without hypnosis, or without being psyched. They should not wonder whether, if they had had a choice, perhaps things would have been done differently. Obviously, some people are more endowed with physical prowess than others. Some are trapped in a lineman's body with dreams of being a quarterback. Coaches, managers, and educators have a responsibility to take all individuals from where they are and help them get where they can go, but within the concept of choice and with the informed consent of the individual, it may not be as far as we dreamed of going without such consent. We want the best for our teams. We want the best in our own performance, but everything has a

---

*The most comprehensive overview of the legal, health, and moral issues related to drugs and sport can be found in the 1973 U.S. Senate hearings on the "Proper and Improper Use of Drugs by Athletes." (157)

cost. What are we willing to pay and for what are we willing to bargain? We have one body, we have one spirit, and the sport experience should provide a means of expression for both body and spirit, but it should not change them beyond recognition or take them out of context of the real world. Our body and spirit serve us far beyond our playing days and they should be more whole, rather than less whole, as a result of our having played.

Children's Sports and the Pro Model

Many discussions centering on the values and abuses of winning relate to youth sports. Professionals and college athletes have served as a model for the structuring of youth sports. However, such models ignore the differences in motivation, values, desired means and ends in youth sports. The pro model with its emphasis on outcome is geared to adults who understand the costs and benefits of the means necessary to achieve victory. Children, on the other hand, are often required to act and think like adults, to forget about the fun and participation benefits, and to focus on the outcome in the same way that adults do. Criticism of "winning" stems largely from the fact that children are asked to participate in a pro model at the expense of being children. The expectations are set by adults who coach youth sports and the parents who have a vested interest in how well their children perform. Organized sport for children has enormous benefits when properly conducted and when the emotional and physical development of the child is recognized as being a period of growth rather than one of full development.

Orlick and Botterill (300) have identified ways in which "every kid can win" in sports even if they lose the contest. A narrow interpretation of "winning" may cause children, in particular, to lose out on many possible successes.

> Besides racking up points, people, youngsters in particular, can win or achieve many immeasurables such as friends, respect, trust, satisfaction, confidence, knowledge, skills, health, fitness, personal well-being, and above all else, happiness. . . . To jeopardize personal happiness or any of these invaluables would seem questionable, yet victory-*despite*-cost orientations appear more and more prevalent in both games and life. (300:27–28)

While these may be idealistic goals for sport and athletics in an adult or a pro model, for children they may be achievable when attention is directed to process rather than outcome. This does not mean winning is irrelevant but that it is kept in perspective. Adult interests have complicated organized sport for children. As Underwood (424:87) noted, "Kids play football because they enjoy it. But adults want kids to play little league football for a lot of other reasons—and that's where the trouble starts." Within the context of sport, when the needs of children rather than adults are paramount, Scott says that it can be a quality experience.

> Such a perspective compels us to rethink some conventional ideas about what constitutes success in age group swimming. Success in the competition is not necessarily success in the sport. Winning races is of value only to the extent that it represents the quality of the experiences the child has had along the road to victory. (If that is not so, if winning is important only in and of itself, our present program is insane. It produces dozens of losers for every winner. (373:19)

The adult who runs the program has to make the decision about what is important for the child and what the outcomes of sport should be. The "goodness" or "badness" of the experience is, in large part, contingent on the adults in and around the program.

> That is not to say that the competition is an evil. Far from it. It is essential. The critical matter is how one approaches it. Highly competitive programs may be either good or bad. In judging a program, the crucial factors at which to look are what kind of person the coach is, how he views his role and how he interacts with the children. It is through the one-to-one personal contact with an adventurer, an alive, aware and sensitive adult that the children's education is nurtured and the vision of their possibilities transmitted. (373:19)

The differences in objectives between children's and adult sport is often blurred by the social emphasis on and the importance of being successful. Such a clouding of objectives and social pressure potentially leads to actions that are inappropriate to the situation. Underwood capsulizes such behavior:

> Such gung-ho parents flock to the kids' leagues. Or become coaches. . . . One coach addressed an errant young warrior as "you stupid bastard." Others simply call their irresolute players "stupid," "slowpoke," "dumbass," or when things are really bad, "cry baby." (424:92)

Even a casual observation by a casual observer would reveal that most "play" is for the prize and that the agon is alive and well. The socialization process begins early, and if you were an eight-year-old who was being addressed by a significant other as "stupid," "slowpoke," "dumbass," or "cry baby" after some flaw in performance, no training in psychology or philosophy would be necessary for you to understand that the only payoff in sport, as in most things, is success. A personal best still takes a backseat if there is someone in front of you when you hit the tape.

As a civilized people we have been committed to saying certain kinds of things like: "Play fair," "Be a good sport," "Don't worry about the other—just do what *you* can do," and "Go on out and do your best." These are things we would like to do and have others do—focus on personal excellence, concentrate on the playing of the game rather than on the winning and losing. This has often been hypocritical rhetoric, especially in youth sports, because most people hate to lose and despite the New Games tradition of "Play Fair-Play Hard-Nobody Hurt" which promotes fellowship and was spawned from a "1960s kids" attitude, failure is almost never rewarded. We are *taught* to believe that failing will bring us and those close to us nothing but shame, obscurity, and discredit. Heroes and winners are recognized and rewarded. Goats and losers are ignored and punished in both subtle and overt ways. The operant conditioning we are exposed to in critical developmental stages is difficult to escape, and the imprints are enduring and transferable to all "worlds" and to a broad spectrum of endeavor.

Success as a cultural value is learned at an early age. Sport is but one medium where the means to be successful are also learned. The socialization process is intricate, but early systems of reward and punishment and the models presented to children have a profound effect in establishing beliefs and values. When children are told to "go out and 'get' somebody" or when coaches close a peewee league ice hockey practice by telling youngsters to line up against someone, drop their gloves, and fight so they "know how," values relative to means and ends are being taught. When winners get ice cream cones or a treat at McDonald's and losers are treated to more practices and "tips" from Dad in the back yard when they get home, there is not much doubt about the importance of winning in the reward system.

There are individuals who argue that there are "lessons about life" to be learned by juxtapositioning the pro model and children's sports. Learning to win and lose, discipline, hard work, dedication, teamwork, status, pride have been cited as important values to be included in the socialization process and have justified the highly organized and institutionalized emphasis in children's sports. While these may be important "lessons," abuse of officials, the teaching of violence to achieve victory, the exhortation of children to employ illegal tactics, and the demeaning of emotionally immature and impressionable "little people" also qualify as "lessons." Such "lessons" must be considered in any moral decision to impose pro model motivations and outcomes on children's sports.

Advocates of the separation of the pro model from youth sports have developed a "Bill of Rights for Young Athletes." (419) Included are the following ten athlete's "rights":

1. Right of the opportunity to participate in sports regardless of ability level.
2. Right to participate at a level that is commensurate with each child's developmental level.
3. Right to have qualified adult leadership.
4. Right to participate in safe and healthy environments.
5. Right of each child to share in the leadership and decision-making of their sport participation.
6. Right to play as a child and not as an adult.
7. Right to proper preparation for participation in the sport.
8. Right to an equal opportunity to strive for success.

9. Right to be treated with dignity by all involved.
10. Right to have fun through sport.

Children who retire from sport or burn out in adolescence are old before their time. Children who come away from age group competition with negative feelings about sport and coaches are unlikely to seek out sport in later life. Early withdrawal from competition precludes a mature person from achieving meaning or pleasure from sport.* A perspective that will prevent "taking the fun out of the game" requires a moral decision by adults involved in children's sports to establish objectives that are in keeping with the developmental level of the child. There are no "goats" or "bums" in kids' sports if you believe "*every* kid can win."

Sex Discrimination

To the extent that sport reflects the values of a larger society and serves to reinforce those societal values as well as the values that participants *bring* to sport, male participation has been seen as highly appropriate and in keeping with the social role of the male. Beliefs and attitudes about the ability and role of women in society is directly reflected by the attitudes most people have held about women's participation in sport. Whether the underlying values are real or stereotypical, sport has the values, or brings out the qualities, most usually attributed to men: competitiveness, assertiveness, individuality, achievement, excellence, discipline, and rationality. Traditionally women have been viewed as possessing antithetical qualities, attributes, and motivations. In addition, society and sport either value or require strength, speed, and size which are not typically attributed to women. The beliefs and attitudes about what men and women *should* be has been a strongly socialized aspect of our value system. What men and women *actually* are or *want to be* have been shown to be dramatically different realities, particularly in the past decade.

---

*Two excellent overviews on the developmental aspects of children's sport and suggestions for objectives and subsequent behavior written for both parents and professionals are: "Every Kid Can Win" (300) and "Youth Sports Guide for Coaches and Parents" (419)

Grounded simultaneously in legal rulings (most notably Title IX* as it relates to sport) and moral decisions about the rights of men and women, a number of issues still exist related to the participation of women in sport. Such decisions as: Should women be provided with equal opportunity to participate in sport and athletics? Should women receive equal funding? Should men and women be governed by the same rules and/or governing body? Should physical education classes be or remain coeducational? Should qualified men or women, boys or girls, be allowed to play on opposite sex teams? Will athletic excellence for men be diluted by the presence or intrusion of women, or by providing women with equal opportunity and/or equitable funding?

If there is a belief that sports are for all people rather than just for male people, then there are beliefs that sport has benefits which are not sex-linked. Such advantages may include the commonly cited objectives of

---

*The key provision of Title IX of the Education Amendments of 1972 reads as follows:

> Sec. 901. (a) No person in the United States shall, on the basis of sex, be excluded from participation in, be denied the benefits of, or be subjected to discrimination under any education program or activity receiving Federal financial assistance.

Amendments P.L. 92-318 (1972) and P.L. 930568 (1974) exempted certain religious, social, and voluntary youth service organizations. The Hatch Bill (S. 1361) has moved to further amend by narrowing the coverage of Title IX. If passed, many affirmative action and equal opportunity provisions of women would revert back to pre-1972 status. Sex discrimination would no longer be prohibited in programs unless they were receiving *direct* Federal funding. Sport related activities affected would be:

> *All extracurricular activities:* Any activity could be restricted to one sex. For example, a student club could be restricted to men only. An honorary society could restrict the number of women it admitted and/ or could have different requirements for each sex.
>
> *All athletic programs:* A school could abolish or diminish its women's program; buy new uniforms for men but have women purchase their own; refuse to give women athletic scholarships, or give them smaller amounts; use all of the money from compulsory student athletic fees for men's programs only; refuse to pay women's travel expenses to games; and exclude women from any sport or team. Women reporters could again be excluded from the press box.
>
> *Physical education classes:* Women would be excluded from coaching classes. Men could be excluded from volleyball classes; women could be excluded from golf instruction.
>
> *Facilities:* A school could have a sauna for men students but not for women. It could refuse to let women's teams practice at reasonable hours, restricting them to prebreakfast hours and/or late evening. (359:2)

Sandler (359) has identified these and other ramifications of the Hatch Bill, if passed, for permitting discriminatory practices. Also sponsoring the bill are Quayle (R-Ind), Hawkins (R-Fla), Denton (R-Ala), East (R-NC), Helms (R-NC), Garn (R-Utah). Attitudes about men and women are reflected in such legislative attempts.

sport, athletic, and physical education programs: optimal total fitness for enhancing the quality of life, awareness of body potential, development of skilled movement, pride in appearance and bodily movements, opportunities for self-testings, meaningful expression, achievement, and excellence. Typically, these objectives have been cited as applicable in an androgynous fashion to people. On the other hand, if one believes and proves these objectives are sex-linked in terms of being more appropriate for one sex or the other, it is possible to practice discrimination in the moral sense of being "right" about such discrimination.

Traditionally, the sex role stereotypes or one's socialization about the differing potentials of men and women has led to a number of beliefs about the sex-linked characteristics of behavior. However, what social scientists have noted in the past two decades is an increasing factual rather than feeling base for the belief that biology is not the root of men's and women's behavior. To the extent that behavior is learned and potentially androgynous, or bisexual, all people are capable of all behavior. Appropriateness of a particular kind of behavior is a function of what we are taught to believe and value. There appears to be nothing innate causing, for example, aggressive versus passive or rational versus emotional behavior in one sex or the other. Humanness precedes sexuality.

From the standpoint that sport involves behavior which is stereotypically viewed as male, it is not uncommon to view women in sport as masculine, inasmuch as they are displaying what society perceives as "masculine" behaviors and values. A long history of mythology has grown up about what men *should* be and what women *should* be. Such views are not necessarily right or wrong, good or bad, but the accuracy of such myths becomes important in making decisions which may lead to discriminatory moral or legal practices. For example, it is believed men are stronger and will always be better than women at a given sport. To a large extent, this is true. Men, by virtue of their biochemical and physiologic make-up tend to have a metabolic, or power, advantage over women. The best man in a sport will always be better than the *best* woman in a sport. Beyond that, however, the myth breaks down because some women will be better than some men by virtue of a skill advantage or by virtue of physiochemical make-up. Women tend to have what is called a "skill" advantage in that their technique is often mechanically sounder in order to compensate for less power. In activities where finesse, balance, or distance (e.g., running and swimming) are primary, women may excel if given the same training opportunities and support system.

Additional mythology has included beliefs by coaches and parents that athletic participation will produce unsightly muscular develement in girls and women. Since testosterone levels are the critical factor in the development of muscle mass, most women and many men will not develop muscle mass regardless of how hard they train. The belief that women are more susceptible to injury has been inhibitory to allowing participation. Injury, however, is not sex-linked but has to do with the level of skill and physical conditioning of any athlete. Any athlete who is poorly skilled or poorly conditioned is more likely to be injured. Since women have not had the advantages of good coaching and good training until relatively recently, injury has been a factor. That women are too emotional to withstand the stresses of competition (as shown by their propensity to cry) has no basis in empirical or social scientific research. As a part of an individual's personality make-up, this may be true, but as a sex-linked characteristic it is an unfounded generalization. Crying by women and anger by men are two *socialized* and acceptable sex-linked reactions to the same phenomenon: frustration. That they are different in expression does not make one better or worse than the other. Making moral judgments of right-wrong, appropriate-inappropriate based on stereotypes rather than on reality is to argue on the basis of interest and from an emotive base. Discrimination based on interest rather than on reality may be suspect in its moral "rightness."

Accurate or inaccurate beliefs about sex differences have had a long-term effect on both programs and activities avalable to women. As Geadelman notes:

> Beliefs about sex differences have affected the kinds of activities offered girls and women. . . . social expectations of appropriate sex roles . . . have had a further impact on program decisions. (128:193)

Some sports (golf, tennis, and swimming) have been seen as more socially desirable for women, since no display of "brute strength" or "unfeminine" movements is required. As "country club" sports with social overtones, these sports have fit in with appropriate roles for women. Sexism is often related to elitism. In that regard, women's sports often do not have audience appeal. Do the men play better? They play *their* game better (stronger, faster, higher), but this does not mean that the women's game is inferior. It is different. However, in a society preferring to see the strongest, fastest, farthest, or highest performance, most women's sporting events are of lesser interest to an audience.

When the participation of girls and women at any level of sport is viewed as an encroachment on male territory, decisions are made to keep them out, to deny them the freedom to choose to play. If they are, *in fact*, encroaching into "Men Only" territory, then sport cannot be considered a human enterprise with values and meanings applicable to humans. As a male enterprise, it may or may not be credible. But to make moral decisions that are discriminatory without establishing *in fact* the viability of sport as a male rather than a human enterprise is to commit a logical error and to base moral decisions on faulty premises. If, however, sport is a human enterprise with androgynous values, all people should be free to choose to play at whatever level of competence that may have or wish to achieve. To believe in the moral underpinnings of a democracy is to believe in equality of opportunity. To believe in the integrity of competition is to support the contract of the structure of the game. In either of these cases, the ability and potential of people may be unequal, but the structure of government or a game *at least* guarantees everyone a chance to try, a shot at the "dream". However, beyond this "chance" is a fundamental political and existential belief in individual freedom:

> A man is said to be free to the extent that he can choose his goals or course of conduct, can choose between alternatives available to him, and is not compelled to act as he himself would not choose to act or be prevented from acting as he would otherwise choose to act, by the will of another man, of the state, or of any other authority. (315:223–225)

Partridge used "man" in the universal sense to mean "person." Man and person often mean the same thing. Woman and person have not always been synonymous. Nonetheless, freedom, choice, opportunity for all parties, and consideration of the "other" as a *person* with equivalent rights may serve as the basis for moral decision making in sport and nonsport settings. To decide or to act without concern for these factors is to cheat the other in a variety of ways, to deny them the opportunity to be themselves as children, men, women, or adults or to discriminate by denying status to an androgynous person.

Lipsyte bemoans the condition of the "Sportsworld" but sees hope when he says:

> One little community recreation program for older people; one totally non-sexist grade school sports program; one high school program that involves every student regardless of skill level; one girls team that doesn't use the JV leftover shoes and the gym at dinner time; a college pool that doesn't discriminate against non-varsity swimmers; a Little League that defuses the pressures of joyless competition; a University classroom that openly approaches the possibility of new games, new methods, fresh approaches—each would be a model for the community, a region, and the country. Each would be another little light to make more people aware of how sports help shape our lives through its cultural impact and dispel the darkness of the Sportsworld, the varsity syndrome, and a system that separates people by calling some athletes and some non-athletes, when this beautiful and good thing we call sports should allow each of us to be an athlete forever. (243:52)

DISCUSSION QUESTIONS

1. Under what circumstances and what ethical rationale would you use to justify the following acts:
   a. Intentionally breaking a written rule
   b. Administering or taking a drug to enhance or continue performance
   c. Allowing or encouraging an injured player to take part in a contest

    d. Playing only the starting players in a game

2. Winning is an important objective for almost any contest. How would you vary the emphasis and focus and what ethical rationale would you use in the following situations:

    a. Co-ed bar league softball league

    b. Division I college women's varsity basketball

    c. Professional football

    d. Olympic swimming team

    e. American Legion baseball league

    f. Youth league soccer

In what ways are these situations similar and different in their competitive focus? What criteria serve as the basis for value judgments related to the conduct of these activities? What responsibilities do the coaches and players each have in maintaining the integrity of a particular sport situation?

DIRECTED READING

Delattre, E.: Some reflections on success and failure in competitive athletics. *In* Sport and the Body, 2nd ed., edited by E.W. Gerber and W.J. Morgan. Philadelphia, Lea & Febiger, 1979, pp. 274–278.

Fraleigh, W.: When the good foul is not good. J. Phys. Educ. Rec. Dance, 53:41–42, 1982.

Harris, J.C., et al.: Ethical behavior and victory in sport: value systems at play. J. Phys. Educ. Rec. Dance, 54(4):37, 98–99, 1982.

Keating, J.: Sportsmanship as a moral category. *In* Sport and the Body, 2nd ed., edited by E.W. Gerber and W.J. Morgan. Philadelphia, Lea & Febiger, 1979, pp. 264–271.

Kew, F.C.: Values in competitive sport. Quest, 29:103–112, 1978.

Pearson, K.: Deception, sportsmanship and ethics. *In* Sport and the Body, 2nd ed., edited by E.W. Gerber and W.J. Morgan. Philadelphia, Lea & Febiger, 1979, pp. 272–273.

Sadler, W.: Competition out-of-bounds. Quest, 19:124–132, 1973.

Suits, B.: The elements of sport. *In* The Philosophy of Sport, edited by R.G. Osterhoudt. Springfield, IL, Charles C Thomas, 1973, pp. 48–64.

Suits, B.: The grasshopper: a thesis concerning the moral ideal of man. *In* The Philosophy of Sport, edited by R.G. Osterhoudt. Springfield, IL, Charles C Thomas, 1973, pp. 198–218.

Thomas, C.: The golden girl syndrome: thoughts on a training ethic. NAPEHE Proceedings, Brainerd, 1980, pp. 136–146.

Underwood, J.: Taking the fun out of the game. Sports Illus., 43:87, 98, 1975.

Bibliography

1. Abernathy, R., and Waltz, M.: Toward a discipline: first steps first. Quest, 2:1–7, 1964.
2. Alapack, R.: Distortion of a human value: competition in sport. J. Phys. Ed., 72:118–119, 1975.
3. Alderman, R.B.: Psychological Behavior in Sport. Toronto, W.B. Saunders, 1974.
4. Aldrich, V.C.: Art and the human form. J. Aesthet. Art Crit., 29:295–302, 1971.
5. Algozin, K.: Man and sport. Philos. Today, 20:190–195, 1975.
6. Allen, D.J., and Fahey, B.: Being Human in Sport. Philadelphia, Lea & Febiger, 1977.
7. Alley, L.E.: Athletics in education: the double-edged sword. Phi Delta Kappan, 56:102–105, 1974.
8. Alvarez, A.: I like to risk my life. Sat. Eve. Post, 240:10–12, 1967. Also in Sport and the Body, edited by E.W. Gerber. Philadelphia, Lea & Febiger, 1972, pp. 203–205.
9. American College of Sports Medicine: Position Statement on the Use and Abuse of Anabolic-Androgenic Steroids. Med. Sci. Sports, 9:xi–xiii, 1977.
10. Anthony, D.W.J.: Sport and physical education as a means of aesthetic education. Phys. Educ., 60:1–6, 1968.
11. Ardrey, R.: The Territorial Imperative. New York, Atheneum, 1966.
12. Asinof, E.: 1919: The fix is in. In The Realm of Sport, edited by H.W. Wind. New York, Simon and Schuster, 1966.
13. Aspin, D.N.: Knowing how and knowing that and physical education. J. Philos. Sport, 3:97–117, 1976.
14. Aspin, D.N.: Sport and the concept of the aesthetic. In Readings in the Aesthetics of Sport, edited by H.T.A. Whiting and D.W. Masterson. London, Lepus Books, 1974.
15. Athletics and education: are they compatible? Phi Delta Kappan, 56:98–146, 1974.
16. Avedon, E.M., and Sutton-Smith, B.: The Study of Games. New York, John Wiley & Sons, 1971.
17. Ayer, A.J.: Language, Truth, and Logic. 2nd rev. ed. New York, Dover Publications, 1952.
18. Baley, J.A., and Field, D.A.: Physical Education and the Physical Educator: An Introduction. Boston, Allyn and Bacon, Inc., 1970.
19. Bammel, E., and Bammel, L.L.: Aesthetics of play. Phys. Educ., 32:192–193, 1975.
20. Banham, C.: Man at play. Contemp. Rev., 207:61–64, 1965.
21. Bannister, R.: The Four Minute Mile. New York, Dodd, Mead and Co., 1955.
22. Bannister, R.: The meaning of athletic performance. In International Research in Sport and Physical Education, edited by E. Jokl and E. Simon. Springfield, IL, Charles C Thomas, 1964.
23. Barrow, H.M.: Man and Movement: Principles of His Physical Education, 2nd ed. Philadelphia, Lea & Febiger, 1977.
24. Beach, F.A.: Current concepts of play in animals. Amer. Naturalist, 79:523–541, 1945.
25. Beets, N.: The experience of the body in sport. In International Research in Sport and Physical Education, edited by E. Jokl and E. Simon. Springfield: Il., Charles C Thomas, 1964, pp. 74–82.
26. Belaief, L.: Meanings of the body. J. Philos. Sport, 4:50–67, 1977.
27. Bell, J.W.: Investigation of the concept-sport as art. Phys. Educ., 81–84, 1976.
28. Bennett, B., and VanDalen, D.B.: A World History of Physical Education, 2nd ed. Englewood Cliffs, NJ, Prentice-Hall, 1971.
29. Bennett, L.A.: Reification of the Human Body in Ancient Greece: A Metabolic Investigation. Unpublished Ph.D. dissertation, University of Oregon, 1976.
30. Bennett, W.J.: In defense of sports. Commentary, 61:68–70, 1976.
31. Berkowitz, L.: Simple view of aggression: an essay review. Amer. Sci., 57:372–383, 1969.

32. Berry, E.: The Philosophy of Athletics: Coaching and Character with the Psychology of Athletic Coaching. New York, A.S. Barnes and Co., 1972.
33. Best, D.: Expression in Movement and the Arts. London, Lepus Books, 1974.
34. Best, D.: Philosophy and Human Movement. London, George Allen and Unwin, 1978.
35. Best, D.: The aesthetic in sport. Br. J. Aesthet., *14*:197–213, 1974. *Also in* Sport and the Body, 2nd ed., edited by E.W. Gerber and W.J. Morgan. Philadelphia, Lea & Febiger, 1979, pp. 345–354.
36. Bettelheim, B.: Play and education. Sch. Rev., *81*:1–13, 1972.
37. Brinton, C.: Neitzsche. Cambridge, Harvard University Press, 1941.
38. Broekhoff, J.: Sport and ethics in the context of culture. *In* The Philosophy of Sport: A Collection of Original Essays, edited by G. Osterhoudt. Springfield, IL, Charles C Thomas, Philadelphia, 1973, pp. 219–228.
39. Broer, M.: The Efficiency of Human Movement. Philadelphia, W.B. Saunders, 1966.
40. Brooke, J.D., and Whiting, H.T.A.: Human Movement: A Field of Study. Lafayette, IN, Bart Publishers, 1973.
41. Brooks, B.W.: Views of physical fitness from four educational philosophies. Phys. Educator, *24*:31–32, 1967.
42. Brown, C., and Cassidy, R.: Theory in Physical Education: A Guide to Program Change. Philadelphia, Lea & Febiger, 1963.
43. Brown, C.: The structure of knowledge of physical education. Quest, *9*:53–67, 1967.
44. Brown, W.: Ethics, drugs, and sport. J. Philos. Sport, *7*:15–23, 1980.
45. Browne, E.: An ethological theory of play. J. Health Phys. Educ. Rec., *39*:36–39, 1968.
46. Buber, M.: I and Thou. Translated by W. Kaufmann. New York, Scribners and Sons, 1970.
47. Bucher, C.A.: After the game is over. Phys. Educ., *30*:171–175, 1973.
48. Bucher, C.A.: Dimensions of Physical Education, 2nd ed. St. Louis, The C.V. Mosby Co., 1974.
49. Burke, R.: Work and play. Ethics, *82*:33–47, 1971.
50. Buytendijk, F.J.J.: The phenomenological approach to feelings and emotions. *In* Psychoanalysis and Existential Philosophy, edited by H. Ruitenbeek. New York, E.P. Dutton, 1962.
51. Byrum, S.: The concept of child's play in Nietzsche's 'of the three metamorphoses'. Kinesis, *6*:127–135, 1974.
52. Caillois, R.: Man, Play, and Games. Translated by Meyer Barash. New York, Free Press of Glencoe, 1961.
53. Caillois, R.: Play and the sacred. *In* Man and the Sacred. Translated by Meyer Barash. Illinois, Free Press of Glencoe, 1959.
54. Caillois, R.: The structure and classification of games. *In* Sport, Culture, and Society: A Reader on the Sociology of Sport, edited by J.W. Loy and G.S. Kenyon. London, The Macmillan Co., 1969.
55. Caillois, R.: Unity of play; diversity of games. Diogenes, *19*:92–121, 1957.
56. Caldwell, S.F.: Toward a humanistic physical education. J. Health Phys. Educ. Rec., *43*:31–32, 1972.
57. Calisch, R.: The sportmanship myth. Phys. Educator, *10*:9–11, 1953. *Also in* Sport and the Body, edited by E.W. Gerber. Philadelphia, Lea & Febiger, 1972, pp. 260–262.
58. Camus, A.: The Myth of Sisyphus. New York, Harper & Row, 1969.
59. Caplan, F., and Caplan, T.: The Power of Play. New York, Anchor Press, 1974.
60. Carlisle, R.: Physical education and aesthetics. *In* Readings in the Aesthetics of Sport, edited by H.T.A. Whiting and D.W. Masterson. London, Lepus Books, 1974.
61. Castell, A.: An Introduction to Modern Philosophy, 2nd ed. New York, Macmillan Co., 1963.
62. Champlin, N.: Are sports methodic? J. Philos. Sport, *4*:104–116, 1977.
63. Cheney, G.: Dance and the problem of departmental affiliation. *In* Issues in Physical Education, edited by G.H. McGlyn. Palo Alto, National Books, 1974.
64. Cobb, L.S.: Philosophical research methods. *In* Research Methods Applied to Health, Physical Education, and Recreation, edited by L.S. Cobb, R.B. Spence, J.F. Williams, and K.D. Benne. Washington, D.C., AAHPER, 1949.

65. Cobb, R.A., and Lepley, P.M.: Contemporary Philosophies of Physical Education and Athletics. Columbus, Ohio, Charles E. Merrill Publishing Co., 1973.
66. Conrad, J.: The fine art. *In* The Realm of Sport, edited by H.W. Wind. New York, Simon and Schuster, 1966, pp. 152–157.
67. Coutts, C.A.: Freedom in sport. Quest, *10*:68–71, 1968.
68. Cowell, C.: Interpreting physical education through contrasting philosophies. Phys. Educator, *20*:147, 1963.
69. Csikszentmihaly, M.: Beyond Boredom and Anxiety. San Francisco, Jossey-Bass, 1975.
70. Day, H.E.: A new look at work, play, and job satisfaction. School Guidance Worker, *27*:4–11, 1971.
71. Dearden, R.F.: The concept of play. *In* The Concept of Education, edited by R.S. Peters. London, Routledge & Kegan Paul, 1967.
72. Delattre, E.J.: Some reflections on success and failure in competitive athletics. J. Philos. Sport, *1*:133–139, 1975. *Also in* Sport and the Body, 2nd ed., edited by E.W. Gerber and W.J. Morgan. Philadelphia, Lea & Febiger, 1979, pp. 274–278.
73. Descartes, R.: Discourse on Method and Meditations. New York, Bobbs-Merrill, 1960.
74. Devaney, J.: Bart Starr. New York, Scholastic Book Service, 1968.
75. Deveraux, E.C.: Backyard versus little league baseball: the impoverishment of children's games. *In* Social Problems in Athletics, edited by D. Landers. Chicago, University of Illinois Press, 1976.
76. Dewey, J.: Art as Experience. New York, Capricorn Books, 1958.
77. Dewey, J.: Interest and Effort in Education. Boston, Houghton Mifflin Co., 1913.
78. Dewey, J.: The Early Works of John Dewey, 1882–1898, Vol. I. Carbondale, Southern Illinois University Press, 1969.
79. Doherty, J.K.: Why men run. Quest, *2*:61–66, 1964.
80. Drengson, A.: Wilderness travel as an art and a paradigm for outdoor education. Quest, *32*:110–120, 1980.
81. Dubois, P.E.: Aesthetics of sport and the athlete. Phys. Educator, *31*:198–201, 1974.
82. Ehrmann, J. (Ed.): Game, Play, Literature. Boston, Beacon Press, 1971. (First published 1968: Yale French Studies.)
83. Ehrmann, J.: Homo ludens revisited. *In* Game, Play, Literature, edited by J. Ehrmann. Boston, Beacon Press, 1971.
84. Eliott, R.K.: Aesthetics and sport. *In* Readings in the Aesthetics of Sport, edited by H.T.A. Whiting and D.W. Masterson. London, Lepus Books, 1974.
85. Ellfeldt, L., and Metheny, E.: Movement and meaning: development of a general theory. Res. Q., *29*:264–273, 1958.
86. Elliott, R.J.: Experience, aesthetics and education. J. Thought, *11*:245–251, 1976.
87. Ellis, M.J.: Play: a paradox for teacher and scientist. Quest, *26*:128–138, 1976.
88. Ellis, M.J.: Why People Play. Englewood Cliffs, NJ, Prentice-Hall, Inc., 1973.
89. Erikson, E.H.: Childhood and Society. New York, W.W. Norton, 1963.
90. Ermler, K.: The Relationship of Existential Freedom to Symbolic Death in Sport. Unpublished doctoral dissertation, SUNY at Buffalo, 1980.
91. Ermler, K.: Two expressions of failure in sport. J. Phys. Educ. Rec. Dance, *53*:37–38, 1982.
92. Esposito, J.: Play and possibility. Philos. Today, *18*:137–147, 1974. *In* Sport and the Body, 2nd ed., edited by E.W. Gerber and W.J. Morgan. Philadelphia, Lea & Febiger, 1979, pp. 102–107.
93. Fairs, J.R.: The influence of Plato and Platonism on the development of physical education in western culture. Quest, *11*:12–23, 1968.
94. Farber, M.: Basic Issues of Philosophy. New York, Harper & Row, 1968.
95. Feldenkrais, M.: Awareness Through Movement. New York, Harper & Row, 1972.
96. Felshin, J.: More Than Movement: An Introduction to Physical Education. Philadelphia, Lea & Febiger, 1972.
97. Felshin, J.: Perspectives and Principles for Physical Education. New York, John Wiley & Sons, 1967.
98. Felshin, J.: Sport and modes of meaning. J. Health Phys. Educ. Rec., *40*:43–44, 1969.
99. Fetters, J.: An experiential body aesthetic. *In* Aesthetics and Dance, edited by C.E. Thomas. AAHPERD, 1980, pp. 8–10.
100. Fetters, J.: Sport, myth and the courage of self-creation. Quest: *30*:36–45, 1978.

101. Fetters, J.: The body aesthetic: a symbolic experience. Proceedings of NAPECW-NCPEAM Joint Meeting, Orlando, Florida, 1977, pp. 254–262.
102. Fetters, J.: The body beautiful: beyond stereotypes. J. Phys. Educ. Rec. Dance, 53(2):31–32, 1982.
103. Fink, E.: The ontology of play. Philos. Today, 4:(Summer 1960), pp. 95–110. *Also in* Sport and the Body, 2nd ed., edited by E.W. Gerber and W.J. Morgan. Philadelphia, Lea & Febiger, 1979, pp. 73–83.
104. Fisher, M.: Sport as an aesthetic experience. *In* Sport and the Body, edited by E.W. Gerber. Philadelphia, Lea & Febiger, 1972, pp.315–322.
105. Fletcher, J.: Situation Ethics. Philadelphia, Westminister Press, 1966.
106. Fogelin, R.J.: Sport: the diversity of the concept. Essay presented at the American Association for the Advancement of Science, Annual Meeting, Dallas, Texas, December, 1968. *Also in* Sport and the Body, edited by E.W. Gerber. Philadelphia, Lea & Febiger, 1972, pp. 58–61.
107. Fox, R.M. (ed.): Philosophy in Context, Vol. 9. Cleveland, Cleveland State University Department of Philosophy, 1979.
108. Fraleigh, S.: Dance creates man. Quest, 14:65–71, 1970.
109. Fraleigh, S.: Man creates dance. Quest, 23:20–27, 1975.
110. Fraleigh, W.P.: An instructional experiment in actualizing the meaning of man as a moving being. J. Health Phys. Educ. Rec., 40:53–58, 1969.
111. Fraleigh, W.P.: A prologue to the study of theory building in physical education. Quest, 12:26–33, 1969.
112. Fraleigh, W.P.: Ethics in professional life. Keynote address for the Working Conference on Ethics, AAHPER, Minneapolis, April 1973.
113. Fraleigh, W.P.: Lecture Notes: PHE 304 Philosophic Perspectives. Brockport State College. September 1973.
114. Fraleigh, W.P.: On Weiss on records and the significance of athletic records. *In* The Philosophy of Sport: A Collection of Original Essays, edited by R.G. Osterhoudt. Springfield, IL, Charles C Thomas, 1973.
115. Fraleigh, W.P.: Some meanings of the human experience of freedom and necessity in sport. *In* The Philosophy of Sport, edited by R.G. Osterhoudt, Springfield, IL, Charles C Thomas, 1973, pp. 130–141.
116. Fraleigh, W.P.: Sport-purpose. J. Philos. Sport, 2:74–82, 1975.
117. Fraleigh, W.P.: The moving I. *In* The Philosophy of Sport: A Collection of Original Essays. R.G. Osterhoudt. Springfield, IL, Charles C Thomas, 1973, pp. 103–129.
118. Fraleigh, W.P.: Theory and design of philosophic research in physical education. 74th Proceedings of the National College Physical Education Association for Men, Annual Meeting. Portland, Oregon, December 27–30, 1970, pp. 28–52.
119. Fraleigh, W.P.: Toward a conceptual model of the academic subject matter of physical education as a discipline. 70th Proceedings of the NCPEAM Annual Meeting. San Diego, 1966, pp. 31–39.
120. Fraleigh, W.P.: Why the good foul is not good. J. Phys. Educ. Rec. Dance, 53:41–42, 1982.
121. Fromm, E., and Suzuki, D.T.: Zen Buddhism and Psychoanalysis. New York, Harper Colophon Books, 1960.
122. Furlong, W.: Danger as a way of joy. Sports Illus., 30:52–53, 1969.
123. Furlong, W.: The fun in fun. Psychol. Today, 10:35–38, 1976.
124. Gallwey, W.T.: The inner game of tennis. New York, Bantam Books, 1979.
125. Gallwey, W.T.: You've got to increase your awareness to improve your play. Tennis Mag., 9:88–97, 1977.
126. Gardner, J.: Excellence: Can We Be Equal and Excellent Too? New York, Harper Colophon Books, 1961.
127. Gaskin, G., and Masterson, D.W.: The work of art in sport. J. Philos. Sport, 1:36–66, 1974.
128. Geadelman, P.: Physical education: stronghold of sex role stereotyping. Quest, 32(2):192–200, 1980.
129. Geisler, N.: Ethics: Alternatives and Issues. Grand Rapids, Zondervan, 1971.
130. Genasci, J.E., and Klissouras, V.: The Delphic spirit in sports. J. Health Phys. Educ. Rec., 38:43–45, 1966.

131. Gerber, E.W.: Identity, relation, and self. *In* Sport and the Body, 2nd ed., edited by E.W. Gerber and W.J. Morgan. Philadelphia, Lea & Febiger, 1979, pp. 128–132.
132. Gerber, E.W.: Innovators and Institutions in Physical Education. Philadelphia, Lea & Febiger, 1971.
133. Gerber, E.W.: Little Ms. Muffet has left her tuffet. Paper presented at the New York State Association for Health, Physical Education, and Recreation Annual Conference. Kiamesha Lake, New York, 1973.
134. Gerber, E.W.: My body, my self. *In* Sport and the Body, 2nd ed., edited by E.W. Gerber and W.J. Morgan. Philadelphia, Lea & Febiger, 1979, pp. 181–187.
135. Gerber, E.W. (Ed.).: Sport and the Body. Philadelphia, Lea & Febiger, 1972.
136. Gerber, E.W., and Morgan, W.J. (Ed.): Sport and the Body. 2nd ed. Philadelphia, Lea & Febiger, 1979.
137. Gerstung, R.: Philosophy of physical education. Phys. Educ., *31*:41, 1974.
138. Gilbert, B.: When games were for fun. Sports Illus., *31*:7–10, 1969.
139. Goodman, N.: Languages of Art. New York, Bobbs-Merrill Co., 1968.
140. Graves, H.: A philosophy of sport. Contemp. Rev., *78*:877–893, 1900. *Also in* Sport and the Body, edited by E.W. Gerber. Philadelphia: Lea & Febiger, 1972, pp 6–15.
141. Griffen, P.: What's a nice girl like you doing in a profession like this? Quest, *19*:96–100, 1973.
142. Groos, K.: The Play of Man. New York, Appleton, 1901.
143. Gulick, L.H.: A Philosophy of Play. New York, Association Press, 1920.
144. Gulick, L.H.: Interest in relation to muscular exercise. Amer. Phys. Educ. Rev., 7:57–65, 1902.
145. Hall, G.S.: Youth. New York, Appleton, 1906.
146. Harper, D., and Hammond, J.: The hypocrisy of amateurism. Quest, *27*:121–130, 1977.
147. Harper, W.A.: Man alone. Quest, *12*:57–60, 1969. *Also in* Sport and the Body, 2nd ed., edited by E.W. Gerber and W.J. Morgan. Philadelphia, Lea & Febiger, 1979, pp. 125–127.
148. Harper, W.: Method. Chapter III *in* Human Revolt: A Phenomenological Description. Unpublished doctoral dissertation, University of Southern California, 1970.
149. Harper, W.A.: Movement and measurement: the case of the incompatible marriage. Quest, *20*:92–99, 1973.
150. Harper, W.A.: Philosophy of physical education and sport: a review of the literature. Exercise and Sport Science Reviews, Vol. II, edited by J. Wilmore. New York, Academic Press, 1974.
151. Harper, W.A.: Taking and giving in sport. Essay presented at the Symposium on the Philosophy of Sport, Brockport, New York, February 10–12, 1972.
152. Harper, W.A.: The philosopher in us. J. Phys. Educ. Rec. Dance, *53*:32–34, 1982.
153. Harper, W.A.: The standpoint of phenomenology. Paper presented at the American Association Health, Physical Education, and Recreation National Convention, Seattle, 1970.
154. Harper, W.A., et al.: The Philosophic Process in Physical Education, 3rd ed. Philadelphia, Lea & Febiger, 1977.
155. Harris, J.C.: Play and Enjoyment. Quest, *29*:60–72, 1978.
156. Hawkins, A.: Creating Through Dance. Englewood Cliffs, NJ, Prentice-Hall, Inc., 1964.
157. Hearings, Subcommittee to Investigate Juvenile Delinquency: Proper and Improper Use of Drugs by Athletes. United States Senate, 93rd Congress, June 18, July 12, 13, 1973.
158. Heidegger, M.: Being and Time. Translated by J. Mcquarrie and F. Robinson. London, SCM Press, 1962.
159. Hein, H.: Performance as an aesthetic category. J. Aesthet. Art Crit., *28*:381–386, 1970.
160. Hein, H.: Play as an aesthetic concept. J. Aesthet. Art Crit., *27*:68–74, 1968–69.
161. Hellison, D.R.: Humanistic Physical Education. Englewood Cliffs, NJ, Prentice-Hall, Inc., 1973.
162. Henry, F.M.: Physical education: an academic discipline. *In* Anthology of Contemporary Readings: An Introduction to Physical Education, edited by H.S. Slusher and A.S. Lockhart. Dubuque, Iowa, William C. Brown Co., Publishers, 1966.

216 Bibliography

163. Henry, F.M.: The academic discipline of physical education. Quest, 29:13–29, 1978.
164. Henry, F.M.: Philosophy of John Dewey and its implications for physical education. J. Phys. Educ., 71:74–75, 1974.
165. Herman, D.J.: Mechanism and the athlete. J. Philos. Sport, 2:102–110, 1975.
166. Herrigel, E.: Zen in the art of archery. Translated by R.F.C. Hull. New York, Random House, Inc., 1971.
167. Hesse, H.: Demian. New York, Harper & Row Bantam Books, 1965.
168. Hobbes, T.: Human Nature. In English Works of Hobbes (1834–43), edited by W. Molesworth. New York, International Publications Service, 1966.
169. Hobbes, T.: Leviathan. New York, Bobbs-Merrill, Inc. 1958.
170. Hobbes, T.: The Elements of Philosophy. In English Works of Hobbes (1893–43), edited by W. Molesworth. New York, International Publications Service, 1966.
171. Hocking, W.: Types of Philosophy, 3rd ed. New York, Chas. Scribner's Son, 1959.
172. Houston, C.: The last blue mountain. In Why Man Takes Chances, edited by S. Klausner. New York, Anchor/Doubleday, 1968.
173. Hubbard, A.W. (Ed.): Research Methods in Health, Physical Education, and Recreation. AAHPER, 1973.
174. Huizinga, J.: Homo Ludens: A Study of the Play-Element in Culture. Boston, The Beacon Press, 1950.
175. Hult, J.S.: The philosophical conflicts in men's and women's collegiate athletics. Quest, 32(1): 77–94, 1980.
176. Hyland, D.A.: Athletic angst: reflections on the philosophical relevance of play. In Sport and the Body, edited by E.W. Gerber. Philadelphia, Lea & Febiger, 1972, pp. 87–94.
177. Hyland, D.A.: Competition and friendship. In Sport and the Body, 2nd ed., edited by E.W. Gerber and W.J. Morgan. Lea & Febiger, 1979, pp. 133–140. Also in J. Philos. Sport, 5:27–37, 1978.
178. Hyland, D.A.: Modes of inquiry in sports, athletics, and play. J. Philos. Sport, 1:123–128, 1974.
179. Hyland, D.A.: The stance of play. J. Philos. Sport, 7:87–99, 1980.
180. Ingram, A.: Art and sport. J. Health Phys. Educ. Rec., 44:24–27, 1973.
181. James, C.L.R.: The relationship between popular sport and fine art. In Readings in the Aesthetics of Sport, edited by H.T.A. Whiting and D.W. Masterson. London, Lepus Books, 1974.
182. James, W.: Pragmatism: A New Name for Some Old Ways of Thinking. New York, Longman's Green and Co., 1907.
183. Jaspers, K.: Limits of the life-order: sport. In Sport and the Body, edited by E.W. Gerber. Philadelphia, Lea & Febiger, 1972, pp. 118–119.
184. Jaspers, K.: Sport. In Man in the Modern Age. Translated by E. and C. Paul. Garden City, NY, Doubleday, 1957.
185. Jeu, B.: What is sport? Diogenes, 80:150–163, 1972.
186. Jokl, E.: Art and sport. In Readings in the Aesthetics of Sport, edited by H.T.A. Whiting and D.W. Masterson. London, Lepus Books, 1974.
187. Kaelin, E.F.: Being in the body. In Sport and the Body, 2nd ed., edited by E.W. Gerber and W.J. Morgan. Philadelphia, Lea & Febiger, 1979, pp. 167–176.
188. Kaelin, E.F.: The well-played game: notes toward an aesthetics of sport. Quest, 10:16–28, 1968. Also in Sport and the Body, 2nd ed., edited by E.W. Gerber and W.J. Morgan. Philadelphia, Lea & Febiger, 1979, pp. 324–331.
189. Kapleau, R.P.: The Three Pillars of Zen. New York, Anchor/Doubleday, 1980.
190. Keating, J.W.: Athletics and the pursuit of excellence. Education, 85(7): 428–431, 1965.
191. Keating, J.W.: Sportsmanship as a moral category. Ethics, 85(1):25–35, 1964. Also in Sport and the Body, 2nd ed., edited by E.W. Gerber and W.J. Morgan. Philadelphia, Lea & Febiger, 1979, pp. 264–271.
192. Keating, J.W.: The ethics of competition and its relation to some moral problems in athletics. In The Philosophy of Sport: A Collection of Original Essays, edited by R. G. Osterhoudt. Springfield, IL, Charles C Thomas, 1973, pp. 157–175.
193. Keating, J.W.: The urgent need for definitions and distinctions. Phys. Educator, 28:41–42, 1971.
194. Keating, J.W.: Winning in sport and athletics. Thought, 38:(149):201–210, 1963.

195. Keenan, F.W.: Justice and sport. Journal of the Philosophy of Sport, Vol. 2 (September 1975), pp. 111–123.
196. Keenan, F.W.: The athletic contest as a 'tragic' of art. *In* The Philosophy of Sport: A Collection of Original Essays, edited by R.G. Osterhoudt. Springfield, IL, Charles C Thomas, 1973, pp. 309–325.
197. Keenan, F.W.: The concept of doing. *In* The Philosophy of Sport: A Collection of Original Essays, edited by R.G. Osterhoudt. Springfield, IL, Charles C Thomas, 1973, pp. 141–148.
198. Keller, H.: Sport and art—the concept of mastery. *In* Readings in the Aesthetics of Sport, edited by H.T.A. Whiting and D.W. Masterson. London, Lepus Books, 1974.
199. Kennedy, C.W.: Sport and Sportsmanship. Princeton, Princeton University Press, 1931.
200. Kenyon, G.: Toward a sociology of sport: on becoming a sub-discipline. *In* New Perspectives of Man in Action, edited by C. Brown and B.J. Cratty. Englewood Cliffs, Prentice-Hall, 1969.
201. Kew, F.C.: Values in competitive games. Quest, 29:103–112, 1978.
202. Kleiber, D.A.: Playing to learn. Quest, 26:68–74, 1976.
203. Kleinman, S.: IV. Sport: whose bag is sport experience? Quest, 19:93–96, 1973.
204. Kleinman, S.: Kinesis and the self concept in women and sport: A National Conference, edited by D. Harris. State College, PA, Pennsylvania State University, 1973, pp. 51–57.
205. Kleinman, S.: Philosophy and physical education. *In* Physical Education: An Interdisciplinary Approach. New York, The Macmillan Co., 1972.
206. Kleinman, S.: Physical education and lived-movement. National College of Physical Education Association for Men Convention, Portland, 1970.
207. Kleinman, S.: The nature of a self and its relation to an 'other' in sport. J. Philos. Sport, 2:45–50, 1975.
208. Kleinman, S.: The significance of human movement: a phenomenological approach. *In* Sport and the Body, edited by E.W. Gerber. Philadelphia, Lea & Febiger, 1972, pp. 175–178.
209. Kleinman, S.: Toward a non-theory of sport. Quest, 10:29–34, 1968.
210. Kleinman, S.: Will the real Plato please stand up? Quest, 14:73–75, 1970.
211. Kohlberg, L.: Stages of moral development as a basis for moral education. *In* Moral Education: Interdisciplinary Perspectives, edited by E.V. Sullivan et al. Toronto, University of Toronto Press, 1971, pp. 23–92.
212. Knoppers, A.: Androgeny: another look. Quest, 32(2):184–191, 1980.
213. Krell, D.F.: Towards an ontology of play. Res. Phenomenol., 2:63–93, 1972.
214. Kretchmar, R.S.: A philosophical description of sport. Paper presented at the American Association Health, Physical Education, and Recreation National Convention, Seattle, 1970.
215. Kretchmar, R.S.: At the heart of athletics. J. Phys. Educ. Recr. Athl., 53:35–36, 1982.
216. Kretchmar, R.S.: From test to contest: an analysis of two kinds of counterpoint in sport. J. Philos. Sport, 2:23–30, 1975.
217. Kretchmar, R.S.: Meeting the opposition: Buber's 'will' and 'grace' in sport. Quest, 24:19–27, 1975.
218. Kretchmar, R.S.: Modes of philosophic inquiry and sport. J. Philos. Sport, 1:129–131, 1974.
219. Kretchmar, R.S.: Ontological possibilities: sport as play. *In* The Philosophy of Sport: A Collection of Original Essays, edited by R.G. Osterhoudt. Springfield, IL, Charles C Thomas, 1973.
220. Kretchmar, R.S., and Harper, W.A.: Must we have a rational answer to the question 'Why does man play'? J. Health Phys. Educ. Rec., 40:57–58, 1962.
221. Kroll, W.: Perspectives in Physical Education. New York, Academic Press, 1971.
222. Kuntz, P.G.: Aesthetic applies to sports as well as to the arts. J. Philos. Sport, 1:6–35, 1974.
223. Kuntz, P.G.: From Ziff to Zen: a defense of the aesthetics of sport. Philosophy in Context, 9:22–32, 1979.
224. Kuntz, P.G.: Paul Weiss on sports as performing arts. Int. Philos. Q., 17:147–165, 1977.

225. Kuntz, P. G.: "Paul Weiss: What is a Philosophy of Sports?" Philosophy Today, (Fall 1976), pp. 170–186.
226. Kuntz, P.G.: The aesthetics of sport. *In* The Philosophy of Sport: A Collection of Original Essays, edited by R.G. Osterhoudt. Springfield, IL, Charles C Thomas, 1973, pp. 305–309.
227. Kupfer, J.: Purpose and beauty in sport. J. Philos. Sport, 2:83–90, 1975. *Also in* Sport and the Body, 2nd ed., edited by E.W. Gerber and W.J. Morgan. Philadelphia, Lea & Febiger, 1979, pp. 355–360.
228. Kurtines, W., and Grief, E.: The development of moral thought: review and evaluation of Kohlberg's approach. Psychol. Bull., *81*(8):453–470, 1974.
229. Kwant, R.: The human body as the self-awareness of being. Humanitas, 2:43–62, 1966.
230. Laban, R.: The Mastery of Movement, 2nd ed. London, MacDonald and Evans, 1966.
231. Laban, R., and Lawrence, F.C.: Effort. London, MacDonald and Evans, 1947.
232. Langer, S.: Feeling and Form. New York, Scribners and Sons, 1953.
233. Lama, Govinda. Foundations of Tibetan Mysticism. York Beach, ME, Weiser, 1970.
234. Lawton, P.: Sports and the American spirit: Michael Novak's theology of culture. Philos. Today, *20*:196–208, 1976.
235. LeMay, S.: Sport and training: some preliminary philosophic considerations. Sport and the Humanities, edited by W.J. Morgan. Knoxville, University of Tennessee, 1979, pp. 56–60.
236. Lenk, H.: Herculan 'myth' aspects of athletics. J. Philos. Sport, 3:11–21, 1976.
237. Lenk, H.: Towards a social philosophy of achievement and athletics. Man and World, 9:45–59, 1976.
238. Leonard, G.: Sports culture scores hollow victories. Rochester Democrat and Chronicle, September 30, 1973, Section F.
239. Leonard, G.: The Ultimate Athlete. New York, Viking Press, 1975.
240. Levy, J.: Play Behavior. New York, John Wiley & Sons, 1978.
241. Lipman, M.: The physical thing in the aesthetic experience. J. Aesthet. Art Crit., *15*: 1956, pp. 36–46.
242. Lipsyte, R.: Sports World. New York, Quadrangle Press, 1977.
243. Lipsyte, R.: Sportsworld: an American dreamland. Proceedings of the NCPEAM/NAPECW National Conference, Orlando, 1977, pp. 45–52.
244. Locke, J.: Essay concerning human understanding. Philosophers Speak for Themselves: From Descartes to Locke, edited by T.V. Smith and M. Grene. Chicago, Phoenix, University of Chicago Press, 1957.
245. Locke, J.: Some Thoughts Concerning Education. Cambridge, University Press, 1913.
246. Locke, L.F.: Are sports education? Quest, *19*:87–90, 1973.
247. Lorenz, K.: On Aggression. New York, Harcourt Brace, 1966.
248. Lowe, B.: The Beauty of Sport: A Cross-Disciplinary Inquiry. Englewood Cliffs, NJ, Prentice-Hall, Inc., 1977.
249. Loy, J.Jr.: The nature of sport: a definitional effort. Quest, *10*:1–15, 1968. *Also in* Sport and the Body, 2nd ed., edited by E.W. Gerber and W.J. Morgan. Philadelphia, Lea & Febiger, 1979, pp. 33–47.
250. Loy, J.R., Birrell, S., and Rose, D.: Attitudes toward agonetic activities as a function of selected social identities. Quest, *26*:81–93, 1976.
251. Ludlan, J.: Informed Consent. Chicago, American Hospital Association, 1978.
252. Luft, J.: Group Processes, 2nd ed. Palo Alto, CA, Mayfield, 1970.
253. Luschen, G.: Cooperation, association, and contest. J. Conflict Resolution, *14*:21–34, 1970.
254. MacLeod, R.B.: Phenomenology: a challenge to experimental psychology. *In* Behaviorism and Phenomenology, edited by T.W. Wann. Chicago, University of Chicago Press, 1964.
255. McBride, F.: Toward a non-definition of sport. J. Philos. Sport, 2:4–11, 1975.
256. McIntosh, P.: Fair Play: Ethics in Sport and Education. London, Heinemann, 1979.
257. McIntosh, P.: Sport and Society. London, C.A. Watts, 1963.
258. McLuhan, M.: Games. *In* Understanding Media: The Extensions of Man. New York, Signet Book, 1964.
259. Maheu, R.: Sport and culture. *In* International Research in Sport and Physical Education, edited by E. Jokl and E. Simon. Springfield, IL. Charles C Thomas, 1964, pp. 9–22.

Bibliography **219**

260. Mandell, A.: Pro football fumbles the drug scandal. Psychol. Today, 9:39–44, 1975.
261. Marcel, Gabriel: If I am my body. In Sport and the Body, 2nd ed., edited by E.W. Gerber and W.J. Morgan. Philadelphia, Lea & Febiger, 1979, pp. 165–166.
262. Maslow, A.: Toward a Psychology of Being. Princeton, Van Nostrand, 1962.
263. Mead, G.H.: Play, the game, and the generalized other. In Sport and the Body, edited by E.W. Gerber. Philadelpia, Lea & Febiger, 1972, pp. 102–107.
264. Meier, K.V.: An affair of flutes: an appreciation of play. J. Philos. Sport, 7:24–45, 1980.
265. Meier, K.V.: An existential analysis of play. Unpublished Master's thesis, University of Western Ontario, Canada, 1971.
266. Meier, K.V.: Cartesian and phenomenological anthropology: the radical shift and its meaning for sport. J. Philos. Sport, 2:51–73, 1975.
267. Meier, K.: The kinship of the rope and the living struggle: a philosophical analysis of communication in mountain climbing. J. Philos. Sport, 3:52–64, 1976.
268. Menninger, K.: Recreation and mental health. In Recreation and Psychiatry, edited by L. Hill. New York, National Recreation Association, 1960, pp. 8–18.
269. Metheny, E.: Connotations of Movement in Sport and Dance. Dubuque, Iowa, William C. Brown Co., Publishers, 1965.
270. Metheny, E.: How does a movement mean? Quest, 8:1–6, 1967.
271. Metheny, E.: Movement and Meaning. New York, McGraw-Hill Book Co., 1968.
272. Metheny, E.: Moving and Knowing. Mt. View, CA, Peek Publications, 1975.
273. Metheny, E.: Philosophical methods. In-Research Methods in Health, Physical Education, and Recreation, 2nd ed., edited by M.G. Scott. Washington, DC, AAHPER, 1959.
274. Metheny, E.: The symbolic power of sport. In Sport and the Body, 2nd ed., edited by E.W. Gerber and W.J. Morgan. Philadelphia, Lea & Febiger, 1979, pp. 231–236.
275. Metheny, E.: This 'thing' called sport. J. Health Phys. Educ. Rec., 40:59–60, 1969.
276. Metheny, E.: The unique meaning inherent in human movement. Phys. Educator, 18(1): 3–7, 1961.
277. Michener, J.A.: Sports in America. New York, Random House, 1976.
278. Millar, S.: The Psychology of Play. New York, Aronson, 1968.
279. Miller, A.: The nature of tragedy. New York Herald Tribune, March 27, 1949, Section E, pp. 1–2.
280. Miller, A.: Tragedy and the common man. New York Times, February 27, 1949, Section II, pp. 1–3.
281. Miller, D.L.: Gods and Games: Toward a Theology of Play. New York: World, 1970.
282. Miller, D.M., and Russell, K.R.E.: Sport: A Contemporary View. Philadelphia, Lea & Febiger, 1971.
283. Moore, G.E.: Principia Ethica. New York, Cambridge University Press, 1959.
284. Morgan, W.J.: An analysis of the Sartrean ethic of ambiguity as the moral ground for the conduct of sport. J. Philos. Sport, 3:82–96, 1976.
285. Morgan, W.J.: An existential phenomenological analysis of sport as a religious experience. In The Philosophy of Sport: A Collection of Original Essays, edited by R.G. Osterhoudt. Springfield, IL, Charles C Thomas, 1973, pp. 78–107.
286. Morgan, W.J.: On the path toward an ontology of sport. J. Philos. Sport, 3:25–34, 1976.
287. Morgan, W.J.: Some Aristotelian notes on the attempt to define sport. J. Philos. Sport, 4:15–35, 1977.
288. Morford, W.R.: Sport: whose bag? I. Is sport the struggle or the triumph? Quest, 19:83–87, 1973.
289. Morland, R.B.: The philosophic method of research. In Research Methods in Health, Physical Education, and Recreation, 3rd ed., edited by A.W. Hubbard. Washington, AAHPER, 1973.
290. Moustakas C.: Creativity and Conformity. Princeton, Van Nostrand Co., 1966.
291. Moustakas, C.: Loneliness and Love. Englewood Cliffs, NJ, Prentice-Hall Spectrum Books, 1972.
292. Morris, D.: The Naked Ape. New York, Dell Publishing Co., 1969.
293. Munro, T.: The Arts and Their Interrelations. New York, Liberal Arts Press, 1949.
294. Murphy, M., and Brodie, J.: I experience a kind of clarity. Intellectual Digest, 2:19–22, 1973.
295. Muson, H.: Moral thinking: can it be taught? Psychol. Today, 12:48–53, 92, 1979.

296. Nietzsche, F.: The Birth of Tragedy. Translated by W. Kaufmann. New York, Random House Vintage Books, 1967.
297. Northrop, F.: The Logic of the Sciences and Humanities. New York, Macmillan Publishing Co., 1947.
298. Novak, M.: The Joy of Sports. New York, Basic Books, 1976.
299. O'Neill, J.: The spectacle of the body. J. Philos. Sport, 1:110–122, 1974.
300. Orlick, T., and Botterill, C.: Every Kid Can Win. Chicago, Nelson Hall, 1975.
301. Osterhoudt, R.G.: A descriptive analysis of research concerning the philosophy of physical education and sport. Unpublished doctoral dissertation. University of Illinois, 1971.
302. Osterhoudt, R.G.: An Hegelian interpretation of art, sport, and athletics. In The Philosophy of Sport: A Collection of Original Essays, edited by R.G. Osterhoudt. Springfield, IL, Charles C Thomas, 1973.
303. Osterhoudt, R.G.: A taxonomy for research concerning the philosophy of physical education and sport. Quest, 20:87–91, 1973.
304. Osterhoudt, R.G.: In praise of harmony: the Kantian imperative and Sittlichkeit as the principle and substance of moral conduct in sport. J. Philos. Sport, 3:65–81, 1976.
305. Osterhoudt, R.G.: Modes of philosophic inquiry concerning sport: some reflections of methods. J. Philos. Sport, 1:137–141, 1974.
306. Osterhoudt, R.G.: On Keating on the competitive motif in athletics and playful activity. In The Philosophy of Sport. A Collection of Original Essays. Springfield, IL, Charles C Thomas, 1973, pp. 192–198.
307. Osterhoudt, R.G.: The Kantian ethic as a principle of moral conduct in sport. Quest, 19:118–123, 1973.
308. Osterhoudt, R.G.: The Philosophy of Sport. Champaign, IL., Stipes, 1978.
309. Osterhoudt, R.G.: The Philosophy of Sport: A Collection of Original Essays. Springfield, IL, Charles C Thomas, 1973.
310. Osterhoudt, R.G.: Toward an idealistic conception of physical education and sport. Phys. Educator, 32:177–179, 1975.
311. Palmer, A.: My game and yours. Sports Illus., 19:28, 42, 1963.
312. Park, R.J.: Raising the consciousness of sport. Quest, 19:78–82, 1973.
313. Park, R.J.: The human element in sports: play. Phys. Educator, 28:122–124, 1971.
314. Park, R.J.: The philosophy of John Dewey and physical education. Phys. Educator, 26:55–57, 1969.
315. Partridge, P.H.: Freedom. In The Encyclopedia of Philosophy, Vol. III, edited by P. Edwards. New York, Macmillan Publishing Co., 1967, pp. 221–225.
316. Patrick, G.T.W.: The psychology of play. J. Genet. Psychol., 21:469–484, 1914.
317. Patrick, G.T.W.: The Psychology of Relaxation. Boston, Houghton Mifflin, 1916.
318. Pearson, K.M.: Deception, sportsmanship, and ethics. Quest, 19:115–118, 1973. Also in Sport and the Body, 2nd ed., edited by E.W. Gerber and W.J. Morgan. Philadelphia, Lea & Febiger, 1979, pp. 272–273.
319. Pearson, K.M.: Inquiry into Inquiry. Unpublished manuscript. University of Illinois, 1968.
320. Pearson, K.M.: Some comments on philosophic inquiry into sport as a meaningful human experience. J. Philos. Sport, 1:132–136, 1974.
321. Phenix, P.: Realms of Meaning. New York, McGraw-Hill, 1964.
322. Phillips, P.: The sport experience in education. Quest, 23:94–97, 1975.
323. Piaget, J.: Play, Dreams, and Imitation in Childhood. London, Routledge and Kegan Paul, Ltd., 1951.
324. Plato: The Complete Works of Plato. New York, Modern Library, 1966.
325. Plessner, H.: Laughing and Crying. Translated by J.S. Churchill. Evanston, IL, Northwestern University Press, 1970.
326. Polanyi, M.: Knowing and Being. Chicago, University of Chicago Press, 1969.
327. Polanyi, M., and Prosch, H.: Meaning. Chicago, University of Chicago Press, 1975.
328. Polanyi, M.: The Study of Man. Chicago, University of Chicago Press, 1959.
329. Postow, B.C.: Women and masculine sports. J. Philos. Sport, 7:51–58, 1980.
330. Progen, J.: Man, nature and sport. In Sport and the Body, edited by E.W. Gerber. Philadelphia, Lea & Febiger, 1972.
331. Ralls, A.: The game of life. Philosophical Q., 16:23–34, 1966.
332. Raths, L., et al.: Values Through Teaching. Columbus, Merrill, 1966.

333. Ravizza, K.: A study of peak experience in sport. Doctoral dissertation. University of Southern California, 1978.
334. Ravizza, K.: Enhancing human performance: an answer lies within. NAPEHE Annual Conference Proceedings, Milwaukee, 1979, pp. 66–74.
335. Ravizza, K.: Potential of the sport experience. *In* Being Human in Sport, edited by D.J. Allen and B.W. Fahey. Philadelphia, Lea & Febiger, 1977, pp. 61–72.
336. Rawls, J.: The practice conception of rules. *In* Sport and the Body, edited by E.W. Gerber and W.J. Morgan. Philadelphia, Lea & Febiger, 1979, pp. 294–296.
337. Reich, C.: The Greening of America. New York, Bantam Books, 1971.
338. Reid, L.A.: Sport, the aesthetic and art. Brit. J. Educ. Studies, *18*:245–258, 1970.
339. Renshal, P.: The nature of human movement studies and its relationship with physical education. Quest, *20*:79–86, 1973.
340. Richter, P.: Perspectives in Aesthetics: Plato to Camus. New York, Odyssey Press, 1968.
341. Riezler, K.: Play and seriousness. J. Philos., *38*:505–517, 1941.
342. Roberts, J.M., and Sutton-Smith, B.: Game training and game involvement. Ethnology, *1*:166–185, 1962.
343. Roberts, T.J.: Languages of sport: exemplification and expression. *In* Sport and the Humanities, edited by W.J. Morgan. Knoxville, University of Tennessee, 1979, pp. 39–55.
344. Roberts, T.J.: Languages of sport: representation. *In* Sport and the Body, edited by E.W. Gerber and W.J. Morgan. Philadelphia, Lea & Febiger, 1979, pp. 332–339.
345. Roberts, T.J.: Sport and the sense of beauty. J. Philos. Sport, *2*:91–101, 1975.
346. Roberts, T.J., and Galasso, P.J.: The fiction of morally indifferent acts in sport. *In* The Philosophy of Sport: A Collection of Original Essays, edited by R.G. Osterhoudt. Springfield, IL, Charles C Thomas, 1973, pp. 274–281.
347. Rokeach, M.: Beliefs, Attitudes and Values. San Francisco: Jossey-Bass, 1968.
348. Rokeach, M.: The Nature of Human Values. New York, The Free Press, 1973.
349. Roochnik, D.L.: Play and sport. J. Philos. Sport, *2*:36–44, 1975.
350. Royce, J.R.: Encapsulated Man: An Interdisciplinary Essay on the Search for Meaning. Princeton, Van Nostrand Co., 1964.
351. Royce, J.: Physical training and moral education. *In* Sport and the Body, 2nd ed., edited by E.W. Gerber and W.J. Morgan. Philadelphia, Lea & Febiger, 1979, pp. 254–257.
352. Sack, A.: Big time college football: whose free ride? Quest, *27*:86–96, 1977.
353. Sadler, W.A., Jr.: A contextual approach to an understanding of competition: a response to Keating's philosophy of athletics. *In* The Philosophy of Sport: A Collection of Original Essays, edited by R.G. Osterhoudt. Springfield, IL, Charles C Thomas, 1973.
354. Sadler, W.A., Jr.: Alienated youth and creative sports experience. J. Philos. Sport, *4*:83–95, 1977.
355. Sadler, W.A., Jr.: Competition out-of-bounds: sports in American life. Quest, *19*:124–132, 1973.
356. Sadler, W.A., Jr.: Creative existence: play as a pathway to personal freedom and community. Humanitas, *5*:57–79, 1969.
357. Sadler, W.A., Jr.: Play: a basic human structure involving love and freedom. Rev. Existential Psychol. Psychiatry, *6*:237–245,1966. *Also in* Sport and the Body, edited by E.W. Gerber. Philadelphia, Lea & Febiger, 1972, pp. 113–117.
358. Sadler, W.A., Jr.: The experience of friendship. Humanitas, *6*:177–209, 1970.
359. Sandler, B.R.: A summary of proposed amendment to Title IX: Implications for Post Secondary Schools. Association of American Colleges: Project on the Status of Women, 1818 R St., Washington, D.C. 20009, 1982.
360. Sapora, A.V., and Mitchell, E.D.: The Theory of Play and Recreation. 3rd ed. New York, Ronald Press, 1961.
361. Sarano, J.: The meaning, or dimension of the body. *In* Sport and the Body, edited by E.W. Gerber. Philadelphia, Lea & Febiger, 1972, pp. 162–164.
362. Sartre, J.P.: Being and Nothingness: An Essay on Phenomenological Ontology. Translated by H.E. Barnes. New York, Washington Square Press, 1953.
363. Sartre, J.P.: Doing and having. *In* Being and Nothingness. Translated by H.E. Barnes. New York, Philosophical Library, 1956.

364. Sartre, J.P.: Existentialism. Translated by B. Frechtman. New York, Philosophical Library, 1947.
365. Sartre, J.P.: Play and sport. Sport and the Body: A Philosophical Symposium, edited by E.W. Gerber and W.J. Morgan. Philadelphia, Lea & Febiger, 1979, pp. 84–87.
366. Sayre, W.W.: Four Against Everest. Englewood Cliffs, NJ, Prentice-Hall, Inc., 1964.
367. Schiller, F.V.: Essays Aesthetical and Philosophical. London, George Bell, 1875.
368. Schmitz, K.L.: Sport and play: suspension of the ordinary. Essay presented at the American Association for the Advancement of Science, Annual Meeting, Dallas, Texas, December,1968. *Also in* Sport and the Body, edited by E. W. Gerber. Philadelphia, Lea & Febiger, 1972.
369. Schrag, C.: Existence and Freedom. Chicago, Northwestern University Press, 1961.
370. Schrag, C.O.: The lived body as a phenomenological datum. Modern Schoolman, *39*:203–218, 1962. *Also in* Sport and the Body, edited by E.W. Gerber and W.J. Morgan. Lea & Febiger, 1979, pp. 155–162.
371. Scott, J.: The Athletic Revolution. New York, Free Press, 1971.
372. Scott, J.: Sport and the radical ethic. Quest, *20*:71–77, 1973.
373. Scott, P.: Aesthetics, education and the aims of age group swimming. Swimmers World, *17*:17–19, 1976.
374. Sellars, W., and Hospers,J. (Eds.): Readings in Ethical Theory. New York, Appleton-Century-Crofts, 1952.
375. Siedentop, D.: Physical Education: An Introductory Analysis, 3rd ed. Dubuque, W.C. Brown, 1980.
376. Siedentop, D.: What did Plato really think? Phys. Educator, *24*:25–26, 1968.
377. Simon, S., et al.: Values Clarification. New York, Hart Publishing, 1972.
378. Singer, R.: Physical Education: Foundations. New York, Holt, Rinehart and Winston, 1976.
379. Slusher, H.S.: Man, Sport, and Existence: A Critical Analysis. Philadelphia, Lea & Febiger, 1967.
380. Slusher, H.S.: Morality as an intimate of sport. *In* Sport and the Body, 2nd ed., edited by E.W. Gerber and W.J. Morgan. Philadelphia, Lea & Febiger, 1979, pp. 290–293.
381. Slusher, H.S.: Sport: a philosophical perspective. Law and Contemporary Problems, *38*:129–134, 1973.
382. Slusher, H.S.: The characteristics of sport. *In* Sport and the Body, edited by E.W. Gerber. Philadelphia, Lea & Febiger, 1972.
383. Slusher, H.S.: To test the wave is to test life. J. Health Phys. Educ. Rec., *40*:32–33, 1969.
384. Smith, N.: Spotlight on dance. J. Health Phys. Educ. Rec., *35*:63–65, 1964.
385. Smith, P.: Sport is a western yoga. Psychol. Today, *9*:48–57, 1975.
386. Spencer, H.: Principles of Psychology. New York, Appleton, 1873.
387. Spiegelberg, H.: Toward a phenomenology of experience. Amer. Philos. Q., *1*:325–332, 1964.
388. Spino, M.: Running as a spiritual experience. The Athletic Revolution, edited by J. Scott. New York, Free Press, 1971.
389. Steel, M.: What we know when we know a game. J. Philos. Sport, *4*:96–103, 1977.
390. Steinhaus, A.: Toward an Understanding of Health and Physical Education. Dubuque, IA, W.C. Brown Co., 1963.
391. Stevenson, C.L.: Ethics and Language. New Haven, Yale University Press, 1944.
392. Stevenson, C.L.: The meaning of movement. Quest, *23*:2–9, 1975.
393. Stone, R.E.: Assumptions about the nature of human movement. *In* The Philosophy of Sport: A Collection of Original Essays, edited by R.G. Osterhoudt. Springfield, IL, Charles C Thomas, 1973.
394. Stone, R.E.: Human movement forms as meaning-structures: prolegomenon. Quest, *23*:10–17, 1975.
395. Stone, R.E.: Of Zen and the experience of moving. Quest, *33*(1):96–107, 1981.
396. Studer, G.L.: From man moving to moving man. Quest, *20*:104–107, 1973.
397. Studer, G.L.: The language of movement is in the doing. Quest, *23*:98–99, 1975.
398. Suits, B.: Is life a game we are playing? Ethics, *77*:209–213, 1975.
399. Suits, B.: The elements of sport. *In* The Philosophy of Sport: A Collection of Original Essays, edited by R.G. Osterhoudt. Springfield, IL, Charles C Thomas, 1973, pp. 48–64.

400. Suits, B.: The grasshopper: a thesis concerning the moral ideal of man. *In* The Philosophy of Sport: A Collection of Original Essays, edited by R.G. Osterhoudt. Springfield, IL, Charles C Thomas, 1973, pp. 148–156.
401. Suits, B.: What is a game? Philos. Sci., *34*:148–156, 1967.
402. Suits, B.: Words on play. J. Philos. Sport, *4*:117–131, 1977.
403. Sutton-Smith, B.: Piaget on play: a critique. Psychol. Rev., *73*:104–110, 1966.
404. Suzuki, D.T.: Studies in Zen. New York, Delta, 1955.
405. Taylor, R.: Metaphysics. Englewood Cliffs, NJ, Prentice-Hall, 1963.
406. Thomas, C.E.: Beautiful, just beautiful. *In* Being Human in Sport, edited by D.J. Allen and B.W. Fahey. Philadelphia, Lea & Febiger, 1977, pp. 73–80.
407. Thomas, C.E.: Characteristics of an experiential aesthetic. Aesthetics and Dance, edited by C.E. Thomas. AAHPERD, 1980, pp. 27–30.
408. Thomas, C.E.: Do you 'wanna' bet: an examination of player betting and the integrity of the sporting event.*In* The Philosophy of Sport: A Collection of Original Essays, edited by R.G. Osterhoudt. Springfield, IL, Charles C Thomas, 1973, pp.291–302.
409. Thomas, C.E.: Personal equations of sport involvement. Proceedings of NAPECW-NCPEAM Joint Meeting, Orlando, Florida, 1977, pp. 262–269.
410. Thomas, C.E.: Science and philosophy: peaceful coexistence. Quest, *20*:99–104, 1973.
411. Thomas, C.E.: The golden girl syndrome: thoughts on a training ethic. NAPEHE Proceedings, Brainard, 1980, pp. 136–146.
412. Thomas, C.E.: The perfect moment: an aesthetic perspective of the sport experience. Unpublished doctoral dissertation, Ohio State University, 1972.
413. Thomas, C.E.: The sport contest as drama. J. Phys. Educ. Rec. Dance, *53*:39–40, 1982.
414. Thomas, C.E.: The sportsman as a tragic figure. *In* Sport and the Humanities, edited by W.J. Morgan. University of Tennessee Press, 1980.
415. Thomas, C.E.: The tragic dimension of sport. *In* Philosophy in Context, 9:33–43, 1979.
416. Thomas, C.E.: Toward an experiential sport aesthetic. J. Philos. Sport, *1*:67–91, 1974.
417. Thomas, C.E.: Where have all the playgrounds gone? Quest, *27*:114–120, 1977.
418. Thomas, D.L.: Sport: the conceptual enigma. J. Philos. Sport, *3*:35–41, 1976.
419. Thomas, J.R.: Youth Sports Guide for Coaches and Parents. Washington, DC, AAHPERD Publications, 1977.
420. Todd, W.: Some aesthetic aspects of sport. *In* Philosophy in Context, edited by R.H. Fox. Cleveland State Univ., 1979, pp. 8–21.
421. Tolstoy, L.: What is Art? Translated by A. Maude. New York, Crowell and Co., 1899.
422. Turbeville, G.: On being good sports in sports. *In* Sport and the Body, edited by E.W. Gerber. Philadelphia, Lea & Febiger, 1972, pp. 255–259.
423. Tutko, T., and Burns, W.: Winning is Everything and Other American Myths. New York, Macmillan Publishing Co., 1976.
424. Underwood, J.: Taking the fun out of the game. Sports Illus., *43*:86–90, 1975.
425. Valentine, E.: Lombardi on winning. *In* Sport and the Humanities, edited by W.J. Morgan. Knoxville, University of Tennessee College of Education, 1979, pp. 61–66.
426. Van Den Berg, J.H.: The human body and the significance of human movement. *In* Psychoanalysis and Existential Philosophy, edited by H.M. Ruitenbeck. New York, E.P. Dutton, 1962.
427. VanderZwaag, H.J.: Sport: existential or essential? Quest, *12*:47–56, 1969.
428. VanderZwaag, H.: Sports concepts. J. Health Phys. Educ. Rec., *41*:35–36, 1970.
429. VanderZwaag, H.: Toward a Philosophy of Sport. Reading, MA, Addison-Wesley, 1972.
430. Van Dyke, R.: Aggression in sport: its implications for character-building. Quest, *32*(2):201–208, 1980.
431. VanKaam, A.: Sex and existence. *In* Readings in Existential Phenomenology, edited by J. Lawrence and L. O'Conner. Englewood Cliffs, NJ. Prentice-Hall, Inc., 1967.
432. Veron, E.: Aesthetics. Translated by W.H. Armstrong. London, Chapman and Hall, 1879.
433. Watson, G.: Social conflict and parental involvement in little league baseball. Quest, *27*:71–86, 1977.
434. Weiss, P.: Nine Basic Arts. Carbondale, Southern Illinois University Press, 1961.
435. Weiss, P.: Philosophy in Process 4. Carbondale, Southern Illinois University Press, 1966.
436. Weiss, P.: Religion and Art. Milwaukee, Marquette University Press, 1963.

437. Weiss, P.: Sport: A Philosophic Inquiry. Carbondale, Southern Illinois University Press, 1969.
438. Weiss, P.: World of Art. Carbondale, Southern Illinois University Press, 1961.
439. Wenkert, S.: The meaning of sports for contemporary man. J. Existential Psychiatry, 3:397–404, 1963.
440. Wertz, S.K.: Zen, Yoga, and sports: eastern philosophy for Western athletes. J. Philos. Sport, 4:68–82, 1977.
441. White, D.A.: Great moments in sport: the one and the many. *In* Sport and the Body, 2nd ed., edited by E.W. Gerber and W.J. Morgan. Philadelphia, Lea & Febiger, 1979, pp. 207–213.
442. White, R.W.: Motivation reconsidered: the concept of competence. Psychol. Rev., 66:297–333, 1959.
443. Whiting, H.T.A., and Masterson, D.W. (Eds.): Readings in the Aesthetics of Sport. London, Lepus Books, 1974.
444. Wulk, G.: A metacritical aesthetic of sport. *In* Sport and the Body, edited by E.W. Gerber and W.J. Morgan. Philadelphia, Lea & Febiger, 1979, pp. 340–344.
445. Young, I.M.: The exclusion of women from sport. Conceptual and existential dimensions. *In* Philosophy in Context, edited by R.H. Fox. Cleveland State Univ., 1979, pp. 44–53.
446. Zaner, R.: The radical reality of the human body. Humanitas, 2:73–87, 1966.
447. Zeigler, E.F.: Application of a scientific ethics approach to sport decisions. Quest, 32(1):8–21, 1980.
448. Zeigler, E.F.: In sport, as in all of life, man should be comprehensible to man. J. Philos. Sport, 3:121–126, 1976.
449. Zeigler, E.F.: Philosophical Foundations for Health, Physical Education, and Recreation Education. Englewood Cliffs, NJ, Prentice-Hall, Inc., 1964.
450. Zeigler, E.F.: Problems in the History and Philosophy of Physical Education and Sport. Englewood Cliffs, NJ, Prentice-Hall, Inc., 1968.
451. Zeigler, E.F.: The pragmatic (experimentalistic) ethic as it relates to sport and physical education. *In* The Philosophy of Sport: A Collection of Original Essays, edited by R.G. Osterhoudt. Springfield, IL, Charles C Thomas, 1973, pp. 229–274.
452. Zeigler, E.F.: Zeigler's reaction to 'theory and design of philosophic research in physical education.' 74th Proceedings of the National College Physical Education Association for Men, Annual Meeting (Portland, Oregon, December 27–30, 1970), pp. 52–57.
453. Zeigler, E.F., Howell, M.L., and Trekell, M.: Research in the History, Philosophy, and International Aspects of Physical and Sport: Bibliographies and Techniques. Champaign, IL, Stipes Publishing Co., 1971.
454. Ziff, P.: A fine forehand. J. Philos. Sport, *1*:92–109, 1974.
455. Zuckerman, M., et al.: What is the sensation seeker? J. Consulting Clin. Psychol., 39:308–321, 1972.

Index

Numbers followed by a "t" indicate tables.

ISBN 0-8121-0871-